Freemasonry in My Life

Sir James Stubbs, KCVO. Portrait by Colin Corfield painted in 1964 which now hangs in Conference Room A at Freemasons' Hall together with portraits of all Grand Secretaries since James Heseltine (1769–1783).

Freemasonry in My Life

Sir James Stubbs, KCVO
Grand Secretary 1958–1980

LONDON
LEWIS MASONIC
IAN ALLAN GROUP

© Sir James Stubbs 1985
First Published in England in 1985

Published by
A LEWIS (Masonic Publishers) LTD, Terminal House, Shepperton
who are members of the *Ian Allan Group*

Printed by Butler & Tanner Ltd, Frome and London

Previous titles by the same author:
  The Four Corners
  The Government of the Craft (Prestonian Lecture 1982)
  Grand Lodge 1717-1967 (in conjunction with A. S. Frere and others)
  Freemasons' Hall, the Home and Heritage of the Craft (with T. O. Haunch)

British Library Cataloguing in Publication Data
Stubbs, Sir James
  Freemasonry in My Life
  1. Stubbs, *Sir* James 1. Freemasons—
  England—Biography
  I. Title
  366'.1'0924 HS400.S7
ISBN 0 85318 143 8

All rights reserved. No part of this book may be reproduced or
transmitted in any form or by any means, electronic or mechanical,
including photocopying, recording or by any information storage
and retrieval system, without permission of the publishers in writing.

Contents

		Page
	List of illustrations	vii
	Foreword	ix
	Acknowledgements	xi
1	Ancestry and early years	1
2	School days	11
3	Oxford—general	20
4	Oxford and Freemasonry	25
5	St Paul's School	30
6	Army life and return to civilian life	36
7	Introduction to Great Queen Street	48
8	1947–1950	58
9	1950–1958	74
10	Grand Secretary: Part One (1958–1967)	90
11	Private life and Lodges	106
12	Celebrating 250 years	118
13	Grand Secretary: Part Two (1967–1980)	127
14	Provinces and visits	154
15	Prestonian Lectureship and retirement	156
16	Farewell Tour	172
17	Conclusion	203

Appendices
   I—Prestonian Lecture 1982
      The Government of the Craft   211
   II—The Badges of the Nineteen Red Apron Lodges   240
   III—Changes in Grand Chapter 1947 to 1980   243

Index   251

Illustrations

	Page
Sir James Stubbs, KCVO: portrait by Colin Corfield (1964)	Frontispiece
My grandfather, Dr William Stubbs (1825-1901), historian and Bishop of Oxford.	2
My grandmother, Catherine *née* Dellar: probably taken when she was in her late seventies: she lived to be 103 and died in 1941.	2
My maternal grandfather, Rev Arthur F. Pope (1840-1921).	3
My maternal grandmother, Kate Pope, *née* Rose.	3
Major James Rose (1820-1909). 23rd Baron of Kilravock.	4
My great uncle, Col Hugh Rose, 24th Baron of Kilravock in conversation with HRH the Duke of York, later George VI, at the Northern Meeting, Inverness, of which he was for some time convenor.	5
Kilravock Castle.	7
Barkway Vicarage, Royston, Herts, my birthplace and home from 1910 to 1926.	9
With my father at Barkway Vicarage in April 1913.	9
Easthampstead Rectory, Bracknell.	18
St Paul's School OTC officers in 1936.	23
Richenda Streatfeild.	32
Wedding group, 6 August 1938.	34
Richenda with daughter Janet in 1945.	35
As OC 3 Company, 21 Army Group Signals.	39
The Installation of RW Bro W. R. S. Bathurst as Provincial Grand Master for Gloucestershire in April 1950.	67
Stratford sub Castle Vicarage near Salisbury.	70
My parents in their garden at Detling, Kent on the occasion of their golden wedding in 1959.	70
Opening of the Wakefield Wing at the Royal Masonic Hospital in 1958 by HM the Queen Mother.	82

With Sir Sydney White after the consecration of Lodge of Ideal Endeavour in May 1955.	86
Alexander Stuart Frere, President of the Board of General Purposes 1959-1972.	92
Gibraltar airport 1955: my first Masonic trip overseas for the installation of Judge Hume Barne.	93
Dinner following a conference in Frankfurt on the plan to unify German Masonry.	94
Wreath laying ceremony at Valley Forge, Pennsylvania in 1976.	96
Sightseeing in Cyprus in 1963: a gathering in the Othello Lodge room.	99
With my son Hugh on a visit to Kilravock for Clan Rose gathering.	107
The Grand Stewards 1983-84.	115
HRH the Duke of Kent arriving for his installation as Grand Master at the Royal Albert Hall in 1967.	122-3
The dais in the Royal Albert Hall during the installation of HRH the Duke of Kent.	125
Talking with HRH the Princess Royal on her last visit to Harewood Court, Hove.	132
Irene Hainworth, private secretary to the Grand Secretary from 1959 to 1981.	152
Photographed at my desk by an American visitor in 1971.	155
With Wendell Walker, Grand Secretary, New York, in Pensioners Court, Charterhouse, 1982.	157
After receiving the KCVO in 1980.	159
Cartoon drawn by John Groves in November 1980 following my Knighthood.	159
The installation of Sir Knowles Edge as Provincial Grand Master for West Lancashire in 1968.	162
With Sir John Welch, Jeremy Pemberton, Cdr M. B. S. Higham and Rev C. E. Leighton Thomson in 1980.	164-5
Quatuor Coronati Lodge No 2076 luncheon to commemorate my retirement as Grand Secretary.	171
Being welcomed by RW Bro Dr E. Sackey, DGM for Ghana in Accra, 1975.	199

Foreword

When the order forms for *The Four Corners* were distributed there was a promise, or threat, included that if its reception justified it there would follow another volume concentrating on Masonry and my experiences at home. *The Four Corners* sold out in a year and I have taken that as justification for starting again, but like Dobson's poem this one has changed as it went along, and has become more truly an autobiography than a further Masonic essay: I can only plead that even professional Freemasons have private lives and antecedents.

My grandfather obtained a Grant of Arms in 1877 and took as motto the curious phrase *Et dixi nunc coepi*. With the help of Dean White of Christ Church my father eventually ran it to earth in the Vulgate, Psalm 77 verse 10 where it bears practically no resemblance to the biblical or prayer book version.

However following his example 'I have spoken (my apology for discursiveness) now I begin.'

James W. Stubbs

Acknowledgements

I have gratefully received encouragement and help from numerous other quarters, notably Alex Frere who, alas, died on the very day I wrote the Foreword to this book, John Skelly of the Oxford University Press who has checked my script for tautology and all the other sins of omission and commission that the OUP is particularly alive to, and to Mrs Betty Huntly who learned only after her retirement from Freemasons' Hall how bad the Grand Secretary's handwriting was: she coped with it both cheerfully and efficiently.

Apart from all those who have made my terms of office at Freemasons' Hall so pleasant I must mention in particular Jeremy Pemberton who not only was a constant source of friendship and support from 1942 till the present time but also was kind enough to read the first draft and make valuable and constructive suggestions: the Craft owes much to his wise control of its affairs.

Illustrations

My thanks are given to the Board of General Purposes for permission to reproduce the illustrations on pages 91, 120-1, 123 and the frontispiece. To A.F. Ferris, PrGM West Lancashire, for kind permission to reproduce the illustration on page 161. The remaining illustrations are from my own private collection the origin of which, in some cases, is not recorded and therefore I extend apologies for not giving acknowledgement by name.

Chapter 1

Ancestry and Early Years

Most British families which have been established in these islands for any length of time are likely to have become crossbred, and the Stubbs family are no exception. On my father's side there is a straight run of Yorkshiremen from the first known, or recorded, William of Birstwith near Harrogate, who acquired nine acres of land there in 1359/60. His son was a forest reeve of Knaresborough, and for the next five centuries that was their area.

My grandfather, another of many Williams struck out in a new direction by going, as a servitor, to Christ Church, Oxford and in due course becoming a fellow of Trinity College: from there he went to a college living, not liking the prospect of a new incoming President in 1850. He remained at Navestock in Essex for 17 years in the course of which he married Catherine Dellar, who taught in the village school and came of a line of agricultural workers in and around the village: so we have north and south united.

In addition to his work as a parish priest my grandfather still found time to widen and deepen his historical scholarship, publishing many papers and holding the appointment of Librarian at Lambeth: after two false starts when he applied for the Librarianship of the British Museum and the Chichele Professorship of Modern History at Oxford, he went back to Oxford in 1866 as Regius Professor of Modern History. He remained there or at Cuddesdon for the rest of his life, except for one interval of five years at Chester. My grandmother with similar short gaps also lived there from 1866 to 1942. Oxford was therefore very much in the blood.

On my mother's side there was rather more variety: her father Arthur Pope after Westminster School and Christ Church became in due course Vicar of Tring in Hertfordshire but gave up the living owing to a self-diagnosed breakdown in health at the very early age of 40. At this point he, rather surprisingly, married a young Scottish lady, Catherine Isabella Ellen Rose, and they settled down, still at Tring, to nearly 40 years of married life. No trace can be found of the Pope family earlier than my great grandfather Ebenezer, an attorney in the Lincoln's Inn Fields area whom I suspect without being able to prove it of having practiced in Great Queen Street. He, Ebenezer, died at an early age leaving a widow, (who promptly married a younger son of the Coventry family), with three children, two daughters who both married into the Church and my great

My grandfather, Dr William Stubbs (1825-1901), historian and Bishop of Oxford: for many generations the Bishops of Oxford in whose diocese Windsor lies were Chancellors of the Garter. He never recovered fully from a cold caught at Queen Victoria's funeral.

My grandmother, Catherine née Dellar: probably taken when she was in her late seventies: she lived to be 103 and died in 1941.

My maternal grandfather, Rev Arthur F. Pope (1840-1921)

My maternal grandmother, Kate Pope, née Rose: she was a 'mutiny baby' but returned to Scotland when very young. Till she married Arthur Pope she kept house for her father (the 23rd Baron) at Kilravock.

grandfather Edward, who went to Westminster School and thence first to Brasenose and then on to Queen's College. He later became an Archdeacon in Jamaica where he married a wealthy widow. When she died he was left with two young daughters and returned to England where he lost no time in marrying his first love my great grandmother Augusta Bigge: as a penniless curate in London he had not been acceptable as a suitor, but the Jamaican fortune obviously made him eligible and his beloved Augusta had remained unmarried. They later returned to Jamaica of which their son, my grandfather, retained vivid memories of a happy childhood surrounded by cheerful black faces, glorious sunshine and bright flowers.

My greatgrandfather, James Rose was the eldest son of a second family: India and the Crimea wiped out his elders and some of his juniors too: he went from Cooper's Hill into one of the East India Company's Cavalry Regiments and spent most of the mutiny chasing Tantia Topi round Western India. In the interim he still found time to marry Anna Maria Twemlow who presented him with four children of whom my grandmother was the eldest.

When my grandfather resigned the living of Tring after a trip round the world of which he wrote a fascinating account (the original of which has mostly disappeared but fortunately not before the New Zealand section had been copied for the archives of New Zealand House), he found himself the trustee of some cousins (referred to at the end of their lives as the Gardner girls). They lived near Fort George and equally near Kilravock where they were on friendly terms with the young Roses. My grandfather, having discovered with the help of Mr Vaisey, Tring's solicitor, the whereabouts of Fort George, went up to visit his young charges, then met my grandmother and promptly married her. Except for a short period when the family moved up to Nairn to look after the mutiny veteran whose health and memory but not his temper were failing my maternal grandparents continued to live at Tring till 1920 when he died and my grandmother remained till the early 1930s when she somewhat irrationally moved to Guildford.

My grandmother was thus some 20 years his junior and took pride in having been a 'mutiny baby': like my Dellar grandmother, also a Catherine, she lived to a ripe old age. The Roses had lived, and indeed still do, at Kilravock Castle ever since it was built in 1460, and can trace a descent at least back to 1280 when the earliest Hugh Rose of whom we can be certain married Marie de Bosco who brought him Kilravock in Nairnshire as her dower (18 out of 25 'Barons' of Kilravock have been Hugh, which makes the family history more complicated).

Returning to the Stubbs's, my father was the tenth child and sixth son of his parents, though of the 11 only six came to maturity: the rest were either still born or died in infancy. By the time of his birth in 1875 the

My great grandfather, Major James Rose (1820–1909), 23rd Baron of Kilravock: after retiring from the East India Company's army he settled down at Kilravock, becoming Lord Lieutenant of Nairnshire.

My great uncle, Col Hugh Rose, 24th Baron, in conversation with HRH The Duke of York, later George VI, at the Northern Meeting, Inverness, of which he was for some time convenor.

family had moved from North Oxford to Kettel Hall in Broad Street, for which the whole family had a continuing affection. (It has now been incorporated into Trinity College from one of whose former Presidents it takes its name.) After a nursery education under the guidance of his sister some twelve years older than himself he went to the North Oxford Preparatory School, now the Dragon School, at approximately the same time as the great C. C. Lynam appeared and laid the foundations for the remarkable educational tradition it has maintained. His elder brother proceeded to Winchester whither my father tried to follow him: but having narrowly missed scholarships both there and at Eton he finally got one at Charterhouse.

'Lynam's' was already well ahead of its contemporaries: the theatrical tradition had set in and my father played Macbeth with such success that he was asked to do Hamlet after he had left for Charterhouse: this venture was not a success and he never overcame his dislike of the play. He also got a very good grounding in Rugby football which survived five years of 'Association' at Charterhouse and enabled him to play in final 'Cuppers' for Christ Church at both codes. He also acquired an excellent grounding in the Classics, together with a number of friendships which continued throughout his long life—or as long as the other halves survived.

When he was at Lynam's my grandfather was made Bishop of Chester and the family moved, not without regrets, to Chester. On his translation to Oxford the family moved south again: the Bishop had accepted the appointment only on condition that he did not have to live at Cuddesdon Palace which he regarded as a white elephant in the middle of nowhere. However the Queen apparently took exception to the idea that he should live in Oxford and Lord Salisbury was charged with the difficult task of straightening it all out. My grandfather ultimately gave way but continued to dislike Cuddesdon though his family (who did not have to work from it) liked it very well. My father's holidays from Charterhouse between 1889 and 1894 were therefore divided between Chester and Oxford: in due course after quite a distinguished all round career at school he secured a Holford Exhibition at Christ Church which was a double source of gratification—he was going to his father's college, and as a Holford Exhibitioner he was following in the footsteps of John Wesley for whom he had a great respect denied to most dissenters (in fact he did not really count him among dissenters at all!). There can be no doubt that he enjoyed his four years at 'the House' from which he emerged with a mediocre degree and no very clear idea as to a profession. My grandfather, however, who had maintained close ties with the City from his professorial years when he was also a Residential Canon of St. Paul's, arranged for him to be articled as a solicitor to Dr Freshfield and he duly started a career in the City. One can only imagine how different it was from undergraduate life and understandably it did not last long for after a few months he discovered a vocation for the Church.

Thereafter followed a period at the Leeds Clergy School of which he always spoke with deep affection (his contemporaries claimed that he always studied the train menus to decide which was the best way to return home to Cuddesdon). In due course he was ordained by the Bishop of St Albans and served curacies at Welwyn and Tring. At the first of these he met his fellow curate, Dick Cattell, a slightly senior Oxford contemporary from Exeter College, a Rugger Blue, Captain of Blackheath and an English International. They served under the redoubtable Dr Headlam, later Professor at London University and Bishop of Gloucester: but after a few years they moved on to Tring, still together, and there fatefully and happily met their future wives Muriel Pope and Cleophe Boyson.

It is now time to return to the Pope family whom we left at the point where my grandfather had met and married my grandmother Kate Rose. They settled in a house still on the outskirts of Tring and produced five children, my mother being the only girl. As the boys were educated, two at Winchester, two as Collegers at Eton, it has been rather a mystery how a retired parson could have managed the fees even in those days: his wife had virtually no private means, and while the Archdeacon had married his wealthy widow in Jamaica, one would imagine that his first family would have had the lionesses' share of the West Indian money. Enlightenment, or at least a partial revelation, came to me quite recently when I

Kilravock Castle, built in 1460 and lived in by the Roses ever since. It is believed that when they had completed the keep of Cawdor Castle on the other side of the River Nairn the masons crossed the river and built Kilravock.

was trying to trace some of the Bigge pedigree as it transpired that his second wife Augusta like her numerous sisters had been left a substantial legacy by an old bachelor great uncle, Philip Rundle (Rundell) of Rundell and Bridges silver and goldsmiths. His was the not unusual, though dramatic story of the industrious apprentice who having lost his first and only love (his master's daughter) in a tragic fire, prospered exceedingly and left over a million pounds. He made generous bequests to various charities mostly in or on the edge of the City, but the bulk went to his Bigge kith and kin. Numerous though they were they seem to have found that their various shares gave them an adequate competence.

My mother came in the middle of the family; being the only girl she probably suffered for it, and certainly passed on to her own children the view that girls must always have preference. After a good many years under the tuition of governesses often shared by her life long friend, Kitty Carr, she was then sent for a few years to West Heath School, at that time situated on Ham Common: this was a very happy period in her life and she made further lifelong friendships some of which have extended into the next generation. When she left school there was of course no question of her taking a job—which indeed in Nairn, where the family had temporarily established themselves, might have been even more difficult than in Tring, and she therefore busied herself parochially and socially. Both her Etonian brothers were excellent tennis players, though her own game was erratic—she admitted to once serving four double faults in a Tring tournament, the eighth service catching her partner, the subsequent Mr Justice Vaisey, in the small of the back! Her experiences of visiting and enjoyment of Sunday School teaching however were to stand her in good stead when she became a parson's wife in 1909. Of the brothers, Harold became a mining engineer in Indonesia, hurried back to England in 1914 and was killed in 1918 after a successful career in the Royal Artillery: Jim, my godfather, became an Indian Civil Servant, retired at an early age and was appointed Bursar of Magdalene College, Cambridge which he served for a number of years, and retired once again to live outside Cheltenham—we were all devoted to him and his two children came to live with us for a year while their parents were still in India: Cuthbert went from Winchester to the Britannia and thence went to sea. He later exchanged into the Royal Australian Navy, married the reason for the exchange, and ultimately rose to become an Admiral. On the way to that eminence he had been the Navigating Officer in HMAS *Sydney* when she rounded up and sank the *Emden* in 1915: his occasional visits to this country, with a splendid Australian twang were always much enjoyed— as indeed were his two daughters' with their respective husbands. The youngest, Hugh, was perhaps potentially the most brilliant. While at school he had won a Westminster Gazette prize for Latin verse and had followed Harold to New College, Oxford with an Exhibition. When at Oxford he acquired a halfblue for tennis, wrote some pleasant verse and became a keen mountaineer. With George Mallory, Claude Elliot, Geof-

Ancestry and Early Years

frey Winthrop Young, Arnold Lunn and others he had already done some notable climbs in Snowdonia, the Lakes and the Mount Blanc Massif: after graduating he went to improve his French at Orthez with a view to the Diplomatic Service as a career, but unhappily lost his life climbing alone on the Pic du Midi d'Ossau.

My grandfather Pope, who had little to occupy his time and a fertile mind, took a great interest in his daughter's marriage settlement—in fact neither party had a great deal to settle: but that did not stop him from arguing vigorously on two particular counts: he was dead set against any investment in mortgages, and took a serious long range interest in the Kilravock inheritance, which at that time was a very faint possibility, though as will be seen later it became a real likelihood during the War. In the end he capitulated and the wedding took place with his blessing at Tring in July 1909. My father had by this time been a curate for nearly ten years and was on the lookout for a living. In due course, and not unassisted by the Rose connection he was presented to the north Hertfordshire living of Barkway-with-Reed (joint benefices were not so usual in 1909, and it is interesting to note that Buckland and Barley have now been tacked on): my parents moved into Barkway vicarage in October 1909, and I was born there three weeks late on 13 August 1910.

The Vicarage was a roomy modern house with indoor sanitation even if it lacked bathroom and lighting facilities, and my earliest recollection is the birth of my sister in April 1913: I am convinced that this was a genuine act of memory not inspired by 'grown-up talk'. My grandmother Pope had arrived as usual to be present at the birth, and on the day itself took me aged two years eight months out for a stroll in the garden. I fell down, scratched my knee and cried: she told me not to cry as I was a big

Left: *My father and myself, April 1913 in the Vicarage garden at Barkway.* Below: *Barkway Vicarage, Royston, Hertfordshire, my birthplace and home from 1910 to 1926.*

boy now and had a baby sister: I thought (as I still do) that her remark was a silly and irrelevant comment, and therefore it cannot have been inserted in my mind at a later date. I can also vaguely recall the Christening, mostly from the fact of my brother (eighteen months old at the most) staggering uncertainly from pew to pew round the font.

Life at Barkway was interspersed with visits to Tring and holidays at Kilravock, and these lasted till 1917 when my father was accepted as an army Chaplain and we moved to Kilravock for a whole year. During this time my youngest brother was born and naturally enough was named Hugh after his many Rose ancestors. Though it is not unusual to remember one's childhood as a series of fine sunny days, while I cannot recollect much in the way of rain, ice and snow figure large: I can still hear the scraping noise of lumps of ice as they drifted down the River Nairn when the January frosts first broke, and as vividly snow storms and blizzards in Hertfordshire.

Life at Kilravock was not greatly disturbed by the war; convalescing officers used to come and stay, for varying periods, mostly Australians whose company we enjoyed. At this time my eyes suffered strain from reading to myself, probably in bad light for it was dark by 3 pm in midwinter and hardly light till 10 am—and therefore I had to have my eyes tested. This involved a course of bella donna drops over several days and consequent visits to Inverness: the drops made it quite impossible for me to do lessons though I could see at long range out of doors. I was temporarily handed over to Campbell the keeper to accompany him on his rounds, thus establishing a friendship that lasted some 30 years and also provided me with a reasonably informed interest in nature.

There was one curious feature about life at Kilravock which impressed itself on me, even at the age of six, when my mother became noticeably pregnant as 1917 drew to a close and was far too busy with the new baby after his arrival to make the Sunday journey to Croy Presbyterian Church. As my grandfather never went it fell to the lot of my grandmother to take me with her to listen to the long service which lasted from 12 noon till 1.45 pm with eloquent prayers and a long and rigorous sermon from the Rev Charles Fraser who on other days of the week was a well known judge of fat cattle. More to the point, however, when we went to tea at the Manse he showed himself an excellent participant in children's games.

My grandmother always placed me in the centre seat of the front row of the gallery in church as if to indicate to all and sundry that I was, at least *pro tem*, the titular head of the clan. With the four senior males variously involved on active service on the Western front, at sea with the Grand Fleet and in India it must have seemed to outsiders a not unlikely prospect: in fact however three out of the four returned unscathed to civilian life, married and had families. Perhaps there was something prescient in my grandfather's intransigence about the marriage settlement.

Chapter 2

School days

My father's year as a Chaplain came to an end soon after the great retreat in March 1918 and we returned to Barkway where life went on much as before right through the armistice and peace celebrations till I went to Summer Fields in September 1919: my father always felt rather bad about deserting Lynam's which he had so greatly enjoyed, but he thought that it had grown much too big for a Preparatory School. I entered with a little French and rather less Latin but a good grounding in English History which had been driven home by my mother's insistence on the dates and wives of the Kings of England. So I did not start in the bottom form, and advanced with fair rapidity. Looking back on my four years there I think that I really enjoyed them and most certainly profited from them: the teaching, especially by Geoffrey Bolton and later by Rev Hugh Alington in the Vth form was magnificent. The competition too was keen, and in my last year certainly the majority of the top form moved on to their Public Schools with scholarships. Summer Fields however was by no means all work: we made plenty of amusements for ourselves in the long winter evenings, and the summer term was filled with bathing in the Cherwell, hammocks and gardens as well as organised games. It was perhaps a pity that the only one I got my colours for, Rugger, turned out to be of little practical use for a Carthusian, but many years later in Hong Kong it reaped its reward, when I met Harold Lee whose hard bullet head had crashed against mine in the scrum when we played Magdalen College School under $14\frac{1}{2}$, and who re-entered my life as the overlord of the Mandarin Hotel. Several long continuing friendships were formed, Peter Monie whose boys followed him there and whom we frequently used to meet as parents and latterly in Australia, Dick Usborne, the authority on P. G. Wodehouse and other contemporary authors who were certainly brought to our notice by Geoffrey Bolton's reading aloud: Edmund Gleadow with whom I shared a bedroom our first term, whose son is also my godson and with whom a desultory correspondence still goes on. The classical teaching was first rate at all levels, and the grammar and syntax drilled into us at that time served us well for the rest of our classical lives: it was from Geoffrey Bolton that I first got the idea that work was worthwhile as well as the need to be accurate. L. A. G. Strong, not yet a well known author, gave us a good foundation in written English too which, I hope, has lasted. It is doubtful whether I would have shone at mathematics whoever had taught me, but they remained a closed book till the glorious moment in 1925 when a credit in School Certificate lower maths relieved me of the need to tackle them in any form again. Summer Fields also did particularly well by us in getting us through most of childhood's diseases with the result that after my first quarter at Charterhouse I hardly missed a day's school.

Form progress up the school was liable to be rapid, with double or even triple promotions quite normal. The result was that when just 12 years of age I found myself, to my own and others' surprise in September 1922, the bottom member of the top (Vth) form and being taught by the formidable though essentially lovable character the Headmaster (known to us all as the Bear). The grounding by Geoffrey Bolton stood us in good stead and most were able to weather the storms that inaccuracy of translation, false sequence of tenses and similar sins provoked. It must have been at this point that I struck out on my own line and said very firmly that I wanted to follow my father to Charterhouse, and not my uncles to Eton: I learned many years later that the Bear had in fact labelled me for a forlorn 12 year old attempt at Winchester! Fortunately my plea was accepted and the following summer three of us were escorted by C. E. Smyth, himself an Old Carthusian, to take the scholarship examination in the great Chamber of the Old Charterhouse, my first impression of the haven where I have now been living happily since 1972. We were all successful, myself 5th, Dick Usborne 7th and Geoffrey Parish 10th though I was almost certainly pushed up by bonus marks for being a 12 year old. All in all Summer Fields had achieved a good result that year even by its own exacting standards, the unusual if not positively unique event of a bracketed first scholarship at Eton by Michael McKenna and Bernard Burrows together with four others on the list and one each at Harrow, Marlborough and Westminster.

What gave me the greatest pleasure however was dividing McKenna and Burrows in the final form examination by coming second: but sadly I derived less pleasure from what should have been a successful cricket season. Having being appointed (for no known reason) captain of the third XI I batted reasonably well against the Dragon School, but had my bowling knocked sideways by the opposing captain—Oliver Van Oss whom I met for the first time. My batting secured me a brief promotion to the second XI for a match at Horris Hill where I managed disastrously to drop three catches and then went on to run myself out before receiving a ball. I therefore resumed my place in the third XI!

Finally our holidays at Kilravock came to an end shortly after 1920 when my grandparents returned south to Tring: we spent one summer holiday there, another very enjoyably at Horton-in-Ribblesdale where my father did a leisurely 'locum' and another less happily at Fairbourne in North Wales. The other holidays were spent almost entirely at Barkway. At first there was very little in the way of co-eval company: most of the neighbouring clergy were either elderly or childless or both, the more substantial houses within walking distance were equally childless till first the Vickers family came to Newsells then the young Crossmans to Cokenach both within a couple of miles, and just as we were leaving in 1926 came the Chapmans to Barkway House at the end of Vicarage Lane. The Vickers were a charming family, each one a little younger than the opposite number among ourselves, and I became and remained devoted to Dinah who was, so to speak, my equivalent. The Crossmans provided two girls a bit younger than me and my brother Tom but just right for my sister. Mrs Vickers soon organised a small school which some half a dozen attended and they were well taught and grounded by Miss Skally. Mrs Chapman, a war widow, arrived with her daughters Elizabeth and Frida with whom we were already acquainted from occasional visits to old Mr and Mrs Hall, her aunt and uncle. The girls were invaluable allies for tennis and a rough form of croquet played on the lower lawn with a pond in close proximity. Together Elizabeth and Frida both remained our close friends until Frida's sadly early death during the war, but fortunately Elizabeth is still with us—being someone of whom I can truthfully say that I cannot remember a time when I did not know her. In due course they married the two Dimsdale brothers who when children were left fatherless too and lived at Little Hormead, which came within range as soon as we had learned to cycle, thus greatly extending our radius of friends. I suppose that there were in fact quite a lot of contemporaries all round us, but we did not seem to know them at all well, and my recollection of Christmas parties is of vast gatherings of complete strangers who all seemed to know each other (possibly from the hunting field) but not us!

As Preparatory Schools went Summer Fields was on the large side, and the change to Charterhouse and a house of just over 50 boys was not as traumatic as it might otherwise have been.

There were unfortunately twelve of us in our first year in Robinites, and at first I was very much the odd man out for games, but the House Captain, Kenneth Nation Dixon, one of the kindliest of persons, realised this and I was put into Second Peripatetics, admittedly the elderly dregs of football but nevertheless cheerful good company, also not unduly worried at losing on occasion by some 18 goals to the stronger sides. I did find the rigorous seclusion into one's own house hard to take: we mixed freely in school hours but any association outside them was frowned upon. Indeed our Robinite Housemaster, Col F. W. B. Smart who deserves more than passing mention, did not like us even to take part in out of school activities such as debates, photography and some other clubs (though not many others existed). Hence we lived as a closed community, always at a greater distance from the school than most and for some time much looked down upon. It did however teach us to get on with our contemporaries and a *modus vivendi* was established; also the scholars of each year were expected to help the weaker vessels with their 'banco' (home work) and I think I can say that we did it gladly.

Col Smart was a delightful, if mildly eccentric character about whom his colleagues were continually inventing stories. 'Was it you, my friend, or your brother who was killed in the War?' was perhaps the best known and most often quoted. (One that I heard from his own lips was a demand to a recalcitrant member of his house not to look at him in that tone of voice.) He had a wife who was kindness itself and two daughters, who were generally away at school, and whom I hardly knew till some of us were invited after leaving school to return for holiday dances. The Colonel despite his outward appearance of vagueness had a very good idea of what was going on in the house, and I was not a bit surprised when years later his elder daughter told me that he was of infallibly sound judgement in sorting out her boy friends.

After two years communal life in Long Room having by then acquired a Senior Scholarship (to much general surprise) and enough School Certificate Credits to bypass Responsions or Little-go, and having seen the last of mathematics, I was promoted to a Study and to the Under Sixth. The pleasure of a study was diminished by having to share it with one of the few Robinites I cordially disliked—he joined the Oxford Group Movement later—but the Under Sixth inspired by Humphrey Grose-Hodge was sheer delight. My previous form masters had been Rev E. E. Bryant, then in his last of 25 years of dedicated service, who debunked much of what we learned at our Preparatory Schools, referring to us scholars generically as 'sheep' or 'salaried idlers'. He was reported, falsely I believe, to have felt himself failing in his duty if he did not get us beaten for idleness by the headmaster, but for all that we were devoted to him. The next year we were divided between Messrs Radcliffe and Gibson and my lot was pitched with the 'Radder', who had also taught my father. He was a gentle and kindly man whose main interests seemed to be good manners and Greek accents. Grose-Hodge really opened up the world of classical culture and scholarship to us, and was prepared to enlarge on any topic. (I was lucky enough two years later to be sent on a Greek cruise by my aunt, and to find him a fellow passenger.) During this academic year we had our first taste of the scholarship of (Sir) Frank Fletcher, the headmaster, reading Homer with him at sufficient speed to keep interest alive.

Meanwhile in Robinites there was a change, athletically at least, for the better: Richard Dyson my fellow classic, Douglas Morton and John Kell were all achieving distinction in different ways, and Robinites was no longer the butt of the description of Charterhouse as consisting of ten houses and a 'totherun'.* Whether it improved in all respects is a moot point: nevertheless the athletes predominated as a class of supermen—and it was most interesting to find on arriving a few years later at Brasenose that by reason of the great number of blues of all kinds presently there that they were taken very much for granted and consequently threw their weight about much less than their younger Robinite equivalents (it is only fair to say that Dyson and Morton were honourable exceptions to this

*Prep. School

stricture). Near the end of my fourth year I became a house monitor together with Noel Carlile and the following years I was allocated a study to myself. Meanwhile we had exchanged the luxuriance of Grose-Hodge for the more exacting pedantry of A. L. Irvine universally known (with deep affection) as the Uncle. He and the headmaster taught us turn and turn about, and were perfect foils for each other: and I could never conjure up the idea of the Uncle teaching Plato or Browning, or of Frank Fletcher taking us through an odious book of classical syntax perpetrated by Buckland Green or the life and works of William Morris. Thus we had the best of both worlds, and Charterhouse featured very high in the University lists (which then meant either Oxford or Cambridge) of Scholarships. I was of course still a year younger than my contemporary scholars, and had reconciled myself to staying on an extra year and, hopefully, picking up a scholarship (possibly a closed one) in December 1928. Apart from Richard Dyson all those competing seriously for awards had got them by January.

The next school quarter was a dark and miserable one only enlivened by a production by Lionel Hale of *Bulldog Drummond* (he had already been largely responsible for a Hamlet in modern dress and totally so for a Rhesus): he cast me as Denny the devoted manservant, and this gave rise to one of the 'Uncle's' numberless good natured jibes to the effect that I was now well cast for life. It was a spirited production, though it was almost spoilt by an epidemic of mumps which ran through the more important characters. Drummond himself (played by John Fletcher) was most suspiciously round in the face for the second performance, but perhaps the star performance of all was the stage management of (Sir) E. G. Tuckwell. My parents had taken themselves off for a winter holiday in Jamaica with my younger uncle at King's House, and without consulting them I decided to get away for a week by having a try for Oxford: filial feeling made me put Christ Church first, even though Richard Dyson was competing there, and the rest of the group followed with Brasenose at the end for no other reason than that Duggie Morton was going there as a commoner and I was on particularly bad terms with him in the house. I enjoyed my week away and calmly went back for the remainder of the quarter without fears or hopes, when quite out of the blue a letter arrived from Brasenose. It was in manuscript from Principal Sampson, and only legible when read at right angles, but it offered me a scholarship. My surprise was only equalled by that of my housemaster and the 'Uncle' (Frank Fletcher at least on the surface was better at disguising his feelings): the latter in fact went down to the Sanatorium and said to the mumpers 'Stubbs has surprised the world'! It is only fair to add at this point that I never for one moment regretted this curious piece of good luck—and that Morton and I never had another discordant word.

When my parents returned there was a rapid three power conference between them, Charterhouse and Brasenose, and as a result it was agreed that I should stay at school for a sixth year (with the implied reversion of the headship of the school and of course of Robinites as well).

I duly became a school monitor and settled into a pleasantly idle summer quarter, there being no leaving exhibition as yet to pursue. Not surprisingly I did not feature very high in the Sixth Form order, the chief surprise however being the remarkable performance of John Hunt, for whom the Uncle had little respect, and it is believed, had written a bad report which had to be retracted. John who was a considerable athlete and a very tidy scholar was not at all fluent in form which may well have created an impression of lack of interest.

My first quarter as head of the school passed off quietly and without incident, but not so the second which coincided with the Dutch Exhibition at Burlington House. There was some agitation in the upper échelons of the school to get permission to go up to London for it, and I extracted a reluctant permission from the headmaster for this purpose, but it was hedged around with conditions which I should have seen were impossible to enforce. I did, however, and this was my mistake, circulate a notice saying that I hoped that all those going would at least put in an appearance at Burlington House (I think about 90% did): but unhappily some travelled back with some junior master(s) and both sides talked. Rumours naturally started and though for some time I tried to brazen it out with Frank Fletcher in the end I was cornered and convicted of deceiving him and abusing my trust. He therefore called for my resignation which I could not well refuse but would not accept my suggestion that Michael Whittington, the Gownboy head monitor, should follow me. Instead he indicated his intention to appoint John Hunt who was not head of his house (Saunderites) and was already about to be Captain of Cricket. I suppose for a short time afterwards I was something of a celebrity, having 'carried the can' for a large number of senior contemporaries. As the quarter was almost at an end, two further ripe scandals blew up, each at the same time, and I made a particular point of showing my (quite real) affection and respect for John Hunt. Looking back I fear that he came out of it worst of all: the burden was too heavy and both his cricket and his work suffered. But as far as I was concerned it cemented a friendship that went on, and was only broken by his untimely death. These events I am pleased to say did not spoil my own friendship with the Saunderite head monitor, Eddie Tuckwell, who like myself was doing a sixth year.

For my final quarter, and now out of the limelight, everyone was kind and sympathetic—A predecessor head of the school described me to his successor in Gownboys as 'a wormy little man' which of course got back to me with the speed of light but that was about all. I was profoundly sorry for John Kell who came down a couple of days after the debacle and hailed me across Under Green as the head of the school: he was much more embarrassed than I, and later wrote me a charming little letter of apology. I worked hard in the Easter holiday including ten days spent at Kilravock where breakfast seldom came on till 10.00 am, and was more than gratified when the examiners (A. R. Ramsay from Magdalene and

Maurice Bowra from Wadham) awarded me the third leaving exhibition.

Shortly before the end of the summer quarter almost by accident Michael Whittington and I agreed to go off on a camping holiday in Scotland later in August after the OTC camp, and this was the first of a long run of holidays by road or canal that were the highlights of our long vacations.

Frank Fletcher and I parted on good terms (he had always been kind and thoughtful) though I was not altogether happy in one sense with his final quotation, 'Nothing in his life became him like the leaving it' in relation to my previous eminence.

Mention of OTC camp brings my mind back to a very fortunate decision made early in my time in the Corps. The Robinite platoon complained that I was always out of step, and it was suggested that I should join the Signal Section where such niceties did not exist. This I did and so fell at once under the spell of P. C. Fletcher who had been a Lancashire Brigade Signal Officer during the war and had been awarded a Military Cross: he possessed a very real insight into the principles of communications. With the elementary equipment at our disposal (which included a 30 Watt wireless transmitter of the oldest possible vintage) he brought us up to a high standard of performance in both buzzer and visual signalling, but more important he made us understand the basic principles: the success in World War II of several of his cadets must, I am convinced, be ascribed to his initial training. I ended up as an Under Officer i.c. Signal Section, a new appointment and one of which I was highly appreciative. Incidentally he and my parents had the common interest of owning ancient Trojan cars.

Membership of the Signal Section had three 'perks', no rifle on parade, a leather instead of a webbing belt, and permission automatically to have a bicycle at school.

Before leaving the subject of Charterhouse I feel I should say something about the principal boy characters of my time: within the house I was under five head monitors, George Berry, quiet and gentle who went from Oxford into the family wine business and was killed in the desert, S. N. V. Sutton a classical scholar and entomologist who spent all his teaching life at Campbell College Belfast, C. P. Hierneiss a Dutchman who went back from Wadham to the Dutch Bar, Cyril Wild who like his brothers had been at Summer Fields with me—and subsequently at Brasenose too; after a distinguished career in business and with the army in the Far East he survived Japanese captivity only to be killed in an aircraft accident in 1946 at Hong Kong: my immediate predecessor was Richard Dyson: a model to all loyal Carthusians of whom I will only say that he may well be thought to have been the best Carthusian cricketer not to have got his colours.

It was a piece of good fortune that much of our final quarter was occupied by preparations for 'the Charterhouse Masque': this performance, first introduced at the School's Tercentenary in 1911 has been

Our next home, Easthampstead Rectory, Bracknell, Berkshire (1926 to 1938). The home which had distinct touches of 'pre-Raphaelite' style about it has now disappeared under the spread of the new town, though the church, equally pre-Raphaelite still survives.

repeated every five years or so—wartime excepted—and consisted of a number of scenes featuring Carthusian worthies or incidents in the school's history. As time went on it had developed and been very much improved from the theatrical and presentation point of view by rewriting by Hugh Trevor Roper (Lord Dacre) and others. A number of us senior boys were entrusted in 1929 with a highly dramatic scene in which Judge Jefferies tries to intimidate the Governors. (For better or for worse it has in more recent performances been entrusted to the teaching staff.) The whole production was in the hands of one of the most remarkable members of Brooke Hall,* Alf Tressler who reduced the absolute early chaos of some 300 performers to precision of words and movement in a few rehearsals simply by his force of personality.

During my years at Charterhouse my father had moved to the Christ Church living of Easthampstead in Berkshire, and we left Barkway with very mixed feelings and found a very different holiday life. The Rectory, the Church and Easthampstead Park itself, where the Marquess of Downshire and his stepmother lived were all Victorian buildings, the product of an earlier Marchioness and a Rector, Osborne Gordon who were both inspired by Ruskin and the Pre Raphaelites: the most outstanding feature in the Church was some excellent stained glass by Burne Jones. Easthampstead as a parish was a curious mixture of town (the western

*Generic title for Masters

end of Bracknell) ribbon development along roads leading to Crowthorne and Bagshot and the ancillaries of two large houses, Easthampstead and South Hill Parks: it was a good deal more advanced liturgically than Barkway, but less so than some of the neighbouring parishes whose more moderate worshippers tended to come to Easthampstead when a more than usually 'spiky' service was due in their own churches. From our point of view as schoolchildren it was a great improvement for there were several families more or less contemporary (with whom we have kept in touch ever since), plenty of opportunities for tennis, mixed hockey and later, dances. When my brothers and I became undergraduates and were home for long stretches of vacation we were in considerable demand as our male contemporaries went mostly into the army or business and so away.

Chapter 3

Oxford in general

Apart from the quotation from *Macbeth* to which I have referred earlier, Frank Fletcher in saying goodbye to me mentioned that Brasenose was a good teaching college. My first five terms were spent in reading for Classical Honour Moderations with Maurice Platnauer and were very much of a continuation of VIth form work; they resulted in a Second Class than which I had never expected anything better. It was not untypical that the last set of Latin verses I had shown up to Maurice contained a line with six and a half feet!

The dozen of us who worked through Mods together produced only one First, and he went over to Law, but a large proportion of seconds of whom two eventually got firsts in the final school of Lit. Hum. (Ancient History and Philosophy, or 'Greats'.) All in all we were very well taught in both schools, and apart from my philosophy tutors with whom I had no mutual affinity whatever (and in one case a cordial personal antipathy) there was a real and successful attempt to make us use our minds. Furthermore Brasenose was richer perhaps than many other colleges in bachelor dons living in, who took an interest in the social activities of the college as a whole not restricting themselves to their own pupils: Dr Stallybrass, known to generations as 'Sonners' as well as Maurice, Michael Holroyd the Ancient Historian and Leif Egeland, the junior law tutor were indefatigable with their entertainment. Indeed Sonners was believed to have had a penchant for finding vacancies in the College for potential blues and for cossetting them when they arrived but I do not recall any of his dinner parties that I attended as being overly athletic. In fact in my undergraduate days I found the College, which was full of blues of all sorts much less athletically hide bound than Charterhouse had been: but more to the point there always seemed to be room, and a welcome, for the thoroughly mediocre player like myself in the second soccer and hockey teams. Sonners was very much a college figure (not that this prevented him later becoming an outstanding Vice-Chancellor) but it was probably true to say that he greatly preferred members of the College to be engaged in College rather than external activities. Accordingly he did not really approve of my two major activities, the O.U.O.T.C. and Freemasonry, though he never allowed them to mar our good relations.

Before embarking on what have been among the greatest influences on my life it is time to say something about the personnel of the College apart from the dons. The overall strength was never as much as 200, with an intake of about 60 each October: most remained up for three years, but the Greats school took four and, besides us, there were always some doing a further extra year such as B.C.L. or medical students with quite a number who had been accepted for the Indian or Colonial Services and were spending an extra year as probationers learning the appropriate language and suitably fitting themselves into the then current phrase 'as blues to govern blacks'. Most undergraduates at that time spent two years in College and then moved out into licensed lodgings for their final year(s). Brasenose had a rather small hall and freshmen mostly dined in a large lecture room, looked after by two superb College servants, Herbert and Ernest Hunt from whom we all absorbed much College tradition and in many cases much college beer as well. 'Freshers Hall' did much to inculcate from the very start the lively College spirit. There was indeed some space in Hall itself for freshmen, and I often dined there though on reflection I think it was a mistake.

Like several other Oxford Colleges (though not I think Cambridge ones) we had a strong territorial connection—ours was Lancashire and Cheshire, and one of the College's source of strength was its succession of fine scholars and athletes from Manchester Grammar School. By and large we were very much a British community with a small number of well liked coloured students and a very few others from around Europe: the Rhodes scholars were invariably of Anglo-Saxon origin and generally fitted into place with the rest of us.

Towards the end of Trinity Term 1930 James Morgan who was doing Mods also mentioned to me that he had become a Freemason and that I might like to follow suit; he also put forward the idea early in the following term that we should suggest to Neville Sabine, a Mancunian classic that we should look for digs as a threesome. Eventually we found a house in St John's Street, much nearer central Oxford than most digs, came to terms with Miss Lawson our landlady and spent two very happy and harmonious years together: James Morgan was already engaged to Cicely Cobb of Lady Margaret Hall, but Neville and I remained, at least intermittentently, heartwhole. Our interests were sufficiently diverse in other respects for us all to have friends in and out of Brasenose, and 28 St John Street was always a very cheerful meeting place: Miss Lawson was prone to describing it as 'a clean hairy 'ouse', but like many others we had to take our baths in College.

It would be both tedious and undiplomatic to the reader, as inevitably someone would be left out, if names were dropped about our contemporaries. But the legal profession is still star-studded with Sonners' pupils, and other walks of life are well adorned by Brasenose men too.

ROYAL CORPS OF SIGNALS

Earlier I mentioned the OTC: I was recruited into the Signal Section by my cousin Bill Stubbs of Corpus with whom I had maintained communication as schoolboys between Radley and Charterhouse. In the Section I found several other old friends, four Carthusians as well as George Marfell from Wrekin with whom I had worked at school OTC camps. The Signal Section provided scope for learning to ride (and drive a six horse cable waggon) in pleasant surroundings 'for free': but it was more concerned with the technical side of communications culminating each year in a setpiece competition against Cambridge. I was selected for the team twice (but honesty compels me to admit that we lost on both occasions) and at the end of my second year found myself the Company Sergeant Major. It was however clear that as the 1931 depression deepened the OTC was going to suffer cuts: in fact the Oxford Signal Section was axed though its opposite number at Cambridge was preserved. For an undergraduate the Territorial Army had little attraction as term time made it virtually impossible to attend drills and the unit's normal activities with regularity. Some of my friends however had discovered an attractive alternative—the Supplementary Reserve Class B where training consisted of attachment to a regular unit for two or three weeks in the year, literally of one's own choosing. I applied for a commission in the Royal Corp of Signals through the OTC Headquarters, filled in the necessary forms and had a medical examination. It is worth recording that I went to the prescribed doctor wearing an Old Carthusian tie: we compared dates and he said that he remembered my father as a contemporary adding 'Don't bother to take your coat off' and thereon I was signed fit for active service. My commission came through dated 13 January 1932 after I had a successful and friendly interview with the Commanding Officer 1st Divisional Signals at Aldershot to which I was allotted for training. Normally there would have been a probationary period of three weeks followed by a fortnight's annual training but in the financial stringency then operating they were amalgamated. It was a step which I never regretted: most of my brother officers in the SR were GPO experts on telecommunication (though I doubt if the word had been invented by then) and most rather older. The young regular officers were helpful and friendly—indeed I still number some of them as friends; no doubt quietly they regarded a classical scholar as an oddity, but a pleasant one.

The unit was still horsed, and a good deal of time had to be spent in riding school and stables, rather less on signal communications. But the new CO Lt Col Barker took a practical interest in us, and I still remember vividly some 50 years later a conversation we had in his car as he drove me to see some kind of demonstration. He had already discerned that I was completely untechnical and remarked that this would not really matter, as the GPO officers, he said, would supply that deficiency, but he said they would take offence and be hurt when told to 'bugger off' by a Brigadier, whereas I would take it 'all in the day's march'. It was advice that I never forgot and never ceased to be grateful for.

The type of training varied of course with the time of year selected (we lost our horses quite soon) and I had an interesting variety from individual trade training among operators to section work in a Brigade Signal Section or as a Despatch Rider at a Divisional HQ office on manoeuvres. My annual trainings went on till shortly before the outbreak of war when for reasons again connected with the OTC I found myself transferred from the SR to the TA.

After my first year Freemasonry began to be a consuming interest, but I will deal with this later in its own right, whilst I round off this brief account of my undergraduate life. I have already touched on the dons with whom I came in contact, and also sketchily, with my undergraduate contemporaries, but there was a third estate of the College realm which should certainly not be passed over in silence: I refer to the College servants whose long service of loyalty to the College supplied a feeling of permanence to us all. Whether it was the Lodge or the Hall staff and messengers or individual Scouts presiding with ample dignity over their respective staircases and helping as much as anyone to bring up undergraduates according to the old traditions of the College, all played their part enthusiastically and with precision. I was fortunate in the two Scouts I had during my two years in College, Benham who moved on to become second in command to Harris in the College Lodge and old Charlie Weeden whose capacity for beer was reputed to have already eaten through two linings of his stomach.

St Paul's School OTC officers in 1936, left to right: F. L. Dawney, A. G. Harbord, R. L. James, L. E. M Savill and myself: the photograph was taken by G. P. Eisen, one of my first pupils with whom I maintained contact for many years both in the Army and in Masonry.

Soon after the start of my second year I was advised from home that one of my Bigge cousins had arrived at Somerville College from Clifton High School for Girls, and also told that I should go and call on her. In those unliberated days this was quite an exercise but I did it, and greatly daring invited Ellen, suitably chaperoned of course, to tea in College. This was the beginning of a happy association not only for the two of us but also more generally between the two Colleges: and the friendships which started in undergraduate days have continued. The social climax in Oxford came, fortuitously but happily, with the College Commemoration Ball at the end of what was for most of us our last term.

But not for me: I had tried unsuccessfully to get various teaching jobs: with only a second in Mods, and little athletic achievements of moment I was not a likely candidate and having failed over half a dozen times I thought I would try to stay up for a fifth year, read another Final school and see whether with this broadened platform I had more success. Principal Sampson, kind as ever, agreed to extend my scholarship—indeed to increase it when Charterhouse cut off my leaving exhibition. Living out of College was known to be cheaper for a graduate as digs were not so strictly controlled, and my father in fact had very little more to pay out. I selected Modern History, partly through *pietas* to my grandfather, partly because some of its more theoretical elements overlapped with Greats, and partly because I reckoned that I could bluff my way through with only a very sketchy knowledge of the later periods. The gamble came off, and I went into the schools with the comfortable knowledge that I had a job waiting for me at St Paul's as assistant to Philip Whitting who had already made his mark on the scholarship lists of both universities.

I got a third second—three years work compressed into one which nearly killed me, and I left Oxford a mere shadow at 9 stone 13. Nonetheless it had been a good year, and the Modern History School with its relatively slow tempo—and I may be forgiven for saying so its relatively much lower standard than Greats—finally rounded off my education, and made me a good deal better prepared to pass it on to others.

Chapter 4

Oxford and Freemasonry

I returned to Oxford from my first long vacation with a rather vague recollection that I had undertaken to James Morgan that I would go, under his sponsorship, into the Apollo University Lodge, with very little comprehension of what that entailed. I had however learned during the summer that my father had taken a similar plunge very recently into the Wellesley Lodge in our neighbouring village of Crowthorne, and that, with my mother's evident approval of his actions, was encouraging. Anyhow I was given and carried our some rather vague instructions, presented myself in broad daylight and full evening dress on a Saturday evening in October at the Masonic Hall then situated in the High Street. There I met Lionel Hale in the same state as myself with a number of other semi-bewildered undergraduates who were given to understand that they were the evening's candidates. Before going into the Lodge Room we were harangued by two other characters, both then unknown to us; the first was the Tyler, Tom Stilgoe who spent the rest of the week as doorkeeper in the Examination Schools just opposite. The other was lame and elderly, known to undergraduates who treated him on equal terms as 'PC', and by their elders with awe and reverence as Very Worshipful Brother Sir Colville Smith. (Incidentally it was claimed that when PC was Master of the Bicester Hounds as an undergraduate Stilgoe had been one of the hunt servants: I know of no positive evidence but neither side denied it.) We were initiated by E. P. Hewetson, a master at St Edward's School and before that a triple blue, including one as a very fast bowler!

SIR COLVILLE SMITH

In due course the natural progression of passing and raising, in similar numbers, took place, and the various leading lights in the Lodge came to be known. PC was the outstanding figure; and calls for further description. He had already been Secretary of the Apollo for many years, apart from one he spent as Centenary Master when without doubt he was also *de facto* Secretary. He had also served some years as Provincial Grand Secretary of Oxfordshire, Secretary of the Royal Masonic Benevolent Institution, Provincial Grand Mark Master for Cornwall (his native county), Inspector General of a group of Rose Croix Chapters in and around the diocese of Oxford (this was I believe the only purely Masonic office he gave up when he became Grand Secretary in 1917). Every other University Masonic body had him either as Secretary or as Treasurer, and because he was indispensable to them they had moved their meetings to Saturday evenings so that he could get down from Freemasons' Hall in London to organise and dominate the proceedings. Outside of Masonry he was the Treasurer of the Bullingdon Club during its periods of activity, and the keeper of its records and continuity on the number of occasions when it was temporarily banned by the proctors. He had also been Treasurer of 'Vincents' the even better known athletes' club and must have been almost unique in controlling two such disparate organisations. He kept a set of rooms in the same block as the Masonic Hall where undergraduate members of the Lodge were made welcome, both after Lodge meetings and at Sunday tea when he kept 'open' house before going to St John's College where he almost invariably dined as a member of the Senior Common Room. After we had gone down from Oxford, and even more so when I went to Great Queen Street, I learned what an awe inspiring figure he was in the Craft, but to the junior members of the Apollo he was always kind and friendly, and one from whom by inference almost more than directly we acquired a lot of Masonic knowledge. In the Lodge itself he was a splendid figure, supported by his two sticks, and with an accompanying stammer that made him all the more impressive, he dominated the scene, which he had largely set himself by the instructions given on Sunday mornings (as soon as the University sermon could decently be deemed to be over) by way of preparation for the next Saturday's meeting. If the practice period passed off well as it often did copies of the 'lectures' would be handed round, and read round the Lodge, so that we learned a good deal more than just Masonic ritual. The real point however was that with the rapid turnover of undergraduates and the large number of candidates always avaliable there was always plenty to do. In this respect we in the Apollo considered ourselves much better off than our counterpart the Isaac Newton University Lodge at Cambridge, where it was not only possible but actually usual practice for non residents to hold office in Lodge. At Oxford the reverse was the case and it was an absolute if unwritten rule that no one not in residence (ie within three miles of Carfax, the city centre) could hold office. So promotion was rapid and I became Assistant Secretary (which meant counting heads for dinner) after only one year, Junior Deacon after two, then Senior Deacon. What happened next was quite contrary to what I have just said. When I was first in London, the circumstances were a little unusual. PC was about to return to the Master's chair in the following year to celebrate a jubilee, the intended Senior Warden (Jack Wolfenden) was on his way to Uppingham to become headmaster, and the Master Elect, T. D. Weldon, another philosopher like Jack was one who regarded rules as guide lines rather than categorical imperatives. So to my great delight, and ultimately to my even greater advantage, I spent a year as Senior Warden, managing to attend all meetings and rehearsals as well. By this time I had become a member of all the University Masonic bodies and was holding office in each: this took up about six of the eight Saturdays of the full University term. Promotion came pretty fast in them all, though there was no bar to office to non-residents such as existed in the Lodge itself. Consequently I went through the most senior office of the Mark and Rose Croix degrees before reaching this position in the Craft.

The other degrees seldom had an attendance of more than 20, and in almost all cases the meeting was followed by dinner privately in one of the Senior Common Rooms. This introduction to good living was doubly pleasant, not only for the excellent food and outstanding wines all for 12/6d but also for the opportunity of getting to know the senior members of the University who were our titular hosts or fellow guests. Magdalen, St John's, Queen's saw us frequently, New College, Brasenose and Balliol less often: to each of them there was access, thanks to a senior member of the college who organised the evening. Speeches were practically non existent and if anything other than port and good conversation occurred after dinner it was generally a few rubbers of bridge. I remember the case of a doctor who was being unusually abstemious, and on being rallied about it explained that he wanted an early night as he had to attend an execution at the gaol the next morning! (That remark could only have been made on one of the rare occasions when we did not meet on a Saturday or possibly after a meeting of the Churchill Lodge which was largely a dons' organisation with a sprinkling of the legal and medical profession, in the city, and dined in much the same way as we did.)

The Churchill and the Apollo interconnected in membership in very much the same way as the Alma Mater and the Isaac Newton did at Cambridge. It was helpful both ways but particularly so for the Apollo which was perennially short of prospective Masters, and as often as not had to persuade them to serve a second year. The Churchill, named after a Deputy Grand Master rather than the great family had started in Henley as a lodge for the 'county' generally but operated without much success: indeed it went into decay almost at once and was revived in 1850, from which it dates its centenary, by W Bro R.J. Spiers, the Deputy Provincial Grand Master of the time who also started the Coeur de Lion Preceptory. By the early twentieth century both had come to be, in effect, University connected bodies.

The junior members of the Apollo quite soon learned of the existence of Grand Lodge from PC; they were perhaps slower to learn about the Provincial Grand Lodge of Oxfordshire as we did not have much contact with the city or county Lodges except at the installation meeting when the Masters came by invitation as they still do 50 years later. We knew however that our well-loved Chaplain, Rev Thomas Trotter Blockley who sat on the Master's right at dinner and always sang the Initiate's song was the Deputy Provincial Grand Master. We later came to know that the Provincial Grand Master was Captain Mark Ulick Weyland, though we seldom saw him. He was universally known as 'Wiggy' from his collection of auburn wigs and he presided with dignity and an aroma of gin, over

Provincial Grand Lodge, and appeared occasionally, it was rumoured, without warning at other installations where he insisted on installing the Master in the strict *Emulation* working or what he believed was strict *Emulation*: so it was small wonder that he left the Apollo to Bro Blockley who followed the *Oxford* Ritual where it was not at complete variance with Wiggy's prejudices! The Provincial Grand Secretary, J. A. Tawney, a banker in the city, was, like his son and myself, a member of Brasenose: he was always kind, and was succeeded by Douglas Amery also of Brasenose who merits more than a passing notice. Amery was a Lecturer in the Economics of Agriculture, and once told us that he had taken up the study by accident when in hospital during the war. His war record in the Hampshires was outstanding and he seemed to have a charmed life till 1917, neither enemy action nor sickness interrupting it. He ascribed his good health to a daily bottle of Burgundy; but in the end however he was very badly wounded by machine gun fire, but said his survival in No Man's Land was again due to Burgundy. It was during his period in hospital that he read, in boredom, an old book on the economic theory of agriculture and, there and then, decided to make it his life's work. He had a great following among the students working for a Diploma in Agriculture (who would probably nowadays seek places at Cirencester, and by whom he was always known as 'The General'). In due course, and on the retirement of Brother Blockley he was appointed Provincial Grand Master, an unusual jump for a Provincial Grand Secretary—but of course one had to understand that the General was an unusual man! I spent several nights camping with the General and his family in the New Forest in my undergraduate days and so laid the foundation for a firm friendship that lasted until his early death in 1955.

I have not mentioned that as well as tails and white ties the Apollo officers wore knee breeches and buckled shoes (white waistcoats too and none of the nonsense about black ones). Douglas Amery who was a Past Master as well as being Provincial Grand Master observed a curious convention in this: if he came as a PM he wore undress regalia—collar rather than chain and knee breeches: but if as Provincial Grand Master full dress, chain and trousers—which is all very logical if one comes to think about it. We dined at the Randolph Hotel in Beaumont Street which was right across Oxford from the Masonic Hall and most of us pulled on a pair of grey flannel trousers over our breeches for the walk through the City, which we accepted as perfectly normal procedure.

To be invited by PC to join the Coeur de Lion Preceptory was generally considered to be a great honour, as he was not only the Provincial Prior but its senior member in rank if not in time; I was therefore fortunate that the privilege came my way in 1934. My mother performed her Lenten penance by making my tunic and mantle out of what she informed me was Nun's Veiling, and later on they were handed to the Preceptory as in the fulness of time regrettably they no longer fitted me but are probably still in use.

Captain Weyland had been succeeded as Provincial Grand Master by Bro Blockley who declined to take on as Grand Superintendent of the Royal Arch and this resulted in a division at the head of the Province which lasted for many years and, in my view, stunted the growth of Royal Arch Masonry.

In most of the other branches of Masonry practised in the Thames Valley, Berkshire and Oxfordshire have been close together, and in some cases Buckinghamshire was included as well. This gave a pleasant parallel with my Grandfather's bishopric of Oxford, and no doubt provides the present day Masonic office bearer with no less a burden than the diocessan.

When I first entered Mark Masonry Canon F.J.C. Gillmor of Reading was Provincial Grand Master and Bro Blockley his Deputy, but when the Canon died Blockley gave up too and there came on the scene in 1934 a comparatively unknown figure though he had been initiated in the Apollo before 1914, Major Robert Lindsay Loyd. He was unquestionably one of the greatest Masons of his generation, but though he rose to the greatest eminence in all sorts of directions he never lost his affection for and interest in 'Berks and Oxon'. He blew a keen wind of change through the Mark Province (his Craft and Royal Arch activities were rather more restricted to Berkshire and London).

Our ruler in the Ancient and Accepted Rite was Lt Col du Pre Powney, whom I am afraid we tended to consider as a tiresome little man. This view was undoubtedly held by PC too, who generally managed whenever he knew that Col Powney was coming to persuade the Grand Secretary General to come too: this move overtrumped the Inspector General even if it did not silence him. As already mentioned, PC was himself Provincial Prior (there were but three Preceptories) and Bobbie Loyd succeeded him with much the same effect as in the Mark.

Masonic life within the University of the 1930s was full and lively; it is true that there was a good deal of wastage in the Apollo itself by members going down and often abroad, who did not pick up their Masonry again perhaps for years. But even though there may be some justification for describing the Apollo as a 'sausage machine' one can adapt Sir Winston Churchill's remark and proudly say 'Some machine some sausages'! Those who went forward into other degrees by and large remained active in all things and though the Lodges etc fell into desuetude during the 1939-1945 war, as they had done in the First World War, there was a sufficient nucleus to be able to revive them by 1948, and by curious coincidence in both cases, a Masonic administrator was at the back of the revival, to which we shall come in due course.

Chapter 5

St Paul's School

When he appointed me to the staff of St Paul's School, John Bell the High Master had told me that I would be teaching the Classical Seventh (St Paul's goes up to the Eighth Form), but I found on arrival that this had been altered and that I was now to be the Form master of Modern Four A, the brightest of the modern side new boys who were not of scholarship class (now it would probably be called the 'B' stream). I purported to teach them Latin, French, History, English and Scripture and as they and I were promoted to Modern Five A the following year we got to know each other extremely well. I also taught two school certificate history forms from which I soon learned how much brighter the classicists were than the modern side, together with two small sets who were either trying the school certificate again in December or having missed it in July were having their first try. They included (Sir) Kenneth Dover now President of Corpus Christi College, Oxford and Alec Forbes who wanted to be a doctor but whom I tried unsuccessfully to turn into a historian: a little later he got a science scholarship at Magdalen College without it ever becoming known that he was Captain of Boats at school: but in due course he got his rowing blue and is now a distinguished physician in the West Country.

My prize pupils however were one stage further on; they had conquered the school certificate and were waiting to go through the mill of the History Eighth. My main purpose was to prepare them in history for Philip Whitting while Eynon Smith took over the task of broadening their minds more generally: I learned a great deal from them and must, I think, have taught them something as no complaints ever came down from Philip. This great man was regularly turning out six to ten open scholars each year, scholars who were not burned out by the time they reached their finals. He had come to St Paul's from Wellington College where one would imagine that his superb talents were wasted and had taken over History Eighth when Cecil Smith its form master had drifted away to become headmaster of Colet Court, the junior school on the other side of the Hammersmith Road. Philip's only concession to himself was that in most years he got some young graduate to help him over the first half of the Michaelmas Term when he had the double burden of the new intake clashing with the final polishing of the scholarship candidates on his hands. When the war came he did not come down to Easthampstead Park like most of the rest of us, but remained in London teaching and doing heavy ARP work for which he was awarded a George Medal. Life, however, after the blitz had subsided was too tame for him and we next occasionally used to hear of him doing something mysterious with the Yugo-Slavs!

During this period of depression the school was very full, and for some time there was no classroom I could call my own, so I and my Modern Four A led a quasi-nomadic existence wandering and squatting in the rooms of colleagues who had a free period. When I finally got a room it was in an ideal situation, small, tucked away round a corner but near the start of the heating system. This last benefit was important as almost all classrooms faced north on the Hammersmith Road rather than south on to the playing fields. The School might with advantage have been planned precisely the opposite way round, but it was said that the Governors of 1880 believed that sunlight was unhealthy and disturbing. However in my five years work there I developed a deep and great affection for 'the red school' and sadly deplored its razing to the ground—and the exile of its personnel to Barnes.

John Bell was at great pains to point out that it was a five day week and there was too a splendid relic, allegedly from the St Paul's Churchyard days, of a November break which was little short of a week and spread over the Lord Mayor's Show and the other celebrations attendant on the change of Lord Mayor. John also pointed out that except for Waterloo every London terminus could be reached by underground without changing. There was also a system whereby one was off duty either Wednesday or Thursday afternoon with an occasional call to take games at the school ground at Ealing; which did not apply to those who took part in the activities of the OTC or the Scouts. I at once allied myself with the former, retaining however my R Signals status and uniform of which the spurs though impressive were rather a nuisance: Sidney Pask was already keeping an eye on a small but keen signal section and I mostly dealt with foot and small arms drill, working up each year to a drill competition and an annual inspection. I suppose that over half the school joined OTC or Scouts, whilst the rest did an hour's drill on Monday afternoons culminating in a run round the grounds, which may well have been the only active exercise of the week for a good many of them.

There was also a small, elite, body who did both Corps and Scouts, and were really the hard core and nucleus of both echelons. After a year or so the chief scoutmaster, Christopher Heath, asked me if I would keep an eye on them as they were in effect working on their own unsupervised; I agreed, with some misgivings, knowing nothing about scouting and not having a high opinion of what I saw of the rest of the school's scouting activities. The Corps Scouts I have to admit were different; they were very tough as well as highly qualified. I think that the lot of them were King's Scouts and most were qualifying for, or already had, a mysterious decoration called the Bushman's Thong. During term they mostly 'did their own thing' but they went camping in the Christmas and Easter

Richenda Streatfeild to whom I got engaged ten days after first meeting her.

holidays, and their scoutmaster was expected to do more than pay them occasional visits. On the other hand my duties with the Supplementary Reserve and the fact that for some years I was supernumerary to the OTC establishment let me off the Corps Camps till 1938 by which time I had been transferred from the SR to the TA General List for service in the OTC.

The Corps Scouts whose leading lights were Johnny Forsyth whom I later met on a Company Commanders' Course at Catterick, John Linklater, who after an exciting war qualified in his middle age as a doctor but died early, Grant the younger brother of one of my successors as head of the school at Charterhouse and Neville Wanklyn who had come to St Paul's from the Worcester training ship and made his name in the Boat Club: I met him too in the war, in a bar in Chester when he tried to drink me under the table with Guinness and rum taken either consecutively or concurrently: I have never, to my deep regret, seen him since. There were various others who came and went, but this was the hard core, and they demanded a winter camp in January 1936, for which I found an approved site near home at Easthampstead. It was very cold but not enough for skating on the nearby lake, and my recollection is that most of the time was spent keeping warm, cooking hot food and going on hikes through the mud in preparation for the next meal. Great good however came out of it as far as I was concerned, for we had a family of close friends, the Houghtons, whose eldest daughter was having a 21st birthday dance at the Pantiles outside Bagshot, to which we were all invited (Stubbs's not Scouts). I saw the scouts through their evening meal, changed into white tie and tails, a chilly business under canvas, and went off with no very high expectations. At the dance I was introduced to Richenda Streatfeild, and we got engaged ten days later: she was in the middle of her training as a Hospital Almoner, and I had just undertaken to do two years as house tutor in one of the two School boarding houses from the following September. So we had a two year engagement, spent in London during term and as we both had quite liberal holidays during them in the country with our parents or paying visits.

I got to like my housemaster Douglas Young less and less and as time went on I was not particularly happy at Colet House; his continual sniping at Freemasonry, which strangely enough he later joined with all the enthusiasm of a convert, very possibly blunted my enthusiasm for schoolmastering, but it certainly did not divert me from my interest in the Craft.

Richenda and I eventually found a maisonette within a stone's throw of the School and, having been married on 6 August 1938 and honeymooned in France we returned to find ourselves in the middle of the Czechslovakian crisis. This disturbing situation now involved preparations for the evacuation of the School and the digging of slit trenches along the edge of the school playing fields. These were filled up again after Mr Chamberlain's visit to Munich and almost unbelievably produced, in the

Wedding group, 6 August 1938, left to right: Margaret Pope, Barbara Stubbs, JWS, RKTS, R. L. James (best man) and Susan Atterbury: in front are Nicolette and Paul Gervis. Taken at Charts Edge, Westerham the Streatfeild family home.

next spring, a magnificent crop of mustard, which according to the surviving residents of West Kensington had been the last crop grown before the School moved, just over 50 years earlier, from St Paul's Churchyard in 1884. Quite apart from the political troubles the School was between High Masters as John Bell had gone to Cheltenham and (Sir) Walter Oakeshott had not yet arrived from Winchester. Maurice Tyson, the Sur Master shouldered the responsibility as he did on later occasions with superb efficiency and unfailing good humour.

A year later evacuation became a reality, and the School moved down to Crowthorne in Berkshire for living quarters and to Easthampstead Park, a few miles away, for teaching. I was there for four terms before being called up to serve with the Royal Signals (had I been only a few months older I would probably have been there for the duration). Meanwhile Richenda organised and took command of a temporary school sanatorium when St Thomas' Hospital where she had been working as a Lady Almoner (later Almoner and finally Medical Social Worker) was too badly bombed to remain an effective working unit, with its prewar quota of Lady Almoners.

A good deal has been written about the evacuation of the School mostly by those who took no part in it, and to this I will add neither my confirmation nor contradiction. Suffice it to say that Walter Oakeshott's inspiration and the loyal support of a diminishing number of masters kept the School alive, and not only alive but probably more flourishing in its smaller numbers than it had ever been before. Those who were privileged to be in the School during hostilities undoubtedly have a warmer regard for it than those who in times of peace regarded it purely as a nine to five educational exercise. At the sanatorium, always known as the 'Ousels', after a false start we were fortunate to have the assistance of Margaret Sharnock as nurse (she had originally come as a night nurse to see me through a bout of pneumonia in March 1940), and both she and Richenda served the School with unstinted devotion throughout the war. Indeed the first time they ever went out both together was on a visit to the bar of the Waterloo Hotel on the evening of VE day! Though actually born in Reading our daughter Janet returned very soon to the Ousels and spent the greater part of her short life there.

Richenda with daughter Janet at Crowthorne in 1945.

Chapter 6

Army Life and Return to Civilian Life

As a start to military service I was posted to the Depot Battalion of the 2nd Signal Training Centre at Prestatyn in North Wales. Having read somewhere that diaries in the Armed forces were discouraged if not positively forbidden I gave mine up with the result that the years 1941 to 1946 provide a selection of vivid but non-consecutive memories, ie. 2nd STC 1941-42, 43rd Divisional Signals 1942-44, War Office Signals Directorate 1944-45, 21 Army Group Signals 1945, and finally the Control Commission for Germany in 1946. These are the bare bones on which I can attach many more pleasant than unpleasant memories. I started in Prestatyn as an unduly elderly subaltern and became a reasonably aged Captain in 43rd Divisional Signals and a young Major in 21 Army Group Signals, and ended up as a noticeably young Lieutenant Colonel in the Control Commission before it began the pains of contraction.

Many friends were made at each stage, some of whom have kept up with us ever since. At Prestatyn Bertie Brett and Clifford Howarth, two very dissimilar characters both of whom ended up very high in the Corps. 'Doy' Randall the brewer of Guernsey and his wife who kept open house for young officers, and in another generation Lt Col Robin Montgomery who left to take up the splendid post of Chief Signal Officer, Pigeons, Major Hobkirk a former Cameronian whose lectures on military law kept NCO courses enthralled, and above all Jeremy Pemberton who arrived to recuperate from a serious motorcycle accident and whose life has been bound up with mine ever since. About Easter 1942 there was a weeding out of the young and fit from what was admittedly, for many, a soft and peaceful existence at Prestatyn, and I was posted after a brief interlude in the 53rd Welsh Divisional Signals to the 43rd who had recently moved into Canterbury and were comfortably billeted in the King's School. For me it was a considerable change from an Officer's Mess of about 100, of which I had for the last six months been Mess Secretary, to a small party of 20 at the most. The STC had been concerned with training civilians virtually straight off the street into soldiers in their first four weeks of service and into R Signals tradesmen in the following few months: in 43rd Div Sigs I saw the finished product, still basically consisting of pre-war territorials but with a constantly changing admixture from various holding battalions. The unit had for a long time been under the command of

Harry Bartlett who though an excellent trainer was a downright bad leader. To the unconcealed relief of all ranks he had got himself promoted to Brigadier and departed a few weeks later, to be replaced by 'Bungie' Gordon, his exact antithesis, who maintained our efficiency and at the same time induced a spirit of real enthusiasm into everything that went on.

'Black Harry' who was very heavy of hand had insisted on living in the Mess instead of with the Divisional Commander Major General (Sir) G. I. Thomas and the rest of the heads of the various branches and services. Bungie went at once to 'A' Mess and used to appear from time to time with us, as an ever welcome visitor. The King's School was bombed soon after I arrived and in the autumn we migrated to Kent College on the northern outskirts of the city.

Life was a mixture of exercises, with or without troops on the ground but always calling for full Signals participation, and the usual military activities of barrack life. I was sent on a Company Commanders' Course to Catterick from which I emerged with the qualification 'technically very fair' which must be about the lowest there was, but a good report in all other respects. This may have been partially due to the fortunate discovery by the Chief Instructor, that we were both members of Brasenose. I went back after some leave to Canterbury to find myself OC Headquarters Company ie. in charge of administration and any other bodies that did not fit legitimately and conveniently into the Signals structure. By now the unit was probably at its peak: Michael Trethowan, John Wheeler and I, all of the same age group together with Humphrey Collins were Company Commanders: Jim Donnison, a product of the original Signals OCTU was adjutant with an outstandingly able Orderly Room Sergeant, who will appear later as W Bro Jimmy Bullen, Assistant Provincial Grand Master, Hampshire and Isle of Wight. We survived a gruelling administrative inspection by G. I. Thomas and very soon after it Jim Donnison invited me for an evening's drinking, during which he told me that he had been medically down graded and was going to the War Office. He invited me to consider the reversion of his job as Adjutant. I had never thought of myself in that connection, though it seemed a natural progression (and Adjutants' pay was not to be sniffed at): so I accepted and very soon took over from him. I can never be sufficiently grateful to Jimmy Bullen for his help not only at the start of my new responsibility but throughout the long months that followed. It was indeed only when he went on promotion to SHAEF that I realised how much his absence would be felt in the unit.

All would have been well but for the promotion of Bungie who left almost exactly as I arrived in the adjutant's office. He was replaced by a lowland Scot who never managed to understand the Wessex mentality; nor was he prepared to counternance our methods far less to leave well alone. He worked himself quite unnecessarily into a state of mental and physical exhaustion, in which he expected his adjutant to do likewise by chasing round the unit which was already doing its work very adequately—and rather better without his interference. He was eventually posted as Chief Signal Officer, Cyprus where no doubt he was more appreciated.

As Adjutant I was also in close touch with the Divisional staff: Michael Trethowan too was well acquainted with them, as was Ron Harrison who was in charge of the Signal Office in succession to Michael. Between us we established a very pleasant personal relationship which was helpful to both sides. In the summer of 1943 I was nominated for a course at the School of Military Administration at Naworth Castle in Cumberland, and to my agreeable surprise emerged from it with top place: it had been a pleasant month's relief from the pressure of adjutantcy and communication work, and whetted my already growing appetite for administration. However I got back to find that a change of CO and of location was imminent: Michael Trethowan explained to me in the kindest terms while he was acting CO that there was no chance of promotion for me in the unit but that most likely a posting away in favour of someone returned from abroad was just round the corner. I had already gone through the whole gamut of mobilisation a couple of times and was beginning to feel that something new was needed, when, out of the blue I was unexpectedly summoned to the War Office. On arrival at the Signals Directorate Major Cecil Crosthwaite gave me a large tea in the canteen of the underground annexe and asked if I was interested in War Establishments, about which I said that I knew nothing apart from that of a Divisional Signals. Undeterred he offered me a job as GSO III in Signals 5 under him. After a brief skirmish more I think for form's sake than with any real intent to block my posting, between the Divisional Commander and the War Office, I made my getaway leaving the adjutancy to Ron Harrison who carried it through the early stages of the campaign till he deservedly got the promotion which Michael had earlier denied me.

It was a considerable change from active army life to what was virtually a civilian existence. The work however was most interesting and gave me a real insight into Civil Service thinking; there had recently been a high powered committee (Godwin Austen) looking at the functions of Signals in the field, mostly in fact the desert, and Signals 5 had to turn its recommendations, which had been approved at a high level, into the skeletal form of various war establishments. Cecil Crosthwaite did it brilliantly up to the point where the proposals had to be submitted to a sub-Committee of the War Establishment Committee itself: I spent weeks at first on my own, after my tutor and predecessor had gone to Baker Street, arguing individual cases, generally before Major Vaughan Morgan (later Lord Reigate) and his colleagues, one of whom was always a civilian from F6 who had the right to break off any engagement in which he was likely to be worsted to take higher advice. By and large however we mostly got what we wanted, sometimes having to sacrifice a pawn (ie, a corporal's job downgraded to lance corporal) in order to save a knight

Army Life and Return to Civilian Life 39

(ie, the principal that all Company Commanders should be Majors): Godwin Austen was about finished when the section was increased in size in order to deal with a preliminary rundown of static establishments and some highly secret special outfits: Cecil then asked if I could suggest someone for a further post of GSO III and I immediately plumped for Jeremy Pemberton, who being still medically downgraded, was adjutant of a training battalion at Catterick.

His arrival, straight into the little blitz, was an immediate success, and the three of us settled down to a triple friendship only terminated by Cecil's death a few years ago. D day came and went; I was the nominal duty defence officer on the night of the allied invasion itself and slept right through it, no one having thought it necessary to disturb me! The flying bombs then came and though we were under some thirty feet of concrete we could hear them through the telephones of less protected colleagues. Though reasonably protected ourselves, we had an unhealthy existence and in the winter months particularly hardly saw daylight for weeks on end. This unhealthy state of affairs was recognised by the War Office authorities who arranged courses of ultra violet treatment, but in spite of this I fell ill in my second underground winter and spent a couple of weeks in hospital with ear trouble. (The hospital was Shenley Mental Hospital which I hasten to add had been taken over by the army for less specialised purposes.) Shortly after this interruption some months of care-

As OC 3 Company, 21 Army Group Signals, taken in Brussels on VE day.

ful strategy on my part came to fruition and I was posted as a Company Commander to 21 Army Group Signals in the last stage of its reorganisation by John Hagon a former War Office colleague. Originally this unit had been 1 HQ Signals and as such had gone to the continent in 1939 but returned to provide communications for Home Forces (at St Paul's School) and being always operational had suffered very little change of personnel. One of my sections, under Andrew Alexander MM claimed proudly that it left 'Brussels repeaters' in 1940 having done a million pounds of damage and returned there in 1944 in time to eat a midday meal that had been prepared for the retreating Germans!

The unit had suffered to a degree in Normandy from COs and Company Commanders who were too technically minded, being much more interested in installing exchanges with their own hands than in ensuring that communications flowed swift and sure in accordance with the Corps motto 'Certa Cito'. John Hagon with the firm support of Major General C. M. F. White, the Chief Signal Officer, set up a general overhaul and my predecessor was the last to go. So I arrived in Brussels as spring broke out but ten days too late for entitlement to the 1939–1945 Star, to find that I was in charge of the whole communications set up for Rear HQ 21 Army Group. My Company was over 600 strong including for operational purposes about 200 ATS whereas my previous one in Canterbury consisted of less than 50. At first both we (No 3 Company), the Unit Headquarters and 21 AG Main Headquarters Signals (No 2 Company) messed together: No 1 was up on the Dutch frontier making good the telephone routes forward (young officers who showed too much interest in the ATS were crossposted to it where building lines along the dykes soon cooled their ardour). On the first of April Main HQ moved up to a lunatic asylum inside Germany and the unit HQ and No 2 Company moved with it, leaving behind some odd details to be absorbed in my already swollen Company: I was given a second in Command Frankie Norris who turned out to be not only a schoolmaster but also my exact twin in age, promotion having been refused for my brightest subaltern, now Sir Kenneth Clucas, KCB, on the ground that at 20 he was too young! Frankie however was an excellent choice as he was a good linguist and knew Brussels and its people well having been there ever since the re-occupation.

In due course the whole HQ coalesced in Bad Oeynhausen and the unit was reorganised on the basis that No 3 Company took over all wireless and No 2 all signal office duties. Our own wireless sections were spread out over a wide area, though the results of their labours were led in by land line to a central building adjacent to the Signal Office. 1945 was a beautiful summer, we had just won the war, and getting out into the countryside round the wireless stations in a comfortable car was sheer pleasure. In addition, however, to my own responsibility for communications both forward and back from Bad Oeynhausen other unusual burdens were added. When hostilities ended a Czechoslovakian Armoured Brigade was sitting outside Dunkerque; it had to be got back for a triumphal entry into Prague and its progress half across Europe carefully monitored, also some communications had to be established to facilitate the return of prisoners across the Elbe, then the dividing line of British and Russian forces. Later on we provided additional communications for the Nuremburg trials, and I have always regretted failing to get there to see for myself how they worked.

Meanwhile the run down of the Army was gathering momentum and senior officers were finding new appointments. 21 AG Signals lost John Hagon to Caserta, and acquired George Walker on the disbandment of 2nd Army HQ. He brought several of his officers with him and the old 1 HQ Signals began to change significantly and regrettably for the worse. Back in Brussels I had done a good turn in providing an extra telephone to a former member of 43 Div Signals, Frankie Sergeaunt and we had met on various occasions, during which he had asked whether I would consider transferring into the Control Commission. The moment seemed opportune for change when George Walker retired with his age and service group to be replaced by Col Lewis from SHAEF. I had served under him for a brief fortnight with 53rd Welsh Div Signals and was under no illusions as to his contempt for my lack of technical skill. So I addressed myself formally to Frankie and found myself posted in a very short time to the Posts and Telegraphs Branch of the Control Commission for Germany (British Element) at Kiel. However I must admit that I left Bad Oeynhausen with regret having thoroughly enjoyed my last, as it turned out to be, purely military assignment, and Bill Lewis despite his low opinion of me technically was always a kind and considerate Commanding Officer.

CCG was a very different proposition and increasingly composed of civilians so far as P and T was concerned mostly from the GPO: the Kiel branch was something of a trial ground for P and T ideas under the able but unamiable Lt Col Hawking. My function appeared to be to clear the local Reichspost of Hitlerism and party members: it was virtually an impossibility as all its staff had been brought willy-nilly into the party (the degree of 'willy' had to be the key factor). Further complications arose whenever I found a German who had held substantial local rank and was thought apt for purging as there would be an outcry from his British professional opposite number that he/she as the case might be was essential to the whole structure of the Slesvig-Holstein Reichpost! After some months of futile though otherwise enjoyable existence I was about to take a 48 hour leave pass to the fleshpots of Copenhagen when I got a frantic call from Frankie Sergeaunt to relieve him at the control HQ of P and T at Bad Salzuflen. Apparently urgent private affairs had caught up with him and he was seeking release from the Commission within a week: Bill Hawking made no objection and if truth were known was probably quite glad to see the back of someone not in the GPO.

So my last stage started as a Lieutenant Colonel (Staff Officer Grade One), a dizzy height to which I had to cling for six months to earn temporary rank as Lt Col with War Substantive rank as Major, which greatly enhanced payments on release.

It is time however to go back to domestic details: during my time in the War Office I had been able to see rather more of Richenda and Janet at the Ousels, and I had also managed to get home from Germany both on leave and while taking a course. All seemed to be going well until one evening I was called to the telephone (how I blessed the 'Engineering Speaker' as a hidden means of communication!) to learn from Richenda that Janet was in Great Ormond Street with what was obviously something very seriously amiss. It turned out to be a tumour on a kidney which was dealt with by Mr Twistington-Higgins who we learned years later was a keen Mason and had also been a friend of my father at a Casualty Clearing Station in 1918. I was given compassionate leave at once by Bill Lewis and though there was really nothing I could do practically it was comforting to Richenda to have me at home for some of the worst time. Tragically the trouble flared up again within six months and Janet died in June 1946 by which time Richenda was again heavily pregnant. Unlike Bill Lewis, Bill Hawking was quite unsympathetic and refused me any extension of a subsequent leave from Kiel though pressed to do so by Signals 5 for whom I was doing a quiet but useful bit of research work on the Pay Warrant: and I must truthfully say that I am glad to think that he never attained any further promotion.

The six months spent at Bad Salzuflen passed very quickly and a good deal of it was taken up on the old job of War Establishments as CCG was beginning to prune itself of unnecessary personnel. I was also responsible for general co-ordination of the work of its various sections in the branch headed by Brigadier Firth, Col Evans of the GPO and a multitude of PO engineers under the vigorous command of L. G. Semple. Another function which called for a considerable amount of tact and diplomacy was that at the same time as the branch shrank in size conversely it expanded in another way—the wives started to appear. In a number of agitated interviews I was asked either to transfer the other half of a liaison to some distant outstation, or to find a specious reason for transferring the officer himself to somewhere else with, of course, suitable accommodation and amenities to which he would be able to welcome his wife. During this trying time Senior Commander Maureen Lenigham (now Leckenby) was always a tower of strength and after an excellent farewell party we bowed out of military life together. At least that was the original intention: but on my final medical examination the RAMC doctors discovered what I had kept to myself for over two years, a hernia which they thereupon insisted upon dealing with themselves, though I was able to persuade them that it could equally well be done in the UK during my release leave.

DOMESTIC LIFE

When St Paul's School returned to London from Crowthorne I was still in uniform: Richenda first set up home with Janet and Nanny White in the attic of Bute House in Brook Green which has since been demolished, the rest of it being occupied by the Junior Girls School. Later Richenda managed to acquire a lease of 43 Rowan Road which had been occupied before the war by Ivan Mavor the school Chaplain and his aged mother but as it had remained unoccupied all during the war its condition was just this side of being classified as derelict. However I managed to get some leave and we moved (about two hundred yards!) in April 1946. Janet went down hill very rapidly and died in June, by which time Richenda was fairly imminently expecting again. Hugh was born in August and I got my release in September.

It is quite surprising now to look back on those days and to realise that we did not think it at all strange to have two living-in staff: Mrs White had stayed with us for several years, and we were just beginning to wonder how we could tactfully tell her that Hugh was outgrowing the need for a nanny, when by good fortune she was called away to look after a widowed brother-in-law. The domestic front however was already being looked after by a series of delightful and mostly very efficient Danish girls who stayed for a year and generally either vetted or actually produced a successor. When Mrs White left all that remained to be done was to double the supply of Danes and to ensure as far as possible that they overlapped with each other. These Danish girls most of whom had grown up under German occupation were cheerful, hardworking and self reliant: having been brought up to strict ideas of curfew they thoroughly enjoyed English emancipation and they spent a lot of their off-time at the excellent club run by the Danish church. One or two of them had friends on Danish ships using the Port of London and we grew accustomed to their return with boxes of eggs, butter, cheese and pungent Danish salami. Bobbie James wife of the new High Master had a succession of Danes also who happily got on well with ours and provided extra company for each other.

MASONIC PROGRESSION

The war years had cut down my Masonic activities a good deal, but not completely. My wardenship in the Apollo in 1934 had qualified me for election to the chair of any Lodge without further preliminaries: I had joined my father's Wellesley Lodge No 1899 at Crowthorne in 1937 and promotion there had been rapid, as he had fallen out on leaving Easthampstead for Salisbury whilst several others ahead of me either disappeared on war service or were evacuated too far away to take office. Consequently I became Master in 1943, with no more meetings till I left the chair twelve months later, to watch Eric Gillmor competently install my successor in a ceremony which I had never seen except as the victim of it. The Masons of Prestatyn were friendly and hospitable and I went several times to St Melyd's No 3840 which had built up a happy relationship with the STC. I had joined Westminster & Keystone No 10 as well in 1938 and during my service at the War Office was generally able to get to its attenuated lunch time meeting and to stand in for one or other of the absentees. No 10 will receive more than passing mention later, since it is as its number indicates of great antiquity and has an interesting history.

When I was released from the Army just a month after our son Hugh was born, we spent a leisurely and pleasant though rather gluttonous week in Dublin before returning to the rigours of civilian and Pauline life. Richenda had by then been persuaded by Walter Oakeshott whose charm was quite irresistible, to become the School caterer having previously helped to bring St Paul's back to London whilst making the school itself habitable: it had become the Polish HQ after being the jumping off ground for the invasion of Europe. Walter then left for Winchester and after another Tyson interregnum, was replaced by R. L. James, who had been a colleague before the war and our best man in 1938. From the outset there seemed likely to be disadvantages as well as advantages in having both a wife and a best man under the same educational roof.

This seems a suitable point to take a retrospective look at my generally passive, though on the whole, enjoyable military career. It may seem surprising to some that a classical scholar with no knowledge whatsoever of physics or chemistry and only a nodding acquaintance with morse code, should have risen in five years from subaltern to become a lieutenant colonel. I genuinely believe that the reason was that both peacetime regular officers and also the output of junior Signals officers from OCTU were trained almost exclusively on communications and the most scientific methods of producing them, to the exclusion from their minds of the trivial and boring details of administration which were given a low priority. Those few who enjoyed such matters and took a deep interest in them could almost always find themselves a niche. Whilst I was fortunate in having learned some basic principles from P. C. Fletcher at school I had been drafted apparently at the time for no very good reason to become Mess Secretary at Prestatyn later to become OC HQ Company in 43 Div Signals and then as previously mentioned by a fortunate accident, Adjutant, where I had nothing technical to do except a wireless frequency allocation every four months: likewise my work in the War Office too was identifiable as pure administration. In 21 Army Group Signals it is true that I was responsible for a wide variety of communications, varying from Despatch Riders to High Speed Wireless, but all the sections under my command (and that went for the ATS too) were highly trained and efficient: my job as I saw it it in every aspect was to keep them happy and to see that whilst working very hard, as they did, they were not abused by maladministration.

Meanwhile the Corps was reaching the point where its senior officers, who had come in at its formation over 20 years earlier, were beginning to fade away even as old incompatibilities were disappearing; also the time was not far off when for the first time the appointment of Director of Signals went to someone who had never been anything else but a Royal Signals Officer. The wind of change was blowing in another direction too: throughout the war there were very few Signals Officers employed in General Staff jobs, and I know of one only who commanded a division, the redoubtable General Penny. This is a strange phenomenon since from his early days posting as Signal Officer to a Brigade or a RA Regimental HQ had allowed the young officer an unparalleled opportunity for seeing staff work going on and for helping it succeed. It is natural but disquieting to think that there must have been some prejudice amongst the senior ranks of the Corps against the acceptance of staff appointments, or was it rather an unwillingness by the Army authorities to accept Signals Officers as anything other than technical experts?

Be that as it may, the fact remains that I emerged from war service no more technically minded or expert than when I entered, but with a good deal of administrative experience. I did realise that even if I picked up a lot of private tuition again I would still be a great deal worse off as an assistant master than as a lieutenant colonel drawing grade one staff pay. Walter Oakeshott had told me that I could not look forward with any probability to one of the two housemasterships at St Paul's and that I had better start applying for headmasterships. This I did, and thanks to some glowing testimonials from both him and Sonners at BNC, plus my Army rank I generally got into a short list but no further: Mercers' School, Guildford Grammar School, Sir Walter St Johns, and finally Abingdon all gave me a run, and I was beginning to recognise some of my fellow contestants as we travelled round—(Sir) James Cobban in particular also a Lieutenant Colonel, also from a great London day school, and also as I discovered later a Mason, who produced at his interview some of his own publications, which the rest of us thought was an unfair bit of one-upmanship.

My return to St Paul's passed off smoothly, and I was gratified to find myself in charge of a higher form than I had ever taught before, Form VIx, the brightest of the second year modern side who were taking their school certificates (now O levels) in two instead of the usual three years: but my heart was no longer in teaching as I found out after a few weeks. The Common Room had changed a lot, not always for the better, and more disturbing I found that the manners of the Paulines had changed quite definitely for the worse. During one of his occasional moments of exasperation Oakeshott had described the school as mid-way between the Old Bailey and the New Jerusalem: so I was not alone in noticing the deterioration.

APPLICATION TO GRAND LODGE

Meanwhile Masonry in Oxford was reviving, and at one of the Apollo meetings in Michaelmas Term 1946, Douglas Amery who was back in action as Provincial Grand Secretary mentioned that Grand Lodge was once more trying to get a Principal Assistant for Sydney White and suggested that I should put in for it. I therefore settled down one evening and wrote out an application, extolling my general experience and virtues as opposed to the legal or accountancy qualifications called for by the advertisement, which I did not possess. I should add here that my application was made several weeks after the closing date, but I covered this speciously enough by my demobilisation. I was aware that there had already been two abortive attempts, one before and one immediately after the war to get the appointment made, and I fancy that both Sydney White and the Board of General Purposes under its new President, Sir Ernest Cooper, were getting desperate. In time I was duly summoned and interviewed, with several others, by Sir Ernest himself, Wallace Heaton, and another figure who remained dumb in the background but subsequently turned out to be H. O. Budd, together of course with Sydney White. It was a friendly but non-committal meeting and I was told there might be some delay: Sir Ernest kindly offered to drive me back to St Paul's but it was not until later that I realised how nearly I must have cooked my goose by telling the Chairman of Gillettes that I always used an electric razor.

Near half term I obtained leave of absence from St Paul's and presented myself for the hernia operation at a military hospital (hutted) near Crawley. Compared to present day practice it was a long drawn out affair, consisting of three weeks flat on my back with penicillin injections every four hours for ten days (one night sister unerringly found the same puncture hole three times running). Moreover there had also been some trouble with the catgut or whatever it was that surgeons used for sewing up the walls, and my surgeon who was an Australian produced a new method which consisted of extracting a long strip of sinew from the outside of my left thigh and using that instead. All went well though my thigh was rather more painful than my ex-hernia, and I was vastly over-tired through my inability to get a decent bout of sleep between punctures.

After a couple of weeks a number of patients, mostly hernias, were moved up by ambulance to Millbank which made visiting a good deal easier and it was at this point that I got a letter from Freemasons' Hall summoning me to a further interview. I quickly obtained local leave from Millbank, cleaned up my uniform, hopefully for the last time, and proceeded to Great Queen Street where the interview took place before the whole of the Officers and Clerks Committee plus Lord Harewood, the Grand Master. It was quite formal and ended with the Grand Master being asked if he had any questions, and after what seemed an interminably long silence he gave me a cheerful smile and asked if I had ever met my Colonel-in-Chief. Fortunately I remembered that she was his wife, the Princess Royal and duly answered in suitable terms. I was then told courteously that in view of my being in hospital I need not wait to be seen by the Board as a whole, and that I could depart. Lord Harewood kindly dropped me off at Millbank on his way to Windsor and a few days later I received a formal letter of appointment. I hurriedly resigned from the school staff and arranged with Sydney White to start work in early February 1947. I found out later that in the interim, he had arranged to see Richenda to point out the domestic disadvantages of being married to a professional Freemason, and nearly 33 years later Richenda re-enacted this move by explaining the same to Caroline Higham. We also took advantage of the gap in change over to make the acquaintance of Miss Haig who was secretary first to PC, then to Sydney White and in the end to me in a career at Freemasons' Hall that spanned well over 40 years.

Chapter 7

Introduction to Great Queen Street

When I started work on the 2 February 1947 it did not take long to realise how completely ignorant I was of the higher organisation of Freemasonry both at home and abroad; nor was my experience at Lodge level much better after five years absence on war service. However I found the staff friendly, extremely helpful and certainly much more capable than Sydney White ever admitted them to be! He had in fact tended to regard their military service as one long and undisciplined holiday away from their proper life's work in Great Queen Street. On the other hand it is but fair to remember that, with a diminishing number of trained staff and an increasing number of temporary additions, he had not only been holding the fort without an Assistant Grand Secretary but had also been organising throughout the blitz and later an underground shelter gratefully used by the occupants of the neighbouring blocks of flats. The shelter and its associated canteen have never been much publicised to members of the Craft but they were well known and appreciated by the people of Holborn. Much closer relations too were established with the Town Hall than before or after the war—particularly when Holborn was replaced by the more distant and less forthcoming London Borough of Camden.

Fortunately by February several of the staff had returned and more were expected shortly, so it was possible to plan for an eventual reversion to peace time staffing; but there remained a vast amount of wartime accumulation of registration, which was being methodically, but ever so slowly, broken down by a team of old gentlemen. The pent up enthusiasm of the war years had gratifyingly manifested itself in to a flood of petitions for new Lodges as shown below:

1941– 7	1945–179
1942– 23	1946–191
1943– 68	1947–190
1944–113	1948–202

as well as a spectacular if not wholly unexpected rise in the number of Grand Lodge Certificates issued:

1941 – 11,688
1942 – 11,855
1943 – 13,834
1944 – 16,657
1945 – 19,538
1946 – 21,223
1947 – 21,958
1948 – 22,859

This was all routine stuff and could be taken in one's stride with the staff as it became available. But a completely new *Masonic Year Book* for the first time since 1942 was a taller order. It was produced, with most of the errors of the 1942 edition cleaned up by Derrick Chanter and printed and bound for us, for the first time, by John Johnson, the illustrious Printer to the University at Oxford with whom and his successors a very happy relationship was established and existed throughout my time.

External relations, with other Grand Lodges were also resuming their old activity, and a resurrection of Freemasonry in continental Europe had started, urged on too precipitately by the United States Grand Lodges, whilst the Grand Orient of France was already making mischief in Germany. Francis Jones who had been at the Hall throughout the war was, at least in his own opinion, the repository of knowledge of Masonry overseas; he had indeed a prodigious memory and an experience that went back to the days of Sir Alfred Robbins, but he spoiled his usefulness by over-reaction to a little judicious flattery, and often talked not too wisely, only too much. Hersey Woods who was almost due to retire had been holding the fort for the Benevolent and Bylaws Departments well as London Grand Rank, both Craft and Royal Arch. He was a tower of strength to a newcomer as his experience went back to the time of Sir Edward Letchworth, and the encyclopaedic knowledge he had gained of Lodges and their leading lights during the time that he was running the Million Memorial Fund had been kept up to date. He had moreover organised several Especial Grand Lodges, from the 'front of the house' point of view, and made his knowledge easily available to the next generation. Registration was in the hands of Ernest Tinney and his body of old gentlemen who as I have already mentioned were plugging away at the returns, but he, poor man, was often ill and we were fortunate enough to be able to re-deploy several of the returned servicemen to his department. The Cash Department headed by Malcolm Grace had kept its head above water throughout the war and had consistently continued to satisfy the auditors: he had several years to go before retirement and was well supported by Stanley Driskell and Walker Curtis who in 1984 is still there. Two other elements of the general office need to be mentioned, both in the forefront of the public eye: the organisation of London which Gerry Winslade had returned to from the army, and Enquiries where George Stubbington aided by old Mr Edwards, dealt patiently and effectively with an increasing number of visitors. With so many diverse departments it may seem surprising to many readers that one shorthand typist coped adequately and punctually with the correspondence but in fact many of the male staff composed and actually typed their own letters. In the first ten years or so after the war I encouraged all the new intake of staff to learn shorthand and typing, which I still believe did them no harm.

When I first arrived the complexity of the whole establishment came as a considerable surprise: still more so the existence of a maintenance staff of over 100 personnel including a part-time regiment of cleaners, and a Library and Museum department working in dignified seclusion on the first floor. The maintenance male staff had to a great extent been recruited from those employed on the building between 1927 and 1933, who consequently knew it well. We were very fortunate that some of them survived into the 1980s. They were led by W.J. Tribe, lately Major RE, who had come back from the Middle East shortly before I arrived, and also by Charles Fry and Mr Fisher on the engineering and electrical side respectively. Sydney White had little use for Tribe, who was on the other hand a firm favourite of W. F. Blay, of whom I shall say more later: Fisher was mainly interested in the additional work he undertook for the Connaught Rooms, and his health was not proof against long hours and entertainment. Charles Fry on the other hand, a genial giant was liked by everyone: he had been Sydney White's right hand in the shelter and a great support to him in other respects as well. He loved the Hall dearly and nothing about its maintenance was too much trouble; almost all the replacements that came to be needed as the building aged were done in accordance with his planning and mostly with the Hall's own labour force. He worked hard to the end, and in losing him we were deprived of a wealth of experience.

Upstairs in the Library there was a very remarkable character, J. Heron Lepper, a polio casualty at the age of eight, twice married and father of a number of children as Irish as himself. He moved on crutches or, outdoors, in an electric chair, never to my knowledge admitting defeat. He had previously worked in publishing and had made himself a formidable Masonic scholar (as part author too of the Grand Lodge of Ireland's history) but remained a kindly though firm critic of the scholarship of others. He always seemed to have time to listen, and for my part I learned much from him. Of his two subordinates Ivor Grantham was a barrister and scholar, whom it was difficult in some respects to get to know, but who turned out to be an admirable foil to Lepper's exuberance and in due course became a most competent successor. On the Museum side Henry Chiltern, ex-soldier and Irish Mason was making himself expert in his own limited field of Masonic 'objets de vertue' and had already done much towards restoring the museum to its pre-war state: he had a staunch ally and henchman in Sgt Barlow the Custodian, also an Irish Mason and one of the leading lights in their military Lodges which at that time were concentrated at Hounslow whilst their parent regiments were sorting themselves out into peace conditions. Last of all came the Grand Tyler, Major Peel of the Life Guards, who was responsible for Lodge lettings, for organising regalia etc when a Grand Lodge party went away, and in an unsatisfactorily vague way for the activities of the porters who moved furniture and Lodge boxes (and could never be found when wanted): the line of demarcation between Major Peel and Tribe was never defined, and Sydney tended to wash his hands of the issue but was known to have said that whenever trouble came in the building the porters would be at the bottom of it. He was not far wrong, but I do not believe it was entirely their fault for they suffered from a succession of indifferent foremen who weakly found it easier to do the jobs themselves than to insist on the porters doing them.

Getting to know the staff and what they did or were supposed to do in their various capacities was not very difficult and really only a matter of time. Getting to know one's way round the building from the ducts below the basement to the roof where there was still a small but flourishing market garden took rather longer and indeed for years I continued to find odd little rooms and corners (in fact I went through one door for the first time in my tenure of office only a few weeks before I retired).

BOARDS AND COMMITTEES

It was altogether another matter of getting to know who was who in the various controlling bodies. These comprised the Board of Benevolence, the Board of General Purposes (with its six Committees), the Grand Chapter Committee and the Grand Master's Council. With the last two I had no contact at first: with the Grand Chapter Committee because I had to wait some time before I qualified in the Royal Arch, the Council because, until it was absolutely necessary, ie when he took a prolonged trip abroad, Sydney White kept me rigidly away from it. In retrospect this was not too bad as it enabled me, since Council generally met just before Grand Lodge, to keep an eye on the administrative build up, to talk to and encourage the scrutineers and generally be about the place, and I could always find out what had been decided even if not what views were expressed. When I became First Principal of the Apollo University Chapter in November 1947 I began to attend Grand Chapter and the Committee, or such part of it as went on beyond the Board of Benevolence with which for some inexplicable reason it met simultaneously.

It was, and till recently continued to be, a small and intimate body with rarely more than seven present. In 1948 and for a number of years it was presided over by Sir Stuart Robertson, KC, a remarkable scholar and athlete who is said to have won three gold medals at the Olympic Games held in Athens in 1898 (for the Hammer, for Tennis where he was conscripted at the last moment, and one for a Pindaric Ode celebrating the revival of the Games in Classical Greek). The first time we met he said 'I've seen you before': this was true since when staying with the Bigge cousins as an undergraduate I had appeared in a bathing dress at his back door in North Devon to collect a surf board and was asked irascibly what I thought I was doing: We became good friends as two of my uncles had been in College with him at Winchester. Informality at these meetings was the keynote: the minutes were neither discussed nor read, and there were generally only two or three items which produced any discussion at all. It was really not till Sir George Boag became President and some more new blood was infused into the Committee that it became more than just an agreeable rubber stamp.

The Board of Benevolence was in a transitional stage as the pre-war Board was indeterminate in size, though in practice comparatively few of the several thousand entitled to do so turned up for meetings. For the duration of the war a caretaker management Committee had been produced, and in 1947 this was given constitutional form, which lasted till the early stages of the Board's transformation into what we now know as the Grand Charity. The new Board was presided over by (Sir) Trevor Matthews of Grindlay's Bank, well described to me by Sydney as 'one of the best men we have got': indeed no praise could be too high. He had able Vice-Presidents in Brothers Cross and MacClymont: the elected members, four from London who were actually balloted for in Grand Lodge plus four from the Provinces who were selected by an arcane process such as was used to select the Provincial members of the Board of General Purposes, comprised the rest of the Board. At the first election there were a good many more candidates than places and some of the old wartime Committee unhappily fell out: it was, to put it mildly, remarkable how many got in who were personally nominated by W Bro Jack Stubbs (who I hasten to add was no relation of mine). There can be no doubt that a vigorous canvass took place though the authorities had in the past often inveighed against this practice. Thereafter very few more 'live' elections to either Board took place between 1947 and 1980, and the few that did caused a good deal of bad blood and did not necessarily produce a result that was in the best interests of the Craft as a whole.

However the newly created Board settled down at once and proceeded to do its excellent work month in and month out. Its only weakness being that, in the earlier years, hardly any of the elected members opened their mouths, the discussion being virtually limited to a dialogue between the two Vice-Presidents, both of whom were old hands. It should be added here that the four Provincial members included the redoubtable Edgar Rutter about whom there is much more to be said in due course in respect of his activities in the Board of General Purposes, in South Wales Eastern Division, and the independent Masonic Charities. He would occasionally speak and, it must be admitted, almost invariably in favour of a more generous grant than the Vice-Presidents had in mind. Harold Brunton had resumed his old function as the Benevolence Clerk replacing Hersey Woods, and continued to serve the Craft magnificently for many years.

In addition to the Board work there were several other Masonic charitable funds run from Freemasons' Hall, the most notable being the London Grand Rank fund (not to be confused with the London Grand Rank Association). In the course of time this fund which was administered through the office by a committee of London Past Masters, appointed by the Grand Master, ceased to be of much practical use as its potential beneficiaries were usually eligible also for the benefits (on a larger scale) of the Board of Benevolence. So a change was worked out whereby all London petitions were first looked at by the Committee, in much the same way as a Provincial Charity Committee would be expected to scrutinise Provincial cases. What can best be described as Masonic first aid was then given before the case actually went forward, a few days later, to the Board itself.

The Frederick Phillips Charity had its special committee also: and in 1947 the fund was still expanding as various life interests were accumulated: Bro Phillips had asked that special consideration should be given to the Masonic hospital but otherwise had left those administering the trust with a free hand. The Charity has been of great advantage in special cases of education where, for example, a wage earning parent has died in the middle of a course of training or there has been some, possibly only temporary, breakdown in normal sources of family income. The Committee has always been composed of senior Masons drawn from a wide variety of professions so as to be best able to cover from the members' own expertise almost any type of case that came before it. Various other funds, as I learned in the course of time, had been established and dealt with cases that fell outside the normal benevolent rules but these were investigated by the department and pushed forward for ultimate decision by the Grand Secretary.

The Board of General Purposes was the mainspring of the Craft's activities, and its monthly meetings likewise were the chief incident in the routine of the office. Its historical development and current form are described in Appendix I, and it will be sufficient at this point to refer to some of the personalities I found on my arrival. Standing out head and shoulders was the President, Sir Ernest Cooper, Chairman of Gillettes and of the Junior Carlton Club, a Canadian who without entirely losing his Canadian outlook had acquired and was still acquiring a wider grasp of Masonic world affairs. I often thought that there was something Gladstonian in his approach to problems both in the theory and the practice of Freemasonry, but he was a lot less prolix than the GOM. Lord Scarbrough once described him to me as having a lot of the Old Testament prophet in him, and one can almost see him dealing with irregular Masonic bodies as Elijah did with the priests of Baal. Whom Sir Ernest loved he also chastened and one needed to be sure of facts and with a ready tongue in any dealings with him. But for all that he was a kindly man keenly interested in the young and intensely proud of his only grandson, David Rutherford who went from Rugby where he had never rowed to Oxford to become a winning President of the Oxford University Boat

Club and only just miss an Olympic place through injury. It was indeed sometimes quite possible to avert Sir Ernest's criticism of one's failings by a well timed question about Oxford rowing!

The Vice-President of the Board changed annually with due regard to Buggin's law, but the Chairman though theoretically subject to re-election each year were in fact pretty permanent. As Sir Maurice Bowra—and possibly others before and since said 'while there is death there is hope': J. E. C. Stubbs, already referred to for his electioneering activities over the Board of Benevolence was Chairman of the Finance Committee but died, comparatively unlamented, in 1950. Meanwhile C. H. Thorpe one of the founding Secretaries of the Royal Masonic Hospital was Chairman of the Colonial Indian and Foreign Committees but did not last much longer. W. Cooper Bailey soon ceased to direct the Procedure Committee as he became Provincial Grand Master for Northumberland and so left the Board: H. O. Budd had just given up the Officers and Clerks to Edgar Rutter. That leaves the two most distinguished characters of the old order, first Wallace Heaton of photographic fame in charge of the Library, Arts and Publications Committee, where he was able to put to good use his skill as a Masonic collector, and Grand Lodge overall owes as much to his sagacity as to his generosity: secondly W. F. Blay, a retired builder and former Deputy Provincial Grand Master of Kent who presided over the Premises Committee, which included at that time, in its sphere of operations, all Grand Lodge's landed property. He had also during the war kindly relieved Sydney White of this responsibility and had to a great extent taken over the day to day running of the Hall.

It should be remembered that in 1947 planning permission, development charges and regulations were in their infancy, and the Masonic authorities were rightly anxious that the visible amenities of the Hall should not be impaired by deterioration or, perhaps worse, by unchecked rebuilding schemes in Great Queen Street. Here Blay was in his element, buying up houses piece-meal on the north side of the street and trying sometimes with a good deal of success to secure with the co-operation of the three Institutions an unbroken block of property. Despite trouble over the condemned and vacant Mark Masons' Hall, which is now part of the Connaught Rooms, where attempts were made both before and after the war without success to persuade the Mark authorities to take over a good site on the north side of the street (history generally repeats itself) his earlier policy succeeded: when Blay died too in 1950 he left comparatively little more to be done. On the other hand the rapid advance of bureaucratic control had probably rendered his work unnecessary, and Grand Lodge found itself the owner of a string of old and virtually worn out properties, heavily protected by preservation orders. Blay and Stubbs together were also closely concerned in the administration of the Royal Masonic Benevolent Institution, which may account for the remarkably generous lease that body had from Grand Lodge for its office accommodation, and for the fact that it still did not own its site for many years after their disappearance.

Other members of the Board appeared more frequently in their official capacities but Robin Bayford did not remain Grand Registrar for long and was quickly succeeded, though sadly for only a short time, by his Deputy Sir Harold Morris with whom it was always a pleasure to work, not least because of the beauty of his handwriting. This latter attraction did not exist in the case of Philip Bull, Grand Director of Ceremonies, but this apart he was benevolence itself both in that office and afterwards when he became Provincial Grand Master for Middlesex and extended his activities, not only to the Hospital but to every conceivable branch of English Freemasonry. There was however no one on the Board who exercised more influence than Edgar Rutter from Cardiff. He had his finger on the pulse of, if not direct controlling, all the Craft's charitable activities having already been Deputy Provincial Grand Master of South Wales Eastern Division for some 15 years. His knowledge of Freemasonry in so many aspects was profound and his intelligence service so efficient that he seemed always to be well ahead of the hunt. Even more to the point he had a considerable influence, probably more than Sydney White as it extended into their social life, with Sir Ernest Cooper. He and Sydney did not hit it off, each mistrusting the other and failing to make the most of their mutual points of contact. I found it unedifying to be warned by Sydney that he was a dangerous man, though I was soon to realise what he meant: Edgar was held to be 'agin the Government' but when he, so to speak, joined it by becoming Chairman of the Officers and Clerks Committee, and still more so when many years later in 1962 Alex Frere and I persuaded him to transfer to the External Relations Committee he became a pillar of the establishment without losing his vitality and readiness of wit. If one must in justice point out a flaw in his character it was one more tiresome to his colleagues than dangerous. His failing was that after a matter was decided following full discussion he tended to revive it—sometimes by after thoughts, but more often I suspect over the dinner table with Sir Ernest. I cannot however overstate my own indebtedness to him or the services he rendered to Grand Lodge, and it was not for nothing that he was in the first distribution of the Grand Master's Order of Service to Masonry.

At this time the Boards were both in varying stages of transition: the new constitution of the Board of Benevolence had brought new members and fresh ideas, while the Board of General Purposes experienced more change than usual in its membership as the old disappeared and were replaced by less antediluvian members.

A NEW GRAND MASTER

The actual 'rulers of the Craft' were similarly affected by change. Lord Harewood, who had become Grand Master so unexpectedly on the death of his brother-in-law the Duke of Kent, who was killed in an air crash whilst on active service, died in May 1947 a bare month after he had appointed a new Deputy Grand Master. In the short period from February to May I had seen little of Lord Harewood but heard much, enough to convince me that he was probably the most knowledgeable if not the easiest Grand Master to work with since the Duke of Sussex a hundred years earlier. He had made a close study of Masonic symbolism as well as organisation and procedure, and the *Aims and Relationships of the Craft* which was published in 1939 owed much to his inspiration. After his election as Grand Master and subsequent installation by King George VI at Freemasons' Hall in 1943 no further promotions in the hierarchy took place for some time and there was not another Pro Grand Master till 1967. However the Deputy Grand Master, General Sir Francis Davies who had continued to be Provincial Grand Master for Worcestershire was ageing fast. His retirement was announced in April 1947, though it may be doubted whether he really knew what was going on around him, and there is some ground for believing that a number of Lodge warrants and similar documents were in fact signed by Lady Davies, this not being discovered till some observant Worcestershire Mason noticed the difference in hand-writing: Lord Harewood appointed the Duke of Devonshire to be Deputy Grand Master, but in fact the Duke found himself Grand Master *de facto* within a few weeks and in his turn he appointed the Earl of Scarbrough as his Deputy, which from the Craft's point of view was a most happy, indeed providential choice. Lord Scarbrough had become a Mason in the Apollo University Lodge among the flood of candidates after World War I, and had thereafter joined Westminster and Keystone Lodge when he left Oxford, but had not taken an active part in Masonry until he went to Bombay as Governor in 1937. He then almost immediately became District Grand Master through RW Bro Bromham stepping down in his favour (only to take over again when Lord Scarbrough's governorship ended). News of his appointment reached Freemasons' Hall in curious circumstances, which are worth detailing, as they indicate the very different attitude the Duke of Devonshire adopted towards his subordinates from Sydney White's: Sydney expected that in his absence all confidential information should go to his private secretary Miss Haig and not to his Principal Assistant, and this attitude persisted almost to the end. The Duke on the other hand made use of the natural chain of command: so it was that one fine summer afternoon when Sydney White was away in the Provinces he spoke to me briefly on the telephone as a complete stranger and said, 'Tell Sydney White that Roger Scarbrough has accepted unconditionally'. I wrote it down and left the message, fortunately in an envelope, on Sydney White's desk—only to be blown up the next day for having quite innocently received it. As in fact the name Roger Scarbrough meant nothing to me at that time I could scarcely be expected to know what an important moment it was.

Meanwhile Brigadier General Darell contined to be Assistant Grand

Master as he had done since 1937, though his health was clearly unreliable. To see the picture clearly it is necessary to go back to the last four months of Sir Colville Smith's life when there was a lot of intrigue and jockeying for position as to his successor. The Board of General Purposes led by RW Bro Russell McLaren wanted Sydney White, who had held office in Grand Lodge since 1919 and virtually acted as Grand Secretary for the last two years of Sir Colville's life, to succeed him. On the other hand there was a vigorous lobby, led by Lord Harewood in favour of Major (Sir) Thomas Lumley Smith, a fellow Etonian and Grand Secretary of the Mark. Relations between the two Smiths had never been very cordial, and the hostility transferred itself to Sydney White. It is as unnecessary as it is unedifying to go into the details of the conflict: suffice it to say that the Board ingeniously outmanoeuvred Lord Harewood who gave in with bad grace. He did however at the same time secure the appointment of Brigadier General Darell as Assistant Grand Master, a new appointment, the obvious purpose of which was to keep the new Grand Secretary in his place. It says much for all the chief actors in this drama (it is a pity that there can be only one protagonist), particularly the Assistant Grand Master and the Grand Secretary that they both rapidly achieved a *modus vivendi* and a firm friendship. It still remains doubtful whether the latter ever subsisted between Lord Harewood and Sydney White but they undoubtedly came to appreciate each others' qualities.

GERTRUDE HAIG

Mention has been made of Miss Haig and this is a good opportunity to look at the career of one who did so much for the Craft in General and Freemasons' Hall in particular. Gertrude Haig had been Secretary to Sir Colville Smith while he was still Secretary of the RMBI and had been brought with him in 1917 to his new office. She was the first woman to be employed by Grand Lodge and used to be described as a 'lady typewriter'. She remained the friend, ally and confidante of three Grand Secretaries only retiring in 1959. She lived on in retirement till 1980, and it was, sadly, my last official duty to attend her funeral in July 1980, a matter of days only before I left the office. She was incorruptible, silent as the grave yet maintaining a keen interest in the staff and its personal and family affairs, which was all the more necessary in the light of the barriers put up by her immediate superiors. While gossip inevitably maintained that she 'ran Grand Lodge' she did in fact never do more than run her own job impeccably and act as a smoothing influence. She was ably succeeded by Irene Hainworth.

Chapter 8

1947–1950

INSTALLATION OF THE DUKE OF DEVONSHIRE

The death of Lord Harewood involved, in due course, the formal installation of the new Grand Master, which was fixed for 23 March 1948. Post war difficulties of travelling made it less than well attended by official visitors from other jurisdictions, but this was compensated for by the great keenness of our own members to acquire tickets. The Duke of Kent's installation in 1939 at Olympia where the seating plan for the Royal Tournament was taken over had been witnessed by over 12,000 brethen: but Lord Harewood's was held at Freemasons' Hall in war conditions. Both had been undertaken by the King himself, and it was confidently expected by the Craft that he would function once more, as indeed he did. Olympia was not available and recourse was once more taken to the Royal Albert Hall, which I believe to be ideal for such an occasion. It provides the occasion with an ideal setting since the various levels of seating as well as the arena itself focus on the magnificent dais in such a way that no one is so far distant from the centre as to feel cut off from the ceremony. Cloakrooms and storage space were indeed then in short supply, though there was at least enough for the Grand Officers and the few official visitors: but the rest had to clothe in the corridors and stow their hats, cases and coats under their seats.

The installation at Olympia had provided enough accommodation for it to be possible to invite applications from the rank and file of Past Masters; but the Albert Hall was appreciably smaller and the Craft's numbers larger in 1948 than in 1939. Hersey Woods put up a plan, which fortunately was accepted, and this was later used again in 1951 and 1967, the basis of it being that every Master of his Lodge had an absolute right to attend, also that a limited number of seats should be allocated to those Grand Officers, who troubled to apply and who were then subjected to a ballot of not very severe stringency. Finally each Master could nominate one of his members for an additional place, but as it could not be guaranteed that there would be room the inference made was that any such place would not be a particularly comfortable one. The plan worked out well, with most Masters taking up their option and it was evident that if they could not do so they exerted themselves to see that a worthy substitute came instead. There was inevitably some discontent among unsuccessful Grand Officers, usually voiced along the lines 'I have always been, and never missed one before', to which the answer (if brutal) was easy.

Sydney White concentrated his efforts on the special stewards, so successfully that both the framework of their positioning and also many of the stewards used in 1948 could be reappointed next time. A great many of them were recruited from the Grand Stewards Lodge, who were already acquainted with Grand Lodge procedure and ceremonial: but the Corps of Royal Albert Hall stewards, with their intimate knowledge of the building and of crowd control, also helped. The seating on the dais behind those actually concerned in the ceremony was left to Hersey Woods and myself, and the rest of the seating was worked out by Brothers Brunton and Browne in particular, both of whom survived to do it twice more. The ceremonial side was safe in the hands of the King, Sydney White and Philip Bull who had all been through it before. This, as I found out later, was far less complicated than the logistical side of getting people ticketed correctly, to their allotted places and finally away. A medical team was provided and St John Ambulance Association gave assistance too from their members who also knew their way round the Hall. One of our best allies, unobtrusive but always ready to help was Andy Woodman head of Benjamin Edgington's, the firm which did so much work at all times for the Albert Hall: I was fortunate enough to strike up a firm and understanding friendship with Andy and still like to think that we worked well together as a team.

The preparations for the meeting broke new ground for me, and not knowing many of those taking part, such as the special stewards, made it all appear rather confusing, but when a further installation took place less than four years later, the experience gained in 1948 proved invaluable. Two incidents stand out from the Duke's installation, as I was not yet a Grand Officer and had a roving commission but with no clearly defined seat. Hence it was purely by accident that I was standing in a convenient entrance in the south east looking at the packed tiers of audience when an agitated Deputy Grand Director of Ceremonies (Kingsley Tubbs) came up and said 'Where is the Grand Master's Standard? It's not in its appointed place': it should have been at the main west approach to be brought in for presentation but the King had either arrived early or got through his welcome quicker than expected, and the Freemasons' Hall housekeeper Hughes, who should have been in charge of the standard had been called away to help dress him in his regalia. (The latter's greeting to the Duke was said afterwards by Philip Bull to have been 'Well, Eddie, I expect you are bloody nearly as nervous as I am'.) Meanwhile Kingsley and I raced round the interminable corridors and more by luck than good judgement found the standard which he proceeded to hand over with dignity and aplomb to the Derbyshire Masons who were about to present it. When it was all over I was walking more sedately, with Philip Bull, down the same corridor when a brother came up to us, seized Philip by the arm and said 'Where did I leave my hat?' Philip replied gently that he was afraid that he did not know. The brother, who was a complete stranger to us both, dropped his arm saying 'Well, you bloody well ought to' and made off.

The King did the installation magnificently and without any hesitancy, and the speeches made were short and to the point, the only blemish came from the ill mannered behaviour of a number of, regrettably, senior Grand Officers who left the dais before Grand Lodge was closed and virtually while the ceremony was going on. The fact that a long list of additional appointments to Grand Rank was being read out and their investiture taking place should not have been used as an excuse for their ill manners. In 1951 to prevent a similar occurrence those on the dais were warned in definite terms that they must stay to the end, and I suspect that Frank Douglas's cold eye would have kept them in their places anyhow.

The medical team had practically no calls on their service as the only fatal casualty occurred on the way back to Paddington. When their OC saw RW Bro Burnett Brown, Provincial Grand Master for Middlesex, (formerly Deputy when the King, as Duke of York, was Provincial Grand Master), who was indeed mortally ill but determined to be present, he said 'If he walks in that procession he will die'. We quickly found a wheelchair and got 'BB' up onto the dais, and back at the end of the meeting in time to have a word with the King.

After this excitement life at Freemasons' Hall reverted back to its normal tenor of routine work interspersed with regular Board meetings. In the following month my position was officially regularised by my being appointed Assistant Grand Secretary, and my evening engagements mounted accordingly. Some were in the official line of duty whilst others were private invitations by Lodges which wanted to get to know me—and in some cases possibly to grind an axe in some gentle way.

LONDON GRAND RANK

When Hersey Woods retired, I took over from him the responsibility of sorting out recommendations for London Grand Rank and London Grand Chapter Rank. There were in those days not as many appointments as there are now—due to the existence of fewer Lodges and Chapters but principally to a lower ratio of appointments, which made the preselection process harder and ensured that a large number of recommendations had to be carried over until the next year or even longer. It was no more easier then, than it is now, to persuade those submitting recommendations that seniority so far from being the only criterion was in fact almost the weakest. In making selections I used always to bear in mind two apothegms, one from Hersey Woods that mathematically only about one in three London Past Masters could ever hope to get the honour, and the other from Douglas Amery to the effect that election to the chair was a Lodge's way of rewarding service up to that point and cancelled out past services; the slate therefore being now wiped clean new service had to be given in order to gain the necessary merit. To these factors I also added one of my own, that even if a set of Past Masters recommended someone as their most worthy colleague he still had to go into free competition with all those recommendations by other Lodges—and on that premise the conclusion was anything but foregone. With the introduction of these three arguments it was generally quite easy to soothe down hurt feelings whether by letter or interview. After I had made my preselections Sydney White would look through them and together we would discuss the relative merits of the border line cases. At that time London Grand Chapter Rank was dealt with on the antediluvian basis of the Grand Chapter Committee calling for a list from each Chapter, of every qualified Past First Principal (perhaps as many as eight or ten from each Chapter) and then solemnly sifting through some thousands of names! In practice it turned out to be not quite as bad as that, because very few Chapters put up all their names, and some none at all. It was quite soon decided to limit the number of recommendations to three, and ultimately to come round to the same system as used for London Grand Rank.

It will be easier to explain other aspects of the work under the headings of the various Committees of the Board of General Purposes.

FINANCE COMMITTEE

The fund of General Purposes was quite heavily in debt following the various property purchases already mentioned. Though there was no great urgency to repay as interest rates in the Dalton era were very low, it was obvious that the debts would have to be repaid at some time, but it was not easy to say where the money was to come from. Income was comparatively static being mainly derived from Lodge dues in respect of individual membership, and registration fees for new members. Rents of properties were a little more elastic as leases fell in, and rents of Lodge rooms could be adjusted with little trouble.

It was over Lodge dues that I witnessed my first power struggle in 1948, by which time the debts had been repaid though the fund was in the red and likely to remain so for a considerable time. We were fortunate that year in having as our Grand Treasurer, Joseph Coates of Northumberland and also of Price Waterhouse who saw the problem clearly and advocated an increase in quarterage (annual dues). For some unexplained reason Edgar Rutter was strongly opposed, possibly he felt that he should be seen to be championing the cause of the Provinces, who were in fact not being subjected to any more increase than London, or that the increase was either ill-timed or unnecessary. What amounted to a battle royal ensued with each of the opposing factions trying hard to get the President on their side. Sir Ernest Cooper was instinctively for the increase as he had already formed the opinion which he was later to enunciate to Grand Lodge as a cardinal matter of policy, that fees should be regarded as capital accretion and that the running expenses of Grand Lodge should be covered by annual payments by the membership of the Craft. This view prevailed and has done so ever since and in the age of inflation has been extended so as to cover increasing costs using less cumbrous machinery.

PROCEDURE COMMITTEE

In matters of Procedure the new *Book of Constitutions* (1940) very much diminished the Committee's work, but there were still several matters which needed to be adjusted. When I arrived a curb was being put on the powers of Masters to call emergency meetings *ad lib*, and to require them to apply for a dispensation to be considered and granted. This was a successful endeavour to limit the rush of candidates as they emerged from the armed forces with a consequent pile up in later years of competitors for office, and this together with a much more liberal attitude to the formation of 'overflow' Lodges kept the position reasonably stable, at least in London. However there were murmurings from the Provinces about the paucity of Provincial Grand Ranks (and the complex nature of the rules governing the matter) and when Major R. L. Loyd became Chairman we worked out a new schedule which lasted with little alteration to 1978. Perhaps its chief improvement lay in divorcing first appointments from promotions, which thenceforward were to be at the individual Provincial Grand Master's discretion and not tied in any way to the number of Lodges in his Province. It must be admitted that this new found freedom went to the heads of some of them, and there was a rather unseemly growth in the number of Past Provincial Grand Wardens, both Senior and Junior, but fortunately it did not last long and commonsense prevailed.

After a winter holiday in South Africa Sir Ernest Cooper came back with his mind full of what he found there in connection with Lodge after proceedings: and he was able to persuade the Board to enunciate to Grand Lodge, which accepted it, that there should be no Fire and no Masonic speeches made in the presence of non-Masons, though tacitly allowing, and even encouraging, the presence of members' ladies who in many cases had prepared and helped to serve the meal. There was nothing at all revolutionary in this proposal, but to have got it formally approved by Grand Lodge was another good example of his tidiness of mind. Another action, this time for my own benefit, related to the office of Assistant Grand Secretary which was a very long way down the table of precedence: Sir Ernest however got it elevated to, roughly, its present position, and in so doing caused something of an uproar in the Provinces, headed by the West Riding! As ranks in the Provinces and Districts followed automatically on those in Grand Lodge, it was in many cases the practice to use the rank of Provincial Assistant Grand Secretary as a sinecure for the least worthy aspirants, or, if it was not a sinecure, to give the working occupant a considerably higher rank as well. Brother Frobisher, Provincial Grand Secretary of the West Riding protested that many (probably a wilful and typical exaggeration) of the least worthy Provincial Grand Officers would be automatically promoted beyond their deserts and over the heads of better Masons (later I met the same level of obstructionism twice when the Grand Rank precedence was altered!). Sir Ernest stuck to his point but allowed a complicated amendment whereby, in this particular instance, the Grand and Provincial Grand Ranks were not kept in strict parallel.

EXTERNAL RELATIONS

The Colonial, Indian and Foreign Committee was a title *anathema* to the strength of Canadian feeling which was never far below the surface in Sir Ernest and quite soon it was realistically renamed External Affairs. It led a busy existence with quite frequent conferences with Ireland and Scotland and, as the occasion required with most of the regular Masonic world. The principal items of discussion were God and Communism: predominantly the latter as it was mainly a matter of trying to restrain our American brethren from charging bull headed at the Iron Curtain, seeking to make pronouncements, which should have been self evident truths and not calling for publicity about the incompatibility of Freemasonry and Communism. In this we were, I believe, successful as a few paragraphs were quietly added to the 1939 *Aims and Relationships of the Craft* and quite quickly these were accepted as an integral part of the original document. When McCarthyism was finally discredited in the USA and throughout the world we heard much less of the need for every genuine Mason to fight Communism. God on the other hand, if one may so indelicately put it, was a trickier problem, and one that can still cause much heart burning. It was and still is common ground that atheists are not acceptable as Masons: but it is beyond the wit of most of us to devise a foolproof and exact definition of atheism, still less of agnosticism; where to draw the line about an answer to the basic question 'Do you believe in God?' will depend quite as much on the questioner as on the respondent. It is my belief that it is the exception rather than the rule for continentals (and probably many in these islands) to believe in the fundamentalist God of the Old Testament. In any case our Hindu, Moslem and Buddhist brethren can hardly be expected to share our beliefs, and furthermore, especially in the Latin races, Freemasonry had in the not so distant past been as much one of the chief vehicles for emancipation as the Roman Church had been the buttress of the established rule. The descendants and admirers of the liberators could hardly be expected to practise, or express, belief in the deity that their old opponents preached. That however did not necessarily make them either atheists or agnostics, but it did make it difficult to say where the line came. Grand Lodge insisted on a stated belief in God and on the presence in Lodge, primarily to give sanctity and binding force to the Obligations, of a Volume of the Sacred Law: there were constitutions which did away with this requirement, or more insidiously replaced the VSL with a Book of Constitutions or a blank white book, and they also skated round the definition of God with the meaningless phrase 'Superior Principle'. The crunch came however in 1950 when the Grand Orient of Uruguay, hitherto believed to have been one of the more respectable bodies in South America was proved, out of its own mouth, to have abandoned the standards of regularity. The United Grand Lodge of England broke off relations with it and has not resumed them, though there may now be some slight evidence of a return to the paths of righteousness, for which our own two* Lodges in Montevideo speak up. But it must be clear to any one who thinks about it that irregularity cannot be cleansed in a moment of time and that the irregulars, even if only a decreasing minority will continue to infect the whole, unless, which is highly improbable, they are ejected.

Grand Lodge's action caused something of a stir in Latin America, and the Grand Lodges (or Orients) in Chile and Brazil were at pains to try to produce evidence that their Superior Principles were indeed God, only under a slight disguise. Chile managed to convince, but Brazil was then and still continued to be a vexed problem: in short that vast country contains two (at least) quite different forms of Masonic government, dating back as a dichotomy to the 1920s. As so often happens particularly among Latins the Supreme Council had a hand in it and established, after a quarrel with the Grand Orient, a rival set of State Grand Lodges. Not least because this seemed to correspond with the United States system, but also because the two US Supreme Councils supported the State Grand Lodges, whose only real ground for existence was the need to provide personnel for their Supreme Council, the new (and schismatic) bodies won almost universal recognition in North America, and having won it they proceeded to blackguard the Grand Orient and accuse it and its leaders of every crime in the Masonic Calendar. The Grand Orient was for years either too proud or too indolent to fight back, and one would like to think also that being secure in its recognition by the three home Grand Lodges it felt that the rest of the Masonic world could go hang. Its rulers when they came to this country or when they met our own District representatives in Brazil were a good deal more impressive than those of the State Grand Lodges, and one cannot but admire the fact that they refrained from digging up the same kind of dirt about the State Grand Lodges, as the latter did about them.

I managed to get a factual account compiled by W Bro Eric White of the manner in which the split in the Grand Orient occurred and how the State Grand Lodges had emerged. It did not however appeal to the Americans even if many of them had bothered to read it, and they continued to lap up half truths and downright falsehoods which came to them from the other side.

Indeed Grand Orient tended to be something of a dirty word in the Masonic vocabulary, conjuring up visions of the Grand Orient of France,

* One has recently returned its Warrant and been erased

and when Masonry was re-established in Holland after the war, under the leadership of Dr Caron he decided to delete the name, and the Groot Ost or Grand East replaced it. It was a slight change of nomenclature admittedly, but very important in showing to the Masonic world that the Netherlands were not to be associated with the irregulars.

PREMISES COMMITTEE

It has already been explained that W. F. Blay was the mastermind of Grand Lodge's property schemes, then conducted through the Premises Committee. It also dealt with what restoration could be effected to bring Freemason's Hall back from its wartime footing and was responsible for making the building, so far as possible, pay its way: and as a result room rents for the seventeen suites were put on the basis of a *per capita* charge for each meeting. But renewal of leases and attempts to gain control of the north side of Great Queen Street were Bro Blay's chief interest, the foremost, being the lease of the Connaught Rooms which was fixed on what were, in those days of cheap money, excellent terms: escalation clauses were practically unknown then and what was a good bargain in 1947 now looks remarkably cheap. Then as now there was occasional agitation for the Craft to take the Connaught Rooms over completely and plunge into catering. Fortunately it was only agitation, and it was generally quite easy to point out to the agitators that for Grand Lodge to go into business on behalf of what at best was only about 10% of the Craft was inviting trouble.

There are probably now only a few of us who remember an obscure theatre called the Kingsway near the eastern end of Great Queen Street. It was pretty well derelict from non-use and bomb damage and in fact alongside it there was a big (empty) static water tank on the site of a war casualty. It was altogether a complex site, a planner's dream (or nightmare) and Blay strove mightily to put all the pieces together. The lady who owned the theatre was hard to pin down, nor did Blay himself ever succeed, but in the end Roland Hanbury Bateman managed to bring all parties to heel, and the Mercantile Credit building is the result. Grand Lodge disposed, advantageously, of some quite useless buildings which were really outside its sphere of interest, particularly as Grand Mark Lodge had moved itself off into Mayfair. We were greatly helped not only by Roland's diplomacy (some of which was rather of the 'gun-boat' type) but also by the Borough Engineer of that time who had a pet scheme to extend Newton Street which used to end on the north side of Parker Street through to Great Queen Street: hence the tunnel now under Mercantile Credit and the ease with which planning permission was achieved and put into practical form.

Blay always insisted on full repairing leases and on a rebuilding clause, the latter in case we ever had the chance to do a comprehensive rebuilding of the north side, and it says much for his persuasiveness that he managed to get away with what appeared to be two rather incompatible conditions.

OFFICERS AND CLERKS COMMITTEE

The Premises Committee also dealt with the wages of the Maintenance staff apart from its three principals, and this in turn tended to lead to annual difficulties and incongruities with the Officers and Clerks Committee.

This Committee met for business once a year, when the salaries and wages of all the clerical staff, the museum staff, Sydney White and myself were discussed exhaustively. It was a day I never ceased to hate as I felt an acute responsibility, which in the army days had been taken off one's shoulders by the Pay Warrant, for the degree of increases that might be allotted. Fortunately the more permanent members who had graduated to come on to the Pension scheme initiated in the days of Sir Edward Letchworth were also on a salary scale which if it changed as it frequently did changed for one and all: but there were others, not on the permanent list who had to be fought for individually, and it was a constant struggle to obtain justice for them. For reasons I never understood, Edgar Rutter, who had just become the Chairman, was opposed in principle to their very existence, thinking that we should have only a permanent staff. It may have been that he felt that he could exert more control over such staff, not realising that there was much work of a purely routine and repetitive nature which could be much more profitably done by middle-aged brethren, retired from their jobs and still wishing for some form of employment than by youngsters straight from school or the forces whose ambition at some time in the future would take them far beyond that kind of work. By quiet persistence I won my own way in the end but it tended to sour our relations for a time and they only became cordial again when he transferred his affections to External Affairs many years later. It must not however be thought that there was any lack of generosity about Edgar Rutter: he was always one of the first to support, even when he did not initiate it, any possible improvement in the scale.

In due course I put forward a scheme for indexing the membership of the Craft; a previous attempt in the 1910s had foundered partly with World War I but more because its proponents had overwhelmed it with

---

Installation of RWBro W. R. S. Bathurst as Provincial Grand Master for Gloucestershire in April 1950. Among those seated are five Provincial Grand Masters together with the Grand Master, the Duke of Devonshire. Front row; left to right: E. R. Dymond (PrGM Herefordshire), P. M. C. Hayman (Dep PGM), 10th Duke of Devonshire (GM), Hon W. R. S. Bathurst (PrGM), G. D. Amery (PrGM Oxfordshire), Ben Marsh (PrGM Worcestershire), George Tryon (PrGM Bristol). Back row; left to right: CdR R. Barrett (Dep GDC), R. Lewis (PrG Sec), P. C. Bull (GDC), the Provincial GDC, JWS (Asst GSec), E. L. Bunting (Dep PrGM Worcestershire), C. R. Baddeley (PDep GDC).

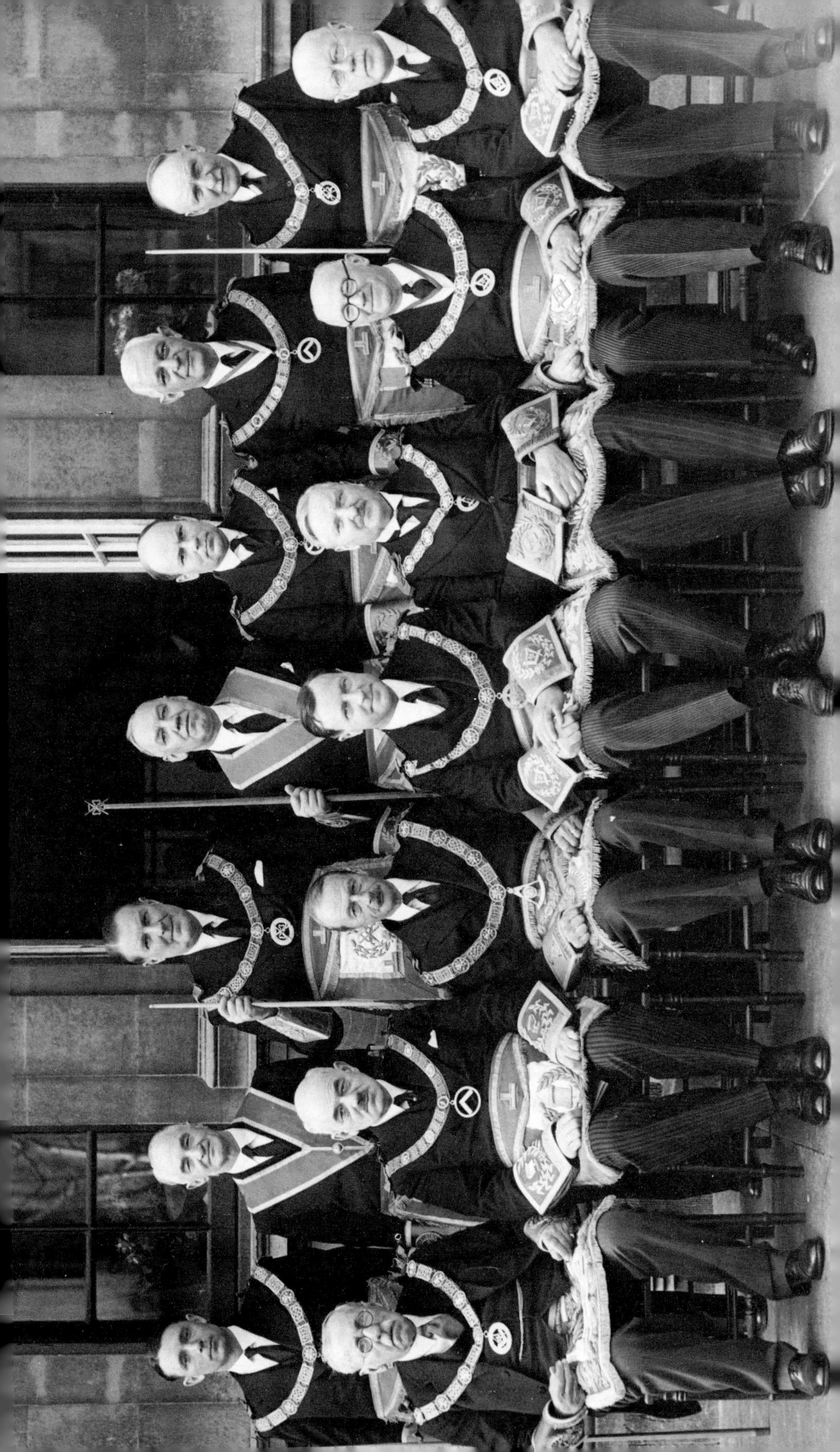

its own weight, trying to get on to a single, though rather large, card the whole masonic *curriculum vitae* with charitable contributions, ranks attained and other Lodges joined. It had never been completed, let alone kept up to date, and successful reference to it was something of a matter of luck. Later on the 'Million Memorial Fund' collecting department had started an excellent card index of all those who had contributed to the Fund, at least to the extent of qualifying for the medal: but unfortunately this too ended abruptly, with the closure of the Fund.

It seemed to me that with the excellent Lodge Register system which dated back to the years immediately following the Union all that was needed was direct reference to the registers with a date to facilitate search. The simplest method was to write a card for every Grand Lodge Certificate issued as this took care of all except the very small number of entrants to the Craft who stuck in the first or second degree. It would progressively take care of the future, and the plan was gradually to work back also through the volumes, year by year, of Certificate registers so that in the end there would be a complete run of the vast majority of members. At that moment the RMBI were asking whether Grand Lodge could take on two young men whose services were no longer required as they had brought their records up to date. They were taken on and set to organise this new venture (one of them is still working at Freemasons' Hall though not on the cards), and we had in 1980 got the best part of 50 years completed. This means in effect that any Master Mason under the age of 70 can immediately be traced to his mother Lodge. I always cherished the hope that when the great bulge of First War intake had been dealt with it would be realistic to look forward—or should I say back?—to the destruction of the old index, but alas.

LIBRARY, ART AND PUBLICATIONS COMMITTEE

The sixth and last committee had the comprehensive title of Library, Art and Publications: this was something of a misnomer as it logically, but not in fact, excluded the museum. It never seemed to get to grips with art, and ultimate control of Grand Lodge's publications lay with the Finance Committee. However it did do valuable work in the museum, not least by inspiring presentations, and occasionally hinting that a portrait of a new Grand Master would be appropriate, but it had been bequeathed a *damnosa hereditas* in the shape of a number of old portraits of dead and gone Masons which had been wished on to Grand Lodge no doubt by sorrowing relatives, but for most of these there could be no other resting place than a store room with their faces to the wall. There is one picture which has an interesting story—John Martin's vast canvas of Joshua commanding the sun and moon to stand still. It would have been in the summer of 1950 that I invited Bill Martin, son of Sir Alec Martin of Christies, to lunch to look over the building: he had been at Oxford with me and I had later been tutor at St Paul's to his younger brother Claude.

After lunch we concentrated on the pictures, about which he was brutally frank, as practically everything we had held to be the handiwork of some artist of repute he ascribed at least one degree lower, including the alleged Hogarth about which Lord Harewood had enunciated some interesting views, until we came to the Martin picture which had been bought several years previously at a Naylor-Layland sale for £29.10.0 by a Mason who presented it anonymously to Grand Lodge. Bill was very enthusiastic, not, as he hastened to point out, because he and the painter were both Martins, but claiming that it was of great value as Martin was just becoming fashionable and this was a very good example of his work. I became slightly more interested when he also mentioned Belshazzar's Feast which I remembered from childhood as an engraving of it was hung in an obscure corner at Kilravock. He also mentioned as a well-known copyist of the late 18th century the Rev William Peters, saying darkly that we probably owned more of his works than we knew.

It was a good many years later that I happened to see a notice of an exhibition of John Martin's work at the Whitechapel Art Gallery: and having an unwontedly free Saturday afternoon I went to it, and on reading the catalogue was interested to find that what was probably Martin's greatest picture was reported as lost without trace, *Joshua*. I enjoyed the exhibition greatly and on Monday morning told Sydney White about it: he was not much interested but said it would be a kindness to the organisers to let them know where *Joshua* was. I did so and was surprised at the immediate reaction, for a Mr Thomas Balsdon, who turned out to be then the greatest expert on Martin and the author of a book about him, turned up with some fellow experts, all of whom expressed pleasure that the lost masterpiece had reappeared and made suggestions that it should be cleaned. This was expertly done and many aspects of detail reappeared. Since then *Joshua* has paid visits to many Martin exhibitions and was figured prominently in the book *The Art of John Martin* compiled and written by my nephew William Feaver.

This Committee also used to confer with the Librarian in producing names of suitably qualified brethren to be put before the trustees of the Prestonian Fund as prospective lecturers; two names were always put forward, it being clearly understood that the second would be 'chosen' to lecture next year. On the publication side a new *Masonic Year Book* had just been produced in 1947, the first since 1942, though some supplements covering the more important changes had been produced at intervals during the War. Later it will be described how we tried to keep down the book size by leaving out less necessary elements and by eventually publishing the *Historical Supplement*, now sadly dated, to take care of the chronological lists of Grand Officers and the erased Lodges and Chapters.

MY FIRST 'SOLO FLIGHT'

Life continued busily for two years but without any particular excitements

Stratford sub Castle vicarage near Salisbury, my fathers last living: the Castle is Old Sarum and he derived much pleasure from being 'perpetual curate of the rotten borough'. The house, no longer the vicarage, was once in the hands of the Pitt family: its east side is late Tudor, with a Queen Anne garden front clapped on to it.

My parents in their garden at Detling, Kent on the occasion of their golden wedding in 1959.

after the Duke of Devonshire's installation in March 1948, but early in 1950 I was then forewarned by Sydney White that arrangements had been made for him to attend the jubilee of the Grand Lodge of Western Australia and that he was also going to make a comprehensive tour of the other Australian Grand Lodges and, if possible, of our remaining Lodges in that country. He had never flown, and did not intend to start doing so at the age of 65, so it was bound to be a long business with sea voyages both ways and some very long train journeys backwards and forwards inside Australia. He was reassuring enough to suggest that I knew enough to get on without him for five months, buttressed by Sir Ernest Cooper and Miss Haig. Everyone was kind and helpful, and I survived the two annual investitures of Craft and Royal Arch, plus several Board and Council meetings. The very first function was the installation of the Hon W. R. S. Bathurst as Provincial Grand Master and Grand Superintendent at Cheltenham. It was particularly appropriate as he had given me my first collar in the Apollo as Assistant Secretary in 1931: the resulting ceremonial however presented some problems. We had gone down by train the previous evening and dined and stayed in a hotel on the outskirts of the town. Next morning Philip Bull and his team departed early to rehearse and do a final check up for the two meetings, leaving me to bring the Grand Master to the Town Hall later on. When he had not appeared for breakfast by 10.30 I became worried and on enquiry found that no one had remembered to call him: and we got to the Town Hall only just in time at the expense, to him, of a hurried breakfast. We were then confronted first with a rickety flight of steps on to the stage, and then by two Principals to assist the Duke, one of whom had a permanently stiff leg and the other had recently had two cataracts removed! Worse was to come, when the Duke found that in the hurry he had left his spectacles behind: Philip Bull offered his but though they were gratefully accepted it was clear that they served little purpose. The audience as a whole fortunately were not aware of the knife edge on which we stood, but the Principals managed to get up the steps and the ceremony thereafter proceeded smoothly. The Grand Master made, as he always did, some charming speeches which quite covered up the faultiness of his ritual.

AWAY FROM FREEMASONS' HALL

Another highlight of that summer was going with Lord Scarbrough to Oxford for the Centenary of the Churchill Lodge No 478: it was a white tie and tails occasion, complicated by the fact that Lord Scarbrough was later attending a state ball at the Palace. Fortunately dinner was being held in Brasenose College and I was able to arrange some accommodation for changing to which we retired after the earlier speeches. Lord Scarbrough got himself into knee breeches and asked me to deal with his garter and a selection of stars, as to which he said that he had no idea which went where, and that Lady Scarbrough alone knew the correct sequence! We managed to get back punctually to London to collect her and the car deposited them in good time at the Palace and then took me home to Rowan Road.

Meanwhile at Headquarters we were getting long letters from Sydney White which were eventually worked up into a travelogue which served as a model for subsequent ones. He himself arrived back in time for the August Board meetings in excellent form, and after ten days in double harness I took myself off on the first of many holidays abroad.

It is perhaps not too fanciful to think of the summer of 1950 as the transition from my Entered Apprentice to my Fellow Craft stage, and I will now pick up the threads of family life and Oxford Masonry.

Our holidays late in August were spent for the most part in Scotland, but we also took one in Ireland, and in 1950 we joined up with Richenda's eldest sister and her husband in the then considerable adventure of a motor tour in France. With only £100 between the four of us we none the less succeeded in living very comfortably for a full fortnight in the course of which we covered most of the Loire Valley, the Massif Centrale and finished up with a couple of nights in Paris. When we came back to London our household was increased by the company of their daughter Nicolette who lived with us for the next year or two while practising her skill of teaching children to dance under Madame Vacani.

My father when he became 70 gave up the benefice of Stratford-sub-Castle outside Salisbury at the end of the war, and after some casting around my parents found themselves a house, rather more derelict than Rowan Road, at Detling in East Kent. The object was to be near his youngest brother Sir Edward who had retired from the Colonial Service and gone first to Wateringbury and later to Bearsted. My parents had no connection with East Kent, and the whole plan fell apart when my uncle died very suddenly a few weeks after they had settled in Detling, with my aunt predictably moving back to London. At that time we had not foreseen a crisis developing so quickly but nevertheless had been apprehensive as to the wisdom of moving into such new territory. They did not, at their age, find it at all easy to make new friends in quite different surroundings: as my brothers who were both bachelors were settled in Clifton and Exeter they would have found a west country headquarters for holidays and vacations much easier, and we in London could have travelled with equal facility in any direction: but it is difficult to avoid the conclusion that it was consideration for my sister, first in St Albans and later in Nottingham, that prevented them from returning to the west country. Richenda's mother on the other hand had settled comfortably, outside Westerham shortly before the war, where she was surrounded by swarms of Streatfeilds.

Freemasonry within Oxford University came to a dead stop so far as the other degrees were concerned soon after 1940, but the Apollo continued to be active, mainly thanks to Clive Saxton who took on as Secretary when Patrick Johnson, a Magdalen Science don, and a Rowing Blue, went to the war. He was greatly helped by Wimburn Horlock when he came out of the forces and by a young Don of New College, David Boult who died all too soon before peace conditions returned. There was therefore a healthy nucleus to build up the other concerned bodies, and I reckoned to spend six Saturday afternoons and evenings in each of the three terms getting to and from Oxford by one means or other for nearly 20 years and held office in one or other of the degrees without a break from 1931 to 1967.

There were various highlights—the Centenary of the Coeur de Lion Preceptory (twin brother of the Churchill Lodge) in 1950, the revival of the Oxford University Ark Mariners Lodge which took place under Bobbie Loyd in a bedroom in the Randolph Hotel, and the centenaries a little later of the Apollo University Royal Arch Chapter, the University Mark Lodge and the Oxford University Rose Croix Chapter, though all efforts to establish a centenary for the Ark Mariners failed—not surprisingly as it had met only three times between the wars! Former members, long since graduated, helped enormously by coming back to meetings whenever they were within reach, and were often able to give guidance to the younger generation. We had been also greatly helped by the removal of meetings to Saturdays which it will be recalled had originated to suit PC's week-end convenience but in the end seemed to suit everyone.

One sad difference from pre-war conditions was that the smaller Masonic bodies were no longer able to dine in Common Rooms and had to rely first on the Randolph Hotel and later at 333 Banbury Road when facilities were established there. It would probably have been impossible for economic reasons to continue our pre-war custom, but in any case the number of dons who could lend their names to a dinner party had sadly diminished. However it was now possible to get all their individual records sorted out, their bylaws brought into line with current practice, and a financial structure implemented to take the place of the so called life membership on which most of them had subsisted. It was said that Jack Gamlen, the University Solicitor, finally came to terms with Grand Mark Lodge with a personal cheque, and I can vouch for having taken their accounts over with a balance (black) in shillings while the Ark Mariners was of a similar size but in red.

Chapter 9

1950–1958

It might have been expected that with Sydney White's return things would have quickly re-established themselves back in the old routine: but such was not the case. During his absence two of the Committee Chairmen, Brothers Blay and Stubbs, had been replaced by Brothers A. Macdonald and George Matthey, in both cases an improvement as the two elder men had outlived their generation and indeed their usefulness. In the course of the summer Dr Bankes, Provincial Grand Master for Middlesex too had died, and it looked very much as if the succession would go, not to his Deputy Norman Moore who had at that time a number of detractors, but to the GDC Philip Bull. This in its turn would result in creating a vacancy of great importance.

The whole matter was thrown more violently into the melting pot in November by the sudden death of the Duke of Devonshire, who had only just returned with Sydney White by sea and land from Malta where he had installed Brigadier Esmond de Wolff as District Grand Master and Grand Superintendent. The rest of the party had flown and been back some time when this tragic event occurred, and one cannot but wonder whether an air journey even in those days might not have saved him much wear and tear. But for his inspired choice of Lord Scarbrough as his Deputy the Duke's death would have been an even greater loss to the Craft as General Darell was already ageing and could clearly not have taken on any further responsibilities particularly as he had become in 1948 Grand Master of Grand Mark Lodge. Whatever may have been his original reservations in 1947 Lord Scarbrough accepted what had come to him so unexpectedly and so precipitately and in March 1951 he was elected for the first of 17 times to the Grand Mastership, appointing Lord Derby as his Deputy and retaining General Darell as Assistant Grand Master. Philip Bull was duly appointed to Middlesex and after some persuasion Frank Douglas accepted office as Grand Director of Ceremonies, which also lasted 17 years. Philip Bull was a bachelor and not over preoccupied with his duties as a lecturer at Imperial College whereas Frank Douglas had heavy business as well as family commitments and stipulated for a third Deputy to help with the ceremonial work, a change which has worked out extremely well.

In his sadly short period of office as Grand Master, the Duke had shown great qualities of leadership at a time when the change over to peace conditions at home and the revival of Masonry overseas both in Europe and the Far East called for it. He would have been the first to admit that he was no ritualist, though the prepared or off-the-cuff speeches that he made at installations and similar functions were delightful and telling; neither did he hesitate to speak with considerable force if he thought fit (eg, in condemnation of dirty stories at the dinner table) and the occasion called for it. Under his direction the Craft settled itself into new circumstances, and though there was no lack of appeals there were no major upsets either in Grand Lodge itself or among the Institutions. Lord Scarbrough had been closely associated with the Duke when they were both in the House of Commons and spoke most eloquently of him at the December Quarterly Communication. It seemed at first however that his tenure of office was going to be ill-starred: the King had himself undertaken the last three installations of the Duke of Kent, the Earl of Harewood and the Duke of Devonshire, and it was an open secret that he was looking forward to the forthcoming one when he fell mortally ill, and was unable to come to the Albert Hall in November 1951. His place was taken by Lord Derby who had just been appointed Deputy Grand Master and who carried out the ceremony with great aplomb and dignity. The procedure was otherwise almost identical with previous installations but was graced with a prayer for the King's restoration to health by the Archbishop of Canterbury. There was moreover a much larger attendance of brethren from other jurisdictions (24 in all) than there had been in 1948.

Earlier in the year, probably inspired by the breaking off of relations with the Grand Orient of Uruguay, as I have already reported, the Grand Master of Chile came to England and spent a long day explaining to representatives of the Board of General Purposes that the attitude of his Grand Lodge in respect of belief in God was substantially different from that of Uruguay: he spoke convincingly though it was clear and difficult to deny that he had the advantage of seeing at first hand the pitfalls into which Uruguay had fallen. He in his turn was followed by the Grand Master of the Grand Orient of Brazil who had accepted an invitation to Lord Scarbrough's installation: which was issued despite the fact that there had already been a lot of argument, especially with various Grand Lodges in the States, about Brazilian legitimacy. We on our side were quite happy about the regularity from the constitutional point of view of the Grand Orient, and Brother Neves was quite as convincing as Chile had been on the religious side.

ATTACKS FROM THE CHURCH

Lord Scarbrough's Grandmastership was beset with difficulties and occasional crises at home, all of which he handled with great skill. Among the most difficult, especially as it affected the non-Masonic world as well as our own organisation was an increase in the number and incidence of attacks from the Churches, established and free. While it can scarcely be doubted that sheer wilful ignorance inspired many of them, the old clerical sport of sniping at those in authority, Archbishop Fisher having been a Grand Chaplain, may have prompted the more malicious: Walton Hannah, who wrote *Darkness Visible* and claimed Masonic experience, perhaps attained the greatest notoriety, and his books were well described as single tickets to Rome where spiritually he at last arrived. But the Masons themselves were not entirely blameless: although, with very few exceptions, they had refrained from rising to the Anglo Catholic bait they had occasionally behaved in religious matters with an insensitivity that was almost as bad. In the years following the war, Church services proliferated and it is difficult to deny that the excuse to appear in semi-public attired in Masonic regalia was one of their attractions; but it is also only fair to remind ourselves that both the Churches in which such services were held and various Masonic Charities profited considerably from the generous collections: furthermore it can be argued, not solely speciously, that if such a service brought to Church just one individual who would not otherwise have gone it was worthwhile. The trouble however came over the form of service; as part of the Bi-Centenary celebrations what was described as a 'Masonic Service' had been held at the Albert Hall. Its liturgy had been carefully chosen to exclude anything that might possibly offend any denominations likely to be represented at it (even so it is handed down that a Rabbi from Birmingham found it sufficiently distasteful to resign from the Craft). This order of service had tended to be adopted by organisers of subsequent but much less representative services, who felt in some muddled way that they too must excise all traces of denominational worship: in justice some fault should be laid at the doors of the various Rectories and Vicarages, whose occupants, equally muddled, but with an eye to the collection and sometimes Masons themselves eagerly concurred. It meant in short that churches were being used for non-Christian acts of worship and were stripped of their essentials, the nadir coming when a Grand Officer who should have known much better prevailed upon an incumbent, invoking the decree of Grand Lodge, which he had no right to do—nor indeed was there any such rule—to argue that the Cross should be removed from the altar.

The authorities at Grand Lodge merely stated that if a dispensation to wear regalia was granted (i) the service was to be undenominational, (ii) there should be no appearance in regalia in public, eg crossing a thoroughfare from church hall to church, (iii) the peacher should be a Mason, (iv) some part of the collection should go to Masonic charity.

Quite rightly the removal of the Cross aroused Christian indignation, probably more widely than a single isolated incident merited: and both the incumbent and the Grand Officer concerned received severe rebukes from the Archbishop and the Masonic authorities respectively. It ended in Dr Fisher, Lord Scarbrough and Sydney White settling down to evolve a new set of guide lines. The main points which emerged were that the 'Masonic Service' of the 1917 pattern was discarded, and it was laid down that the format of a service 'which Masons are particularly welcome to attend' (or words to that effect) was in all cases to be dictated by the parson in whose church it was to be held. In fact the incumbent became totally responsible, and we at Freemasons' Hall did not issue a dispensation for regalia to be worn till we were satisfied that he was agreeable to the form of service.

This went some way to disarm criticism, but more was to come after Sydney White's time, for Lord Scarbrough could see no virtue in what he called 'dressing up to go to Church', and said in effect that if that was what made people hold such services they had better not hold them. I was told to issue a general letter in which he said that he was not going to issue dispensations for regalia save in the most exceptional cases, and that he hoped Provincial and District Grand Masters would follow his lead: many did, though some stolidly persisted. Such services in the London area withered and died, and I can remember thereafter very few cases where I heard of a 'service which Masons are particularly invited to attend' being held: yet on the other hand I attended several out of London, in connection with the 250th Anniversary at Wells, a bicentenary at Bridgwater, and indeed Lord Scarbrough's own memorial service in St Paul's, which was packed full—but regalia was not worn.

Lord Scarbrough similarly was the power behind a pronouncement by the Board of General Purposes in September 1962:

Relationship of Masonry and Religion
The Board has been giving the most serious consideration to this subject, being convinced that it is of fundamental importance to the reputation and well-being of English Freemasonry that no misunderstanding should exist inside or outside the Craft.

It cannot be too strongly asserted that Masonry is neither a religion nor a substitute for religion. Masonry seeks to inculcate in its members a standard of conduct and behaviour which it believes to be acceptable to all creeds, but studiously refrains from intervening in the field of dogma or theology. Masonry, therefore, is not a competitor with religion though in the sphere of human conduct it may be hoped that its teaching will be complementary to that of religion. On the other hand its basic requirement that every member of the Order shall believe in a Supreme Being and the stress laid upon his duty towards Him should be sufficient evidence to all but the wilfully prejudiced that Masonry is an upholder of religion since it both requires a man to have some form of religious belief before he can be admitted as a Mason, and expects him when admitted to go on practising his religion.

The Board hopes that Grand Lodge will agree that this is a valid statement of the Masonic position, and in the practical application of these principles will lay down:
(i) that Masonic rites, prayers and ceremonies be confined to the Lodge room, and that dispensation to wear regalia (which term includes white gloves) in public be granted only in exceptional cases.
(ii) that there be no active participation by Masons, as such, in any part of the burial service or cremation of a Brother and that there be no Masonic prayers, readings, or exhortations either then or at the graveside subsequent to the interment, since the final obsequies of any human being, Mason or not,

are complete in themselves and do not call in the case of a Freemason for any additional ministrations. That if it is wished to recall and allude to his Masonic life and actions, this can appropriately be done at the next Lodge Meeting in the presence of his Brethren, or at a specifically arranged Memorial Service;

(iii) but that while no obstacle should be put in the way of Masons wishing to take part in an act of corporate worship, only in rare and exceptional cases should they be granted dispensation to do so wearing regalia; moreover that the order of service should in all cases be such as the officiating Minister or his superior consider to be appropriate to the occasion. (*Extract from Report of Board of General Purposes, adopted 12 September 1962*)

While this was actually sparked off by an argument, mostly with our members overseas on the subject of 'Masonic Funerals', the earlier paragraphs deal in a downright way with the heading of the statement. Unfortunately some old rituals, and indeed early editions of the *Book of Constitutions*, had published a liturgy for funerals and it was not clearly understood that this was only properly used in the absence of any minister of religion, a distinct possibility abroad in past generations, particularly where for reasons of hygiene the law demanded immediate interment. We in the English Constitution were not helped by the fact that the Grand Lodge of Scotland appear to condone if not actually encourage, public funeral processions in full regalia overseas. In countries where funerals are occasions of pomp and circumstance and brethren tended to belong to two or more Constitutions embarrassment inevitably arose, and it was sometimes difficult not to think that candidates, where they had a choice selected the Constitution which offered the best funeral rites; though it is all very well to consider one's inevitable destiny, this seems to be carrying it a little too far.

Later on with an insouciance that verged on pure genius Lord Scarbrough took no notice of a poorly mounted television programme which purported to show an initiation ceremony in full detail, and so good was his example that it was indeed a nine day's wonder, as on the tenth I received not one letter of protest from Masons, and remarkably few during the previous nine. The Board, which at first was a little agitated at the prospect, was well advised by the two Grand Wardens, Lord Townshend and the present Pro Grand Master now Lord Cornwallis not to rise to any baits.

PROBLEMS WITH REGALIA

Within Grand Lodge itself dissension started—and indeed still rumbles to this day—about the use of full dress regalia by Grand Officers. It is a complicated story, in which gratitude, vanity and misapplication of the Constitutions all play an important part; nor is it simplified by the fact that at the lower level there are two types of regalia with no indication whatsoever in the Constitutions as to which is appropriate to which occasion. It was however quite clearly laid down what Grand Officers should wear, and one might be excused for thinking that that was the end of the matter; sadly it was not. Starting at the top, several Provincial Grand Masters were in the habit of wearing their chains with undress regalia which was then irregular and probably copied from their Deputies: it was however much more comfortable and saved wear and tear on their heavily ornamented and outrageously expensive aprons. Among the rank and file of Grand Officers in a good many Provinces it was (possibly always had been) the custom to wear 'full dress' regalia at installations and it was argued, not entirely without reason, that they could not often get up to Grand Lodge meetings to wear it, that Provincial Grand Lodge occurred but once a year, and that as the regalia had in many cases been presented by their brethren gratitude and courtesy alike demanded that it should be displayed at least at Installations. The same arguments did not apply so much in and around London, where very broadly speaking, the higher ranking Grand Officers never wore full dress though the lower were apt to.

A straightforward attempt to get some sense into the Rules, which might also have meant that they would be followed, was foiled by RW Bro Bathurst from Gloucestershire who turned his powers of Masonic erudition against the authorities. Consequently the Board's highly sensible amendments were referred back to it by Grand Lodge in a series of amendments and counter-amendments, and in the end what is substantially the present set of rules were evolved.

The upshot is that it is now left to the individual Grand Officer to wear which he likes except on certain occasions laid down in the rules, with the important proviso 'unless impracticable'. A Lodge cannot through its Master or Secretary tell Grand Officers what regalia to wear, nor indeed can the Grand Secretary; all he can do is to indicate what he or the senior Grand Officer concerned is going to do, and leave it to the individuals' common sense: I for example have never worn full dress regalia in any private Lodge.

The 'unless impracticable' clause was inserted partly for airborne visitors who could not be expected to add heavy apron collar and gauntlets to their baggage, but also in the faint hope that this slight opening of the door would lead to a greater use of undress regalia on all occasions and that ultimately none but the acting Grand Officers would appear in full dress—which would in fact be the property of Grand Lodge. One tiny amendment, much later in time, should be mentioned at this point. Gauntlets had always been an infernal nuisance to the wearer, and were almost the most expensive items: at Charitable festivals they were quietly doffed as soon as we sat down, and the Connaught Rooms must have reaped a rich harvest when they were clearing up. W Bro Alan Jole came forward with the suggestion that 'may' should replace 'shall' in the Rule which dealt with their wearing with full dress regalia: Grand Lodge accepted it without demur and possibly without full comprehension with the result that Gauntlets have practically disappeared from the Masonic scene.

At the time the whole regalia episode was rather unedifying as it seemed to indicate that Grand Lodge was a lot more interested in sartorial detail than in the true purpose of Masonry, and I still have cause to fear that over the 30 years that have elapsed since the 'Bathurst rebellion' little progress has been made in the true direction of simplicity and economy.

THE MASONIC INSTITUTIONS

Shortly after the Coronation an appeal was started for Westminster Abbey and Sir Ernest Cooper urged Grand Lodge to support this by means of payments under covenant, arguing that the Abbey had recently shown itself as the centre of the Commonwealth as much as, if not more than, a denominational building. Grand Lodge accepted enthusiastically, and it can be argued that this had two effects, it brought the notion of payment by covenant to the attention both of individual members, and of the Board of General Purposes, and it was one of the early examples of Masonic giving outside the orbit of Freemasonry. Quite soon after this and following expert legal advice, the Fund of General Purposes started an ingenious scheme of covenanting its investment income to the Fund of Benevolence, and so making its tax payments *nett* instead of *gross*!

The subject of covenants naturally leads us to the Masonic Institutions which were already moving in that direction despite some diehard objections to the whole concept. The two educational charities were feeling the pinch of rising costs, and were at the same time aware that the numerical total of calls upon their funds were dropping and furthermore that the improvement, if such it was, in the public sector of education was leading widows, particularly those with daughters, to seek 'out-education' grants rather than places in the four schools.

The Royal Masonic Institution for Girls at this point found itself likely to have a number of lean years with festivals sponsored by small provinces, and Sydney White was cajoled into accepting the presidency for 1954: the view was that his great popularity in London, coupled with his name in the Provinces and abroad would redress the balance. Unfortunately it overreacted: a superb total was reached, which would probably have been even greater but for an uneasy feeling in the inner councils of the RMIG that if too much was attained the target for future festivals of all the Institutions would be set impossibly high and the ultimate end product over the years would be embarrassingly less. The Festival in itself was a great success and undoubtedly at the time was a matter of real pride and pleasure to the Grand Secretary—the third in succession to preside over a Girls' festival and, I trust, the last. In the longer run however it was not so happy as Sydney White, on the spot in Great Queen Street, almost certainly took more practical interest in what was going on than a distant Provincial Grand Master, and did not leave it to the expert handling of the Secretary, whom he did not much like anyhow. He had unfortunately surrounded himself with a small band of helpers, notably W Bro R. H. Allen, who harried the Lodges relentlessly and brought back glowing or dismal, but far from objective accounts of what they achieved. By the end of 1954 when the loose ends had been tied up Sydney White had engendered bad blood with the management of the RMIG, had found holes to pick in their administration and started what can only be described as a profitless revolution. Both he and the Secretary were Chartered Accountants and an official report on the Institution by a third did nothing to create a peaceful atmosphere: indeed it might be true to say that the troubles of 1954 were still lingering on in the 1980s.

The Royal Masonic Institution for Boys was dominated by Edgar Rutter, and its Secretary Col Jones realised that his best hope of success lay in following his lead assiduously. Between them, and at about the same time as trouble was breaking out in the RMIG they evolved a scheme for closing the senior school, extending the Junior (Col Jones got on well with the headmaster of the latter and not with the former's) and greatly expanding out education. The residential school would have become little more than a refuge for boys for whom a place could not be found elsewhere. Looking back in the light of 20 or more years experience it now does not seem either a revolutionary or a totally bad scheme, but it failed to win acceptance for two reasons: first it was badly presented by Rutter and his following who did not seem to have taken sufficient trouble to prepare the way, relying no doubt on their prestige. Second it appeared to be in advance of its time as may be seen from the fact that within a generation all they suggested—and more—has come to pass. It was loudly condemned as 'Socialism from South Wales' and things rapidly reached such a pass that Lord Scarbrough felt bound to step in and appoint a Committee of Enquiry into the Institution and the schools at Bushey. It consisted of Sir Gerald Upjohn, then a High Court Judge in the Chancery Division who presided with J. F. Wolfenden (later Lord Wolfenden) and George Turner, who had between them held successfully some half dozen headmasterships, and I was detailed to act as its Secretary. We produced a report in a remarkably short space of time, which recommended that the school (that is the senior one, the junior one was barely mentioned) should have a new headmaster as by implication if not by positive statement relations between Norman Sinclair and the RMIB management in Great Queen Street were irreparably damaged, and that there should be a governing body independent of the Board of Management, and finally that a Bursar, based on Bushey should be appointed (again implicitly) to prize the day to day management out of Great Queen Street.

The report was generally well received, even if grudgingly so, by the Board of Management. An excellent headmaster who was not a Mason, was selected, a Governing Body, the membership of which was nominated by some learned bodies and by the Board of Management and the Grand Master was finally established. Its Chairman was Lord Cadogan, a recent Senior Grand Warden, and pending the appointment of a bursar I was called upon to act as its Secretary. I almost said Secretariat as no provision was made for clerical assistance in Freemasons' Hall, and to have used any which could have been got from the RMIB would have been, metaphorically speaking, to welcome a 'mole' with open arms!

Nevertheless we struggled along, and the Chairman and I achieved a good deal of progress: the appointment of R. L. James (who appears earlier as my best man and who was by then headmaster of Harrow) as a governor was a masterstroke, not least because he could beat the other Welshman, Edgar Rutter at his own game and had the added advantage of really knowing about education. Another valuable member was Dr W. C. Costin, of St John's College, Oxford who held the balance of common sense and good will between them and was a splendid ally to the Chairman. Meetings were vigorous, not to say sometimes acrimonious, and Edgar Rutter used to accuse Lord Cadogan of using the 'language of the hunting field'!

The Upjohn Report, so far as it went, may be said to have achieved what it was meant to do: but there was still something radically wrong with the make up of the RMIB as a whole, and it is not unfair to say that

Opening of the Wakefield Wing at the Royal Masonic Hospital in 1959 by HM the Queen Mother. Lord Scarbrough has just presented Sir Malcolm Hilbery and Matron is making her curtsy: along the line are HH the Maharajadhiraj of Patiala, R. E. Lawson (House Governor), JWS, Sir Ernest Cooper and Frank Douglas.

it was a disease of a chronic nature affecting all the Masonic Charities. Put simply, it was that they were controlled entirely by their subscribers, for in the early days when there tended to be more petitioners than vacancies or money there was a complicated voting system based on subscriptions. There had not been actual elections of candidates since before 1920, but the subscribers baulked of their authority in this respect still controlled the management of the Institutions according to each one's individualistic rules. A breach had been made by 'Upjohn' in the RMIB and quite soon there was agitation in both RMIG and RMIB for a reorganisation of the government of the Institutions themselves. Each of them settled in its own way for a new constitution which took a few faltering steps towards democracy but without abandoning the archaic 'purchase' system. I was however no longer concerned; the Boys had by now acquired a bursar, rather too closely linked to Great Queen Street for the liking of some, and I had never been brought directly into the machinations whereby the RMIG changed its rules (though not noticeably either its personnel or its habits). The RMBI, whose Secretary Col Cecil Adams was streets ahead of his confrères in ability and the respect of the Craft, remained untouched by revolutionary tendencies for much longer, while the Royal Masonic Hospital despite internecine struggles between conflicting elements at Ravenscourt Park continued to present for the time being a united and successful front to the Masonic world at large.

Although it is fair to say that the fortunes of the two educational charities changed very much for the better with a change of secretaries, what was changing much more basically was the relative importance of them as against the RMBI and the Hospital. Smaller families born to younger parents who had themselves a better life expectancy meant that there were fewer candidates for the benefits of either of the two Institutions. It was also a fact that the improvement in local education made it more likely that a widowed mother would see the advantages of out-education, and of keeping the family together, over that provided by the schools. It was undoubtedly sad, but to my mind inevitable, that Masonic boarding school education would shrink: the Junior Schools at Weybridge and Bushey were the first to go, even though a generation earlier they had been the last to come and Weybridge faded out with little excitement, but the closure of the Junior School at Watford was the occasion for a good deal of rather spurious local agitation. The RMIB authorities however stood firm, and having stood firm found the next step, closure and disposal of the Senior School a few years later less traumatic. Thus in 1984 the Craft is left with its best-found school, at Rickmansworth, the sole survivor, and it is to be hoped that it will survive, diluted though it may be with non-Masonic and fee paying pupils; and there seems to be much, if not everything, to be said for making it fully co-educational. These are words that neither the young schoolmaster at St Paul's or the Secretary of the Upjohn Committee ever thought he would put down on paper.

1957 AND THE GERMAN PROBLEM

All this however is carrying us far ahead, and it is time to return to the mid fifties. As Sydney White grew older, it became more and more a subject for discussion that a third senior officer should be inserted into the hierarchy of the office. Curiously enough Rule 22 puts the appointment of Grand Secretary at the pleasure of Grand Lodge till he is 65, and thereafter at the pleasure of the Grand Master: this was an innovation of 1940 which seemed meaningless, but Sydney explained it as having been put in at the instigation of Lord Harewood who felt that only an individual, and not the amorphous body of Grand Lodge, would be prepared to get rid of a Grand Secretary who had outlived his usefulness as he had himself witnessed in the declining months of Sir Colville. After much discussion an advertisement was inserted in the major dailies; it produced a very large number of quite useless applications, most of which failed to qualify in the terms of the advertisement, but a handful, of good ones. The short-listed candidates were interviewed, and the choice was made of Alan Jole, freshly home from the Sudan Civil Service. He brought a very much needed Civil Service training into the office and soon made himself indispensable as Sydney White continued to allow himself to become more and more entangled in the politics of the Institutions. He was in any case slowing down and although the process was in itself slow it became more and more noticeable. By the summer of 1957 when a full scale conference was mounted in a final attempt to solve the German problem he was far from well. It now seems almost certain that at this ripe old age he contracted mumps from his grandchildren! He never regained his full health and from September until his death in March 1958 he was more often in hospital or 'convalescing' at home than in the office.

The German problem requires some detailed explanation; basically and from the earliest days there has been two types of Masonry current with not a great deal in common between them. Within these two types there were several Grand Lodges, all tolerant of each other but not, one would suppose, particularly friendly. The fundamental cause was not far to seek: Germany itself even after 1870 contained several independent (at least nominally) States, and before 1800 and 1866 there had been dozens of them. In some cases such as Prussia there were elements quite separate geographically from the Prussian homeland, but looking for their culture (which included their Masonry) to it. Some great city States such as Hamburg had derived their Masonry from the British Isles, others from France and the Low Countries just as Prussia for the most part had taken its from Scandinavia. Neither the creation of the German Empire nor the emergence of the Weimar Republic had made much difference, though it is worth bearing in mind that when Masonic relations were restored some time after Versailles the Prussian Grand Lodges had been loath to do so.

Later when Masonry was suppressed by the Nazi regime, the Prussian Grand Lodges which, like Scandinavian Masonry, were Christian, had tried quoite unsuccessfully to prolong their existence by coming to terms with the regime on the basis that they were simply cultural and beneficent organisations. It availed them naught except possibly a few months' respite, but on the contrary put them in very bad odour with the 'humanitarian' Grand Lodges when Masonry started to revive with the end of the war in Germany. The *raison d'être* of the conference in the summer of 1957 was to bring the hostile sects together, if by no other means than telling their leaders that there was not going to be full recognition of German Masonry till that happened. In a sense the humanitarians, the United Grand Lodge of Germany (NB the singular is important) were sitting pretty: it was led by Dr Theodore Vogel who had a considerable following in his own and other countries and they had shown much more elasticity of mind than the stubborn successors of the Prussian Grand Lodges with the almost equally stubborn Scandinavians in support. The Scandinavian Grand Lodges themselves, secure in their own system, were not particularly anxious about recognition outside their immediate circle. It came therefore as quite a surprise that the leading figure in that conference should be the Swedish Chancellor, Count Rolf von Heidenstam, who displayed a real talent for negotiation which brought the two German parties much closer to each other than ever before. He also astonished us all by making the speech of the day in English, French and German successively, without flaw or hesitation!

The Germans retired, both sides apparently well satisfied, after an amiable dinner at the Mitre, Hampton Court. The next we heard of their relations was the publication of a tortuous document entitled '*Magna Carta*', which was designed, if all parties could be got to accept it, to produce a kind of super Grand Lodge, or more realistically an umbrella under which they could all shelter without loss of independence. This statement of intent sufficiently resembled the general concept of a Grand Lodge for it to receive the recognition of the Masonic world generally under the title of the United Grand Lodges (NB the plural) of Germany.

FAREWELL TO SYDNEY WHITE

This conference was Sydney White's swansong; though actually in its proceedings Sir Ernest Cooper played the principal part it is but fair to say that without Sydney's lead, and particularly without his experience of, and popularity with the Scandinavians the conference would probably never have been convened. Looking back I am surprised how little thought I gave to his decline as I took on more and more of the routine work, as well as the historical research I had been undertaking for some time which culminated in the *Historical Supplement to the Masonic Year Book*. To the very end he refused to allow any of his business with Lord Scarbrough to be delegated, and I established relations with the latter only in our joint production of a consultative document for preliminary discussions on the formation of a Grand Lodge or Grand Lodges in India. In

With Sir Sydney White after the consecration of Lodge of Ideal Endeavour No 7379 in May 1955. I had been called in at the last moment to act as Junior Warden.

the late summer of 1957 there was a slight flare-up between Sir Ernest Cooper and myself, which I am glad to say cleared the air and in fact resulted in greatly improved relations being established. It came however as a distinct shock when in December on our way up to Blackpool to help Sir Allan Adair install the new Provincial Grand Master, Laurence Rutherford, to be told by Frank Douglas that Sydney White was determined that I should not succeed him if he ever came to retire. Frank made it plain that he and Sir Ernest were on my side, and that if nothing happened soon they and Sir Cullum Welch who was President of the Board of Benevolence and had just finished his year as Lord Mayor would get themselves commissioned by the Grand Master to tell Sydney that he must retire, the implication being that when that happened his views as to the succession would have scant respect. In spite of being thus alerted there did not seem to be anything very much I could do about it except make myself more than usually useful and efficient. What was going on in Sydney's head I never discovered; my own belief is that he, like Elizabeth I, violently disliked any prospect of a successor. It may well be on the other hand that he had come over ten years to accept me as part of the subordinate office furniture and that someone he knew less well and was less accustomed to would be more acceptable.

And so I went on into 1958, undertaking all the ordinary routine for the early months of the year, Grand Lodge accounts, Installations, lists of Grand Officers for the ensuing year. These were all achieved with little excitement or variation from the usual, thanks to the unfailing support of Miss Haig. Rumours however had begun to circulate from the hospital from which Sydney had discharged himself over Christmas that his days were numbered. His death finally occurred on Sunday, 9 March quite soon after Lord Scarbrough and Frank Douglas had gone down one afternoon to see him at his home at Bickley, and had returned clearly convinced that they would not see him again. He died peacefully, as he would have wished in his own home.

There were many obituary notices, which between them managed pretty successfully to paint a picture of a great Grand Secretary, but these have long since disappeared into filing cabinets, and 26 years later we may perhaps with advantage take another look at them. When Sir Colville Smith succeeded Sir Edward Letchworth in the dark days of 1917, there was an Assistant Grand Secretary, W Bro Resbury Few, there was also, following the translation of PC a vacancy in the RMBI.

Resbury Few took this up for the comparatively few years that were left to him, and the way was clear for a new appointment even if the time was not particularly propitious with the nation in arms. Sydney White, he once told me, against the advice of his professional (Chartered Accountant) colleagues applied for and got the advertised job as Chief Clerk: he then became Assistant Grand Secretary five years later, by which time he had thoroughly reorganised the office and was already engaged in the preliminaries of the Million Memorial Fund Appeal. By sheer industry and ability he made himself practically indispensable to a chief who was not notably interested in the minutiae of office work, but who was *persona grata* with the rulers of the Craft and those who managed its affairs. With them, in his earlier days, Sydney must have had immense difficulties of mutual understanding, nor did these difficulties completely cease till after Lord Harewood's death. He had two major disadvantages to start with, no active military service and no public school training, but on the other hand he understood the financial structure of Grand Lodge, and his qualification as a Chartered Accountant inspired confidence where it counted most in the long run, the rank and file members of the various Boards and Committees.

Most of all however he was known to be incorruptible and almost impervious to flattery; qualities which when linked to a burning faith in the goodness and usefulness of Freemasonry, and an expanding experience of all the aspects of Grand Lodge work made him so indispensable that despite the efforts made at the time of Sir Colville's death to dislodge him, he got the appointment that he had so well earned. For the next 20 years he gave his energies unstintingly to prove how wise that choice had been.

It would be idle to deny that he had a strong liking for the centre of the stage, for he was a masterly exponent of ceremonial and ritual and enjoyed every moment of it; but it was not solely the joy of being the star, it was also the satisfaction of doing a job well and better than anyone else.

To his staff he was almost invariably courteous and considerate though he had his human likes and dislikes, but he kept as rigid a line between him and them, as there had been between Sir Colville and himself. I feel sure that Sir Colville never offered him a seat, when they had discussions in the office, for he assuredly never offered me one, even when I came in one day with a badly twisted ankle and aided by a stick. Many of the staff had grown up under his command and this applied particularly to the maintenance staff whom he had seen at work on the new Freemasons' Hall and who had come over, almost to a man, to serve Grand Lodge when the building was completed. Most of them and the army of cleaners, many of whom were local women who had used the Hall as a wartime shelter were devoted to him.

Some of his practices and habits were almost Victorian, his refusal to fly, disapproval of tax avoidance by covenants, and unwillingness to delegate responsibility, so that he never really took a holiday.

The funeral took place on the following Thursday quietly, but attended by the whole hierarchy of Grand Lodge, the members of which gathered for lunch (we had to send out for a bottle of gin as no liquor could be found except a half bottle of purely medicinal brandy) in the flat which Sydney had occupied during his working week and which had therefore been empty for several months. After lunch they all came down stairs. I was summoned and forthwith appointed Grand Secretary: Lord Scarbrough and Sir Ernest both made encouraging remarks to an accompaniment of 'hear, hears' from the others.

Lord Scarbrough made a point of returning to see me the next day with some kindly advice which he said he had not wished to embarrass either of us with at the time; meanwhile Sir Ernest arrived and took me to lunch next door, insisting that I should sit in the place Sydney White had always occupied and which I proceeded to do for the next 22 years! Frank Douglas then invited us at very short notice to dinner, which meant that we had arrived.

There was very little to clear up as Sydney and Miss Haig between them had kept everything in perfect order, though I discovered a week or two later in a strongroom to which I had never penetrated a tea-trolley full of old papers which was obviously his 'filed, too difficult' collection, fortunately most of them had answered themselves though a certain number of skeletons emerged. Miss Haig, who had stated forthrightly that she would go at once if I was not appointed, wished to retire after one more year making 42 years of outstanding service to Grand Lodge, then helped enormously during the next few months and was assiduous in ensuring a smooth handover too when it came. The two senior clerks, Malcolm Grace, the Cashier, and Francis Jones the expert on External Relations and the main gossip centre of the Hall had just retired, so a good deal of staff redeployment had to be undertaken with Alan Jole, who had on his arrival taken over my old office in the middle of the clerical area and was in a good position to know what changes would be for the best: I had myself moved to a larger office adjacent to the then Grand Secretary but felt rather isolated from the staff generally. It was never to be used again for the Second in Command, who was in fact much better situated where I had started in 1947.

Chapter 10

Grand Secretary—Part One (1958-1967)

My 22 years as Grand Secretary divide themselves into two periods, before and after the death of Lord Scarbrough in 1969, more realistically than with the change of Grand Master and the 250th Anniversary celebrations of Grand Lodge in 1967, for he had remained a dominant figure as Pro Grand Master, a title that came back into use with the election of a Royal Grand Master.

Both the Grand Lodge Proceedings and the chapter in the publication *Grand Lodge 1717-1967* which I wrote give an adequate annalistic account of the first period, and I will not go over the old ground in the same way, but rather refer to incidents, personalities and trends that set the pattern at that time.

In 1958 after Sydney White's death the leading personalities apart from Lord Scarbrough, were Sir Allan Adair, Sir Ernest Cooper and Frank Douglas. Sir Allan Adair had already made a great name for himself as Assistant Grand Master in London and in the Provinces, his natural infectious enthusiasm at once raised the tone of any meeting he attended, and his evident capacity for enjoyment made all those present enjoy the occasion too. He was, and indeed in 1985 still is, a magnificent ritualist and a master of ceremonial. Sir Ernest Cooper was ageing by 1958, and suffering from English winters so different from the Canadian ones of his youth, was finding it more and more necessary to spend the early months of the year abroad. He still however had a very firm grasp on the affairs of Grand Lodge and the Board of General Purposes, whilst both in Europe and America he was a greatly respected figure. His fellow President, of the Board of Benevolence, Sir Cullum Welch had just come to the end of his Lord Mayoralty and was clearly going to be able to devote more time to the affairs of his Board and to Freemasonry generally. Frank Douglas was the King Maker *par excellence*: from his activities in the City he had a very wide circle of acquaintances and a highly developed intelligence service. There could be no adverse opinions as to his success as Grand Director of Ceremonies, to the performance of which he gave immensely of himself whilst at the same delegating to his competent body of Deputies. He dearly loved pulling strings, and still more pretending that he was pulling them, and a good example of this came when Sir Ernest announced his retirement in compliance with doctors' orders.

The office of President was of cardinal importance, particularly so with a new Grand Secretary; Frank took the point that the two had to be compatible and sympathetic, and set about the search for a possible successor. His first choice was Lord Crookshank who had been Provincial Grand Master for Lincolnshire since 1954, and whom he thought might possibly be ready to step down from that office. Lord Crookshank however was devoted to Lincolnshire, part of which he had represented in Parliament for many years, but, a more serious complication, he was a prominent member of the Supreme Council 33°, which he realised he would have to relinquish. He wanted to do this even less; in fact he did not really want to be President at all, and used all his parliamentary skill to avoid the change. It was just as well as he fell ill and died a few years later. I then came forward with the suggestion of Alex Frere, a Past Grand Treasurer, at the time Grand Superintendent in and over Buckinghamshire. I did not then know him very well but realised how able he was and well accustomed to taking decisions. I therefore mentioned his name to Frank who, by good chance, happened to be going by sea to the States and found him on board too. It soon became all Frank's idea, a mild case of self deception which I was not disposed to uncover. So in April 1959 Sir Ernest retired and Alex Frere started a long and important tenure of office which lasted till 1972, covering the 250th Anniversary and the change of Grand Master. It was a continuing pleasure to work with him, and I believe that he would agree we formed a good team; devoid of difficulties or inhibitions. Another change was imminent: Miss Haig wanted to retire having seen me safely installed and seemed to be irreplaceable: however I obtained authority to advertise (without involving the name of Grand Lodge in the first instance) and baited the notice as attractively as possible with an invitation to write to a Box Number for further information. Quite a number of enquiries resulted, one or two of which withdrew their interest at once on learning that the post was involved with Freemasonry, however a reasonable field remained and I interviewed about half a dozen. The first, by sheer accident, was unquestionably the best and I appointed Irene Hainworth, who came from the hard school of the ATS (AA), had been secretary to the Headmaster of University College School and more immediately, to Sir Wavell Wakefield. I never regretted the choice, nor I think did anyone with whom she came into close contact until she retired shortly after me in 1982.

OVERSEAS VISITS

The major foreign trips in which I took part between 1958 and 1980 have already been described in *The Four Corners*, but there were a great number of shorter ones in Europe some of which deserve a mention at the same time as the reasons for them.

It will be recalled that Sydney White would not fly: nor was he at all partial to foreign travel, though he was persuaded, over and above his great Australian tour, to go to Newfoundland and later to Ontario and

Alexander Stuart Frere, President of the Board of General Purposes 1959 to 1972. This portrait by Colin Corfield now hangs in the Board rest room at Freemasons' Hall with other portraits of Presidents.

Gibraltar Airport 1955: my first masonic trip overseas for the installation of Judge Hume Barne. Left to right: JWS, Jack Ellicot PGD, T. B. Langton Dep GDC and (from 1978) PrGM Hampshire and Isle of Wight, Frank Douglas GDC and later Assistant Grand Master.

finally on a convalescent trip to Brittany. In 1955 the occasion arose when it was necessary for a deputation, led by Sir Allan Adair, to go to Gibraltar to install Judge Hume Barne as District Grand Master and Grand Superintendent, and Sir Allan and Frank Douglas insisted that someone should go as secretary. This was to be my first trip, and the forerunner of many, abroad for Grand Lodge, and it was a short but pleasant interlude. The Judge who had retired to Gibraltar from his judicial appointment in Egypt and who had been made District Grand Master without much notice to himself or his future District was full of new ideas, which were much needed after 28 years of absentee control by RW Bro Colonel Ellis. He had however a great antipathy to going to bed and we had to establish a duty roster to sit up listening to him till about 4 am. A subsequent deputation was led by Lord Scarbrough himself in 1960 to install the Judge's successor, Anthony Mena who was the first Gibraltarian to hold the office. The European Grand Lodges were very kind in inviting me, generally with my wife also, to visit them and sometimes, as in the case of Scandinavia and Finland, it was possible to combine these visits with a summer holiday. We all three, my son Hugh being then about 15, went up the Norwegian coast in the regular mail steamer and returned via Oslo, Stockholm and Helsinki having taken in Copenhagen on the way out where we had many friends. A second visit to Stockholm was arranged for the purpose of presenting King Gustaf Adolf

Dinner following a conference in Frankfurt on the plan to unify German masonry. Left to right: JWS, RKTS, Richard Mueller Börner (Three Globes Grand Lodge) and Dr Theodore Vogel (United Grand Lodge).

VI with regalia as a Past Grand Master, when the party consisted of Lord Scarbrough, Lord Zetland the Representative of the Swedish Grand Lodge and myself. The Grand Master was most emphatic that we should be prepared with formal morning dress as well as white tie and tails for Lodge meetings: morning dress, including top hats, was not the easiest thing to stow in an aircraft, but we just about managed. There was a slight anti-climax when His Majesty received us in a light grey flannel suit, but the more specifically Masonic part was a real treat. In three evenings we saw and heard in perfect English the main elements of all the Swedish degrees, and I got the distinct impression that Lord Scarbrough, who was not an English Knight Templar, ended up slightly more exalted than Lord Harris the Grand Master himself.

The deputation in 1958 to the Grand Lodge of California for the dedication of the new Masonic Temple has already been described elsewhere together with my own visits to Canadian Grand Lodges and our own three Lodges on the Canadian mainland. Later that year my wife and I went to Frankfurt for a long weekend with Bro Hans Hoffmann as interpreter so that I could find out what exactly were the implications of the *Magna Charta* with which Dr Vogel was trying, successfully as it turned out, to bring the two main rival bodies of German Freemasonry together. I satisfied myself and subsequently the Board of General Purposes that the overriding body which was going to be established, with full power of foreign relations, was sufficiently close to the normal concept of a Grand Lodge for it to be capable of recognition, thus solving the problem that the European Conference in London of the previous year had underlined.

In due course the United Grand Lodges (plural) was recognised however ungrammatical it may sound, but there remained a fissile tendency even after the two main bodies had been joined on almost equal terms by the headquarters organisation of the American Lodges in the South and the British in the North. Over and above the inherent differences between the Humanitarian and the Swedish Rite systems the United Grand Lodges have been troubled with insidious approaches to their Lodges, particularly in the Rhineland, by members of the Grand Orient of France. One cannot but feel some sympathy with the rank and file of the German brethren who have so many variations of practice and language within their own organisation if they accept or even incline to overtures from yet one more. The position becomes aggravated by the paucity of regular French Lodges on the French side. Still it cannot be denied that if the German authorities put their whole heart into stopping intervisitation it could be done, a few examples of condign Masonic punishment *pour encourager les autres* would work wonders. I believe that this is a good example of the strength of the British system of devolution of Masonic power and responsibility. A Provincial organisation would know much more of what was going on, and would be better able to stop what was undesirable than a distant Grand Secretariat, whose powers anyhow under the *Magna Charta* were seriously circumscribed. Meanwhile I have no doubt that the Grand Orient will continue to make trouble wherever it can.

About the same time as German Masonry was evolving the Grand Loge Nationale of France was suffering one of its periodic crises: its Grand Master, Cheret, the prewar Grand Secretary was becoming deeply involved in negotiations with the irregular Grand Lodge of France and had to retire: he was succeeded by Ernest van Hecke, little known at the time but one who like his successor Louis de Rosière strove valorously to keep the GLNF on the right path, but at the same time was always ready to extend a welcoming hand to erstwhile members of the two irregular Grand Lodges who wished to 'come clean'. I was invited to go over to Paris to accept Honorary membership of the Centre des Amis Lodge, which indeed I still enjoy and this was the first of several, mostly short, visits to regular French Masonry, the most exciting of which was in 1967 when Lord Scarbrough attended the dedication of their new premises at Neuilly. He was accorded the highest honours including a formal embrace by Louis.

Some years earlier when I was working one Saturday morning, as we all did except Sydney White, I was asked to receive a visitor from Belgium, which I did with some diffidence knowing that it had been the Grand Orient of Belgium which nearly a century before had preceded the Grand Orient of France into its course of ungodliness. Charles Wagemanns duly appeared and genuinely made the point that he and many of his generation disagreed with the principles, or lack of them, of the Grand Orient and wanted to make themselves regular. I explained to a ready listener that it might be a long process with many discouragements on the way, but that I also believed that their best course was to break completely with the parent body and set themselves up anew, being totally independent and basing themselves purely on English principles. Charles always created a most excellent impression wherever he went, and in a surprisingly short time the Grand Lodge of Belgium was pretty generally accepted and recognised; so much so that in 1967 he was selected to make one of the principal speeches at Grand Lodge's 250th anniversary celebration being by then our Representative near the Grand Lodge of Belgium.

It will be remembered that the last Masonic action of the Duke of Devonshire had been to install Brigadier Esmond de Wolff in Malta; 34 years later he is still there, though lately retired as District Grand Master. He ran the District magnificently, managing to keep on good terms with the Irish and Scots, and even with the Roman Church. Being a realist he appreciated that the introduction of Maltese, who would almost by definition be lapsed Catholics, into the Craft could only exacerbate the suspicions and deepen the hostility of the clerical authorities: he therefore stood firmly against any such introduction. In his earlier years the Armed Forces and the Dockyards provided plenty of initiates, and Malta itself

Wreath laying ceremony at Valley Forge, Pennsylvania in October 1976. Left to right: Dep GM Pennsylvania, JWS and RW Bro J. L. McCain, Grand Master of Pennsylvania beneath a statue of George Washington.

was a popular retiring place to which many experienced Masons went, anxious not to lose touch with the Craft. Unhappily as time went on all these sources dried up, and it cannot now be denied that Malta is as overpopulated with Lodges as it is underpopulated with Masons actual or potential. Some of the Masonic bodies are transferring to England where, like those from Pakistan before them, they can hope to have several years of activity before the old Malta membership dies out and they eventually become like any other Lodge whether it be in London or the Provinces. The latest information is that the District has been dissolved.

I never managed to make contact with the Port of Hercules Lodge in Monte Carlo apart from an enjoyable lunch party, but to our other two outposts in Europe I paid several visits. In Greece Star of the East Lodge No 880 had suffered very badly with the rest of the island in the earthquake of 1953: and though a grant in aid had been made by Grand Lodge it had proved difficult to find out precisely what was going on; indeed the Lodge which worked in Greek had few English speakers or correspondents and was very much of a mystery. On my way back from India after the establishment of the Grand Lodge of India which is described a little later, I broke my journey in Cyprus and Greece with the idea of going across the country by road and ferry to meet the Zanthiot brethren and see what more could be done to help them. By a great stroke of good fortune the Master in 1961 was one of the very few who spoke English. Commander Alexander Bultzo, Royal Hellenic Navy, was both Master of the Lodge and Member of Parliament for the Island. He had been brought up by an English nanny and had served in British ships for most of the war (he had even survived a radar course in our language). Alex met me at the airport with all arrangements made for our long trip past Patras to the ferry point and thence by a three hour trip in an ex-landing craft to the island. We had plenty of time to talk *en route* and after our conversations and an actual visit to the Lodge at work in the makeshift building I was fully convinced that what they needed was a good deal more financial help for their rebuilding scheme, (the original help had largely gone on the relief of personal distress) as there was literally only one building left standing in Zante City and great damage had been done by fire following the earthquake. It was also evident that in their isolated state, linguistic as well as geographical, anything that could help in supervision was going to be worthwhile. The money, on my explanation of the circumstances, was readily forthcoming, and for supervision we were fortunate in having Alex Bultzo. I was more than dubious as to what had actually happened when he was installed, so I arranged for him to attend a consecration when he was in London, a few months later and contrary to the usual practice and with the ready consent of the Master Designate I did a full installation and inner working purely for his benefit and guidance.

Later I had time for a short visit to the Grand Secretary of Greece as I wanted more information about the set up of the Grand Lodge, for occasional correspondence in English was getting us nowhere. It seemed to our authorities that the governing body bore a strong resemblance in many respects to a Supreme Council, and as such contravened our Principles of Recognition. He was a gynaecologist and we met in his surgery where, surrounded by his professional working tools, we had a satisfactory talk, from which it emerged that the root trouble was caused solely by the names and not the functions of the governing body, whom I later met (not in the surgery) and found both co-operative and anxious to clear the air.

Alex got hold of copies of the *Emulation Ritual*, and the *Lectures* and proceeded to produce an accurate translation of them all into modern Greek, a mammoth task indeed. A couple of years later Sir Allan Adair, Col M. G. Edwardes, Rev Tom Nevill and I paid Zante another visit following a Consecration in Cyprus: by then Star in the East had qualified for a Centenary Warrant. We had been staying in Nicosia in readiness for a fairly early start by air to Athens, thence by the usual bus and ferry: but Robin Roe, the Grand Inspector, persuaded three of us (Sir Allan prudently stayed in bed) to go with him to see Kyrenia and St Hilarion in the dawn which meant leaving about 5.30 am. All went well and we returned to the hotel, had breakfast and packed, leaving for the airport in good time, but there we experienced a terrific thunderstorm which delayed our departure by about two hours and meant that we missed the bus from Athens. There was nothing to be done except hope that Alex Bultzo who was meeting us at the airport would have something up his sleeve. True to form he had hired a taxi to take all five of us and our baggage to the ferry, some 120 miles, but warned us that there would be no time for any meals or 'comfort stops' as the ferry would wait for no one. The road to Patras has several level crossings, and at one of these while waiting for the train we managed to attend to our discomfort and still had time to collect some oranges: and by the time we reached Patras we had made up sufficient time to get some very sweet and sticky cakes. Sadly, dinner in Zante was not till after 11 pm, a very long gap from our 7.30 breakfast, though when it came it was well worth waiting for.

All was not well when we arrived, as there is also a Greek Constitution Lodge in Zante, and the Grand Master of Greece hearing that our Assistant Grand Master was to be in the island for our Centenary had decided to invite himself. He claimed that as Grand Master he was going to take precedence over *our* Assistant Grand Master in one of *our* Lodges. Mike Edwardes and I were determined this should not happen and spent most of the day arguing the point with the Greek Grand Director of Ceremonies, whose English conspicuously deserted him when his arguments failed. Finally I ventured almost my only word of modern Greek, which I believed to be 'No': it appears that I badly mispronounced it and said something almost unbelievably obscene with the result that the GDC disappeared and both he and his Grand Master were seen no more. Nor did the members of the Greek Lodge as a whole turn up at the Centenary meeting, which passed off very happily in a Lodge room which had been entirely rebuilt and refurbished since my previous visit. Our return to Athens was less dramatic, and we were entertained to an excellent lunch at the Yacht Club in Piraeusby by the Deputy Grand Master who had obviously not heard of the earlier contretemps.

My first visit to Cyprus had been in early winter and lasted just long enough for me to be taken over to Famagusta and shown the Twin Churches, where Othello Lodge then met. Old Famagusta is full of churches in a more rather than less derelict condition, but these two were sufficiently well preserved to function as a Lodge room and as a supper room. Unhappily being in a Turkish area they soon ceased to be available for Masonic use, most of the Othello members being Greek, and the last time I was able to get into them they had every appearance of being the work place of a Turkish signal organisation. I was also taken over the Venetian Castle in the magnificent Hall of which Lord Harewood had consecrated the Lodge during his Pro Grand Mastership. Another visit, this time in early summer, was paid to help consecrate Apollo Lodge, the aftermath of which in Greece has already been described. By then tension was rising in the island, but we had among the consecrating officers both a Greek and a Turkish Grand Officer, and it was both interesting and

Sightseeing in Cyprus in 1963: a gathering in the Othello Lodge room, one of the twin churches in Famagusta. This followed the consecration of Apollo Lodge No 7886, Limassol, and was followed by the centenary of Star of the East Lodge No 880 in Zante a few days later.

encouraging to see them go out into the warm darkness after the ceremony to ascertain the cause of rumours that were circulating as a result of unmistakable small arms fire in the distance.

Those two visits had greatly increased my interest in the island, and in 1967 when both Richenda and I were very tired after the Masonic and social activities of the 250th celebrations we decided to spend our summer holiday there. We were told on all sides that it would be impossibly hot and humid, that we would probably be shot, or at least shot at, that the food would be both uneatable and inedible—but none cavilled at the wines. In fact for seven successive years we spent every summer holiday there, in some cases combined with a short trip elsewhere till the revolution of 1974 made travel round the island too difficult. In the course of time we established a pleasant routine which involved a late arrival at Nicosia airport where W Bro Costas Nicolaides welcomed us, a night at the Ledra Palace where we woke up to hot sun and the smell of jasmin, hiring a car and setting off in various orders to Famagusta, Kyrenia, Platres and Paphos. We toured the forest roads and found small cafes which produced excellent omelettes and beer or wine at any time. We explored Buffavento and Kantara Castle, but never succeeded in getting to the topmost level of St Hilarion as it was held as a watch tower by the Turks. Almost every time as the Lodges themselves were in recess we enjoyed a social evening with the Masons and their ladies at the principal meeting places. Indeed once we celebrated the birthday of George Meikle the Grand Inspector in company with the Grand Master, whom I unfairly cajoled late in the evening to sign 30 warrants, charters or patents. Occasionally we were also entertained by the members of the Greek Constitution: one of these gatherings particularly stands out in my mind. We were staying in Paphos, well known as a potential trouble centre, during one of the more disturbing periods, and George Meikle in fact had rung up to warn us against taking a particular route up to Platres the next day. Our hosts had sent their wives out of town to the problematical security of various Orthodox monasteries inland, so Richenda was the only lady present: dinner took place outdoors on the edge of the harbour and was progressing well though the language barrier was ever present. I had got to the end of such small talk, Masonic or otherwise, as our joint vocabularies could muster, when I thought I would try a new line, and asked the Master to whom I was sitting next, whether in the old days he had ever known my uncle, Sir Edward Stubbs, who had become Governor of the island after the Storrs débâcle. The Master ruminated for what seemed a long time, obviously translating question and answer into Greek and back again, and when the answer came it was electrifying, 'Yes, he gave my father five years for sedition': After a further long time, while Richenda in particular looked at the greasy waters of the harbour just below and wondered how deep they were, he then went on in resigned but friendly tones 'but he spent the time well, translating your Milton into Modern Greek'. Thereafter the rest of the evening passed off in a very friendly way with a lot of admirable Cyprian wine.

This also reminds me of a rather similar incident a year or two later, when we were dining with the Meikles and several others (it was probably another of George's birthday parties) in the Turkish area of Limassol on the apron of a garage which was used in the evening as an *alfresco* restaurant. It was a moonlight night with some cloud; conversation had suddenly flagged and a clear English woman's voice was heard from a nearby table 'I thought I saw Grivas in town today', this when he was being much hunted. A cloud passed over the moon, a very loud bang occurred and every light in the town went out. When the moon reappeared there was heard a good deal of scraping of chairs and table legs on concrete, and several shamed-faced diners appeared from under their tables. The town lights remained out and we found on returning to the hotel that owing to a power failure candles were in evidence and the lifts and lights not working: but such was the power of Grivas' name.

Our Cyprian holidays continued in much the same pattern up until 1973 and we had one planned for 1974 too but were prevented by the civil war. Later I did pay two subsequent visits of an official kind, once to consecrate a new Lodge at Paphos, and once to support the Pro Grand Master (Lord Cadogan) in establishing a new District Grand Lodge and installing George Meikle as the first District Grand Master. In both cases the pleasant sensation of being free to wander where we liked had gone and we were restricted to the Greek part of the island.

A few other holidays had a touch of business about them. We went to Eastern Canada once after the annual meeting of the Grand Lodge of Canada (in the Province of Ontario) at Toronto, driving round the Gaspé Peninsula and New Brunswick, where we visited VW Bro Charles Hope and his family at St Andrews. A visit to Sri Lanka on a package tour involved meeting a number of Masons of Colombo and Kandy, and sadly the funeral of RW Bro Jennings Senior, the father of the present District Grand Master: another package tour took us to the Seychelles where I was able to meet and give some help to a number of brethren who were trying to get a Lodge started—successfully in the end—in that delightful but unlikely area.

THE GRAND LODGE OF INDIA

Much of the history of English Freemasonry has followed the pattern of the British Empire, with development and devolution. The process went on throughout the 19th century with Canada, Australia and New Zealand setting up their own Grand Lodge(s) with less or more support from home. I have already touched on the question as it affected India, which is likely to be the last case and which was of particular interest to Lord Scarbrough as a former Governor of Bombay. Together we composed a document which laid out the advantages and disadvantages of Masonic independence without at all favouring either and got the agreement of the

Grand Master of Ireland (Raymond Brooke) and the Grand Master Mason of Scotland (Lord Eglinton and Winton) to issue it to all the Lodges in India. They also agreed to waive the terms of a concordat which their predecessors had entered into in 1905 and under which a two-thirds majority of the interested Lodges was a prerequisite. It was felt, and the outcome found them right, that in this particular instance it would be better to let each Lodge decide for itself and await the result of a poll before taking an irrevocable decision. At the same time a strong Committee was set up in India under Lt General Sir Harold Williams (Bill), a great figure both in Irish and in English Masonry, to help the Lodges and to advise the rulers at home of what they found out from their enquiries. Events moved rapidly and by September 1960 a ballot had been taken in all Lodges, which showed a narrow margin so far as the English were concerned of 96 to 85 in favour of independence: the other two Constitutions showed not dissimilar results though the strong, largely Parsee Scottish Masonic Community in Bombay was almost universally opposed.

Following the poll, which fortunately showed that there were very few Lodges in which there was a close division of opinion, it was decided that the inauguration of the Grand Lodge of India would take place on 24 November 1961 and that high ranking representatives of all three Grand Lodges would take part. The Grand Master to be, His Highness the Nawab of Rampur had his feet in both the English and the Scottish camps and was acceptable to the relatively small number of Irish Lodges. It remained to invent a ceremony for an occasion which had, so far as any of us could discover, no parallel. When a new Province or District is established by our Grand Master, as has happened with West Kent at home and Trinidad, Zambia and Cyprus abroad, there is nothing to do except announce it and go straight on to install the newly appointed Provincial or District Grand Master. This procedure seemed hardly adequate for the new occasion, so I had settled down during the summer months to devise what was in effect going to be a consecration as well as an installation. It had to be divided so that the representative of each Grand Lodge had a fair share, Scotland for the Consecration, Ireland for the Constitution, the formal pronouncement, and England for the Installation. The three Grand Secretaries met and agreed on the wording and Frank Douglas assumed overall responsibility for the ceremonial.

In due course, some travelling by sea and some by air, we gathered in Delhi as guests of the Nawab of Rampur and his family; each of us was allotted a car from his fleet, and a member of his entourage to look after our needs. There was inevitably a lot of rehearsing, though my own active part in the ceremony itself was minimal. However for all of us except W Bro Lt Col M. G. Edwardes who had seen service there in his early days, it was our first experience of India and all the more fascinating for that. Bill Williams organised a visit by air to Agra and Fatehpur Sikri as an interlude in our Masonic labours, and the long and involved ceremony the next day (after a deplorable rehearsal!) went without any worse hitch than that the censer had disappeared when Howard Potts went out to collect it. It was discovered two floors down in the Ashoka Hotel where the meeting was held—in the kitchens! His Highness and Bro Sundaram the Grand Secretary had planned their side of it to perfection so that when we heard, only a matter of days later that they had quarrelled irrrevocably and that the Grand Master had resigned, we were all deeply saddened. Fortunately I had struck while the iron was hot and early in the morning the day following the installation had persuaded both Grand Master and Grand Secretary to put their signatures to a Concordat which settled the relations between the two Grand Lodges and, in particular, safeguarded the rights of those Lodges which had opted to remain under the United Grand Lodge of England. The Concordat also made it clear that England would warrant no more Lodges in India, and that India would not warrant any Lodges outside India, whilst similar documents were drawn up for Ireland and Scotland. I brought ours back with me and it was duly completed by the signatures of Lord Scarbrough and Erskine Simes as Grand Registrar.

The Concordat had purposely left vague the question of financial arrangements between the new Grand Lodge and our Districts, and between Lodges of the two parent bodies. It was hoped, overtrustingly, that goodwill and fraternal feeling would solve any 'little local difficulties'. In some cases this worked out happily, but when I returned to India on a more extensive visit in 1968 I found that there was still a lot of dissatisfaction on both sides. In Bombay I spent a long morning trying to act as an arbitrator and found on that occasion that W Bro Mr Justice Madon who later became Grand Master of India was most understanding and co-operative on the Indian side. At a lower level there seems to have been very little trouble between the Lodges where different Constitutions used the same building, and here as in New Zealand I was pleased to see that the juniors set a good example to their seniors.

Very soon after the installation the party broke up, some went straight home while I interrupted my journey by way of Cyprus, Athens and Zante, and between flights at Beiruit.

In due course the Lodges that helped to form the Grand Lodge of India sent their warrants home, some of them in a very fragile and wormeaten condition, to be endorsed, cancelled and returned as historical evidence of their origin in English Freemasonry. It only remains to add that within a short space of time a Grand Chapter and a Grand Mark Lodge were formed on much the same pattern, and that when Richenda and I toured India in 1968 we were able to take part in the celebration of seven years of Masonic independence.

MORE INDEPENDENCE

The smoothness and goodwill with which the Indian Masonic sovereignty was achieved compares favourably with what had happened in earlier cases, and indicates that it is perfectly possible for more than one jurisdiction to flourish in a given area, proving that co-existence can be to the advantage of all parties. To try to stamp it out merely stiffens resistance and encourages a determination to maintain the *status quo*.

It is an established historical fact that when an independent Grand Lodge is established in territory which has previously been under the Grand Lodges of England, Ireland and Scotland, much more often than not some Lodges prefer to cling to their old allegiance. As a result we have small 'pockets of resistance' in Canada and Australia, a larger one in New Zealand and as already indicated a much larger one in India. Over the years I tried to visit all of them and to give reassurance, if it was needed, that we at home would give such Lodges our unstinted support if pressure was applied to them by the newly formed National Grand Lodge(s) to reverse their decision of loyalty towards their Mother Grand Lodge. Pursuing this policy I went to Montreal and Halifax where there are still English Lodges: it may be noted on the other hand that there has never been any attempt in Newfoundland, once our oldest colony and now the Dominion of Canada's tenth Province, to establish an independent Grand Lodge: we still have four Lodges in Australia, all of which I have visited together with a good proportion of the two score and more in New Zealand. On the other hand it has to be borne in mind that the situation in South Africa is quite different in as much as there was never any agreement at the time of the recognition of the Grand Lodge of Southern Africa that the 'home' jurisdiction would not warrant any more Lodges.

The genesis of the Grand Lodge of Southern Africa is so different from that of others that some explanation by one of the few survivors from that time is called for. During the Second World War the Lodges in South Africa under the Grand East, then still the Grand Orient, of the Netherlands were almost the only part of it not to be overwhelmed by German or Japanese invasion. In any case they accounted for quite half of its strength and this proportion increased when the Far Eastern Lodges asserted their independence and soon afterwards disappeared with the collapse of Netherlandic authority in the East Indies. Accordingly the South African Lodges formed a very important part of the Grand East, as was demonstrated by the fact that they were ruled in a kind of dominion status, by their own Deputy Grand Master. Soon after the election of a Brother Davidson as Grand Master trouble flared up in Europe as he clearly wished to assert himself by drawing into his sphere of operations Masonic bodies such as the Grand Lodge of France which had never been recognised as regular. His methods (he was a patent agent by profession) were tortuous, but his aims were clear: he wished to be the Grand Master, under whatever title, of Europe. The Lodges in South Africa were well aware of this and of the likelihood that, if his plans went forward and he carried the Grand East with him that body would be disowned by the rest of the regular Grand Lodges in Europe, and possibly in the world at large. They would thus fall under the same ban, which would make their situation in South Africa, cheek by jowl with the English, Irish and Scottish Lodges quite untenable. The Deputy Grand Master, Dr Botha, came to Europe to get first hand information at the Hague and received much encouragement in London. The result was that on his return to Cape Town he threw off his allegiance to the Grand East, proclaimed an independent Grand Lodge and was elected Grand Master. He had already been warned in London that recognition would not be accompanied by the customary agreement by those concerned with Lodges in South Africa not to warrant any more: he was so eager, as indeed he had to be unless his Lodges were to be left unrecognised, to gain recognition that he accepted. Ironically only a few months later Bro Davidson fell from power and no more was heard of the 'Grand Lodge of Europe': Dr Botha's action thus proved to be precipitate, but I remain convinced that the Netherlandic Masons in South Africa are better off in the independence they now enjoy, even if it is slightly curtailed as I have shown, than they would be tied to the Grand East of the Netherlands. I believe that the situation is quite well recognised and appreciated by those who count in the Masonic world, and that Craft membership generally in the Republic loses nothing by the continued right of the other three jurisdictions to warrant new Lodges. This is only a theoretical problem: South Africa has more pressing practical ones, such as the admission of Africans, the use of Afrikaans and the sustained hostility of the Reformed Church.

Chapter 11

Private Life and Lodges

Promotion to Grand Secretary did not intrude too greatly into our private lives, though Richenda, who had been working for St Paul's School from the early days of the war and had seen the school's successful evacuation to Crowthorne, Berkshire and back, was anxious to return to medical social work. She was persuaded by the High Master, Tony Gilkes, to stay on long enough to see them through the 450th anniversary celebrations in 1959 which culminated in a visit to West Kensington by the Queen and the Duke of Edinburgh. Soon after that she left for a refresher course in 'almoning' and, after a short stretch of temporary jobs, did two long stints at St Thomas's and Fulham Hospital as it gradually absorbed or was absorbed by the new Charing Cross.

The following note from the *Pauline* shows how much she was missed:

Mrs Stubbs

Mrs Stubbs, to whom we said goodbye last term, had been our catering manager ever since the war. During the whole of it she ran the School sanatorium at the Ousels. Her management of the Tuckshop at Easthampstead in the later years, and her organisation of the central lunch there, had revealed her remarkable powers; and when, after our return, obligatory school lunch was decided upon, she was naturally given charge of the undertaking, with management of the Tuck shop as well.

Few people realised the extent of her responsibilities; the kitchens serve seven hundred lunches or so on five days a week, and the Tuck shop is crowded three times daily and expected, and always found, to be equal to every demand. Each department has its staff—about thirty persons in all—whose welfare must be considered.

Mrs Stubbs became a legendary figure. It was not just that routine requirements were punctually met; she welcomed the extra and the exceptional; the individual who needed a special diet; the society that wanted a tea; the occasion that called for an organisation which might mean the staff arriving at six in the morning, and she herself being here almost all night. She provided for them all, with her own combination of cheerful vigour, unassailable efficiency and unobtrusive devotion. She seldom refused a request, certainly not on the score of difficulty (as with another notable administrator 'the merely difficult takes so long, the impossible a little longer'), and she was immediately and completely at the service of any one, young or old, in genuine distress. To her own staff she could do no wrong.

Her central position which brought her into touch with every part of the

School, and her prodigious efficiency, made her a pivotal figure in a surprisingly wide range of matters, and her intelligence service—the best in the School—made it wise and always profitable to consult her.

We shall all miss her vigour, cheerfulness, efficiency and absolute reliability; those who have known and worked with her for many years take leave of her with affection and deep regret.

As far as she was concerned the change of work involved longer travelling and the loss of school length holidays, but as Hugh was growing up he became more used to looking after himself during his times at home. He had followed his uncles and myself to Summer Fields in 1954 and to Charterhouse in 1959, where he suffered a little at both from following his Uncle Hugh, my youngest brother who was the classical scholar *par excellence* of the family, but fortunately at Charterhouse he made up for it by common sense, efficiency and a capacity for organisation. From Charterhouse he proceeded to Exeter University and in due course qualified as a solicitor. He was taken on by Freshfields in 1972 which my father, as already previously recounted, had left for the Church in 1899.

JUBILEE MASTERS' AND OTHER LODGE MEMBERSHIPS

It might have been thought that my evening visits to Lodges and Chapters would have increased; this was not really so, though it became more necessary to choose between rival invitations, and in the early days to assess where a visit was needed and where it was no more than a matter of curiosity in the members to see what the Grand Secretary was like. There were however a few new memberships that came up, so to speak,

With Hugh on a visit to Kilravock for a Clan Rose gathering in June 1970.

with the rations. The Royal Alpha Lodge No 16 which is in a very real sense the Grand Master's 'private army', had in force till recently a bylaw which would have been totally irregular elsewhere, to the effect that the Grand Secretary was automatically its Secretary. This was still its rule in 1958 and I found myself elected a member and also invested as Secretary at the first meeting after my appointment! Whilst the bylaws were modified in 1963, the practice continued, and subsequently Michael Higham took over, on my retirement in 1980, thus enabling me to go through the Chair, not a very laborious process, two years later.

The Bard of Avon Lodge, in the Province of Middlesex, was almost equally eclectic though with a strong natural bias towards the Masonic hierarchy of Middlesex. I became a member in 1958, while the Lodge was still meeting in the pleasant surroundings of the Mitre Hotel, Hampton Court, and when the Mitre closed its doors on the Craft we moved to Cole Court, Twickenham, which, after the initial shock of change, has proved equally pleasant. Very shortly after my appointment I was asked by Sir Ernest Cooper to join the Jubilee Masters' Lodge, which I had visited periodically, of which Sydney had been a Past Master, and of which Sir Ernest was at that point the Master for the second time in 1958. He was installed in March by Lord Scarbrough himself to mark the Lodge's 60th anniversary, and as I was present, with every intention of enjoying a quiet evening with so much 'top brass' about, I felt that I could not possibly be needed for anything. It was, and still is, an unwritten piece of Masonic protocol that when one of the four chief rulers of the Craft is present and speaks, as inevitably he does, lesser men like Grand Director of Ceremonies and Grand Secretaries are exempt and consequently hold their peace. My peace on this occasion was shattered on being called upon by Lord Scarbrough himself to reply to a toast of his own invention at virtually no notice. I got by with it, but ever afterwards made the rule clear to all concerned.

I was proposed for membership at the next meeting, and placed on the agenda for election in November: by this time I had found myself pledged to attend the Grand Lodge of Scotland's Annual Festival on or near St Andrew's day, which coincided with the Jubilee Masters'. I regarded this coincidence of dates as a mild nuisance though unavoidable, but I suppose my suspicions ought to have been aroused by the interest which both Sir Ernest and Frank Douglas were showing in making sure that I went to Edinburgh. On my return from a very enjoyable evening in George Street, the first of several, and during which I made a speech the southern accent of which completely foxed the shorthand writer, I found two messages awaiting me, the first was no surprise—that I had been elected to membership of Jubilee Masters: the second was a real bombshell as, at the same meeting, I had been elected to the Chair to follow Sir Ernest! Small wonder I had been kept away.

However this was the start of a happy relationship with the Lodge which reached its highest point perhaps when I was invited to become

Master for the second time in 1973, when the 75th anniversary was celebrated. It was a great occasion, attended by the Grand Secretaries of Ireland and Scotland, as well as by Dr Jackie Wallace the Irish Deputy Grand Master who made one of his best and most inimitable speeches. I have always enjoyed the meetings which bring together a very good cross-section of London Masonry.

Attendance at the Wellesley Lodge in Berkshire had become increasingly difficult, and the Lodge's nature had changed a good deal too since my father and I were in office in it together before the War. I therefore decided to resign, but wishing to maintain a live link with Berkshire I first joined the Berkshire Masters' Lodge which I have been able to attend fairly regularly in addition to my years as Master in 1974.

Westminster and Keystone Lodge No 10 which I had joined in 1938 requires more mention than just a casual reference to attendances during the War. As its number implies it is one of the oldest on the roll, and it must be a matter of conjecture whether in 1722 it joined Grand Lodge as an already established Lodge or was one of those formed by the five year old Grand Lodge, in which case it must have been one of the very first: for myself I incline to the first alternative. Its early years were spent in the City and Soho, but in 1792 it moved to Westminster and adopted its present name in lieu of the Tyrian. The move was not a success and by 1854 the Lodge was reduced to the lowest possible numbers and in grave danger of having to hand back its warrant. Fortunately a number of young Masons from Oxford were seeking to form a University Lodge in London at that time, and it was suggested to them that they would do better to join, take over and revitalise No 10. The plan succeeded and the link thus forged has continued to the present day, and to a lesser degree with the Isaac Newton at Cambridge. It was made still stronger by Sir Colville Smith having been for many years Secretary of both it and the Apollo. Consequently when I became a member I inevitably found many friends, and when later I reappeared after the War as a member of the next Grand Secretary's staff my appointment as Assistant Secretary seemed natural. This office I held except for a period as Senior Warden and Master till Denis Burnett Brown retired to the country and I succeeded him as Secretary in 1957 only giving up the office when I in turn retired in 1980. Even then it fell into the hands of Michael Higham for a short period, and I could not but feel sad that he abandoned it so soon in favour of being Director of Ceremonies exchanging office with Jeremy Pemberton. It has had a distinguished list of members, and Lord Scarbrough who had been one in his early days used to say that the absolute, if not the perfect, Mason was a member of the Apollo, No 10 and the House of Lords as well as being at least a Provincial Grand Master:* at

* The list included Lord Robins (Rhodesia), Lord Lewellin (Dorset), Lord Rathcreedan (Oxfordshire), and Lord Crookshank (Lincolnshire): the last two were in turn Treasurers over a long period, and it was Lord Crookshank who sent me a postcard, while the country was in the middle of the 1950 General Election:—'Attlee has done what Hitler never managed to do—made me miss a meeting of No 10'.

an influential, though slightly lower level, in 1980 it contained the President of the Board of General Purposes, the Grand Secretary, the Deputy Grand Secretary, the Grand Treasurer and an Assistant Grand Chaplain as well as one of the most senior Provincial Grand Masters. I particularly enjoyed sharing the Secretary's table with Lord Widgery LCJ who had his own idiosyncratic method of keeping Lodge Accounts. He became Master just before being elevated to the Bench, and I remember, at his installation, reading out to him the exhortation 'patiently to submit to the decisions of the Supreme Legislature' on the evening of a day when he had been unsuccessfully addressing the Law Lords! A continuing strand of membership was provided by four successive William James Thompsons (together with the younger son of the second). The latter and his younger son both left the Lodge a handsome legacy which we decided to invest in claret and port, and we have been drinking the original purchase and its successors ever since despite the disapproval of Lord Crookshank who favoured putting the earlier legacy away safely in old Consols.

SCHOOL LODGES

On coming out of the army I had joined the Charterhouse Deo Dante Dedi* Lodge No 2885 which I had visited years earlier with my father as guests of his contemporary Harold Haig Brown. The Lodge had been bombed out of the Old Charterhouse where it had always met and was settled in 1946 at the Piccadilly Hotel, to judge by the noise a few feet only above the tube. It still had a good many of the older members who went back to an unhappy era at the end of the previous war, when Arthur Marriott Powell, a Carthusian stormy petrel, had tried unsuccessfully to force the Masonic authorities into accepting a kind of prayer meeting for the armed forces, alive or dead, as an adjunct to all Lodge meetings. A certain amount of bad blood was engendered, and almost alone of the school Lodges Charterhouse did not qualify itself as a Hall Stone Lodge; in justice it must be added that they made the very handsome gift to the Charterhouse War Memorial Chapel of the North East Porch whose door is surmounted by an elaborate escutcheon or device of Masonic symbols. My first two or three years in the Lodge were not particularly happy ones as I seemed to bear the brunt of various arguments with the Grand Secretary's Office, particularly with an elderly Grand Officer and member of the Chancery Bar, Norman Armitage, whose certainty that he was right was only equalled by the frequency with which events proved him wrong! There were however new members coming in and others coming back from the forces, notably J. P. R. Hale who came from a long and distinguished Carthusian's family and Howard Potts, a Past Grand Steward who had miraculously survived as a Japanese Prisoner of War on the Siamese Railway. I knew very little at the time about what was

*The motto of the school founded in 1611 by Thomas Sutton and the original name of the Lodge, to which Charterhouse was added a few years later when School Lodges began to proliferate.

going on in the higher councils of the Lodge, and was surprised to be invited to lunch at the Savoy by Howard and still more to be asked whether I would undertake the Mastership in the following year. I adduced Norman Armitage as a good reason for declining: but Howard said that this had occurred to the minds of the Past Masters and had only strengthened their determination, and that in any case when tackled the old man had protested his pleasure at the suggestion with the irrelevant comment that my father and he had been in the Classical VIth together.

I was already installed in the Chair of No 10 at the time, but calculated that I should be out of it by the time of the Charterhouse Lodge installation. In fact I was still further clear because in the spring of 1952 I was called up as a 'Z reservist' to do a 14 days training course at Catterick with the result that the installation had to be postponed.

(The 'Z' training was a pleasant holiday though Catterick in early May was still in the grip of winter. My chief recollections are of the very gingerly way we were all handled, rather as if we might break out into open revolt, and of nearly electrocuting a brother officer who incautiously tried to adjust an aerial as I was pumping full power into it; and the fact stood out clear that our methods of handling signal traffic at 21 Army Group Rear HQ in Brussels was vastly superior to the latest modifications and improvements being taught in 1952.)

I was however installed in the end and started a busy year of visits to the other School Lodges, almost all of which I managed to get to, with the result that when Public School Lodges Festivals were revived by Tom Langton in 1957 I already had a wide acquaintance with most of their members. The Lodge was able to get back to Charterhouse E.C. in 1957 and has met happily, though expensively, there ever since.

One of the chief ingredients for success in a School Lodge, particularly if it meets on School premises, is to have among its members some of the School staff. There is almost always someone of this category, a long serving master or the bursar, sometimes even the headmaster, who will be a focal point. The three School Lodges that I have been most closely associated with, Charterhouse, St Paul's and Clifton have been very fortunate in this respect: Sir Frank Fletcher, George Turner, Oliver Van Oss and Brian Rees at Charterhouse, even if they did not achieve great prominence in the Craft; John Bell and Robert James at St Paul's with the perennial Tom Martin, whilst Clifton was greatly strengthened by Jock Crawford and Hugh Davie, who after they retired, settled nearby and kept in close touch with both Lodge and School. On the other hand lack of such connecting links, and in the cases of the Public School Lodges the actual distance from London, which tended to make the School draw on a northern or midland population for its pupils have always been weakening factors.

Sydney White was said quite unjustifiably to be opposed to closed shop Lodges and in particular to School ones, and to have inherited this prejudice from PC; but I know of no grounds for this view in either of them.

PC in fact was the first Master of the Old Cliftonian Lodge, and Sydney's son Jack is an active member of the Old Tonbridgian. Sydney did however say to me on more than one occasion that he thought it was a pity for anyone to belong only to his School Lodge as in that case he never really extended his Masonic acquaintanceship or experience. With this I wholly agree, but it is equally true of other closed Lodges, *viz* Hospital, Regimental or Legal.

Tom Langton's efforts at Radley in 1957 bore splendid fruit and the festivals have gone on in unbroken series ever since and are just about to start their third round with Charterhouse in 1986. A great change was instituted by Marlborough in 1971 when the Lodge decided to invite ladies too: this of course involved finding something for them to do during the Lodge meeting, and a good deal of ingenuity has been brought to bear. We have been almost invariably fortunate in the weather; the arrival of the new Assistant Grand Master, Fiennes Cornwallis, at Malvern was greeted with a terrific clap of thunder but the rest of the day remained pleasant enough. It could very well be argued that the thunder was not aimed at him, but was a mark of divine displeasure that for the last time ladies had not been invited.

Two highlights of my membership of Deo Dante Dedi were the initiation of my son Hugh, to whom I gave the Charge, and also his installation eight years later, from opening to closing, by myself: the latter took just over 90 minutes, with nothing left out, and in that respect at least was a model performance. Lord Cadogan, Frank Douglas and Sir Allan Adair attended the three degree ceremonies, but David Pascho's suggestion that the Great Architect might drop in for coffee after dinner came to nothing! Acting on views previously expressed Hugh joined the Lodge of Antiquity and became its Master in 1984.

LODGE OF ANTIQUITY

In 1960 after several attendances at its meetings as a visitor, I had been invited to join the Lodge of Antiquity No 2: like No 4 it works without a warrant having been one of the founding four Lodges of Grand Lodge in 1717. It bases itself firmly, if mythically, on its connection with Christopher Wren and the rebuilding of St Paul's Cathedral after the great fire of London. Alex Frere was already one of the leading personalities in 1960, and it is difficult to avoid the suspicion that I was brought in as a counterbalance to the Studd family, of whom there were no less than five in the Lodge (as the Treasurer's name was Tubbs clear articulation was always essential). I had an uneventful year as Master in 1964 and was sitting back pleasantly idle when a crisis materialised in the latter half of 1966.

It became clear that when Grand Lodge celebrated its 250 years in 1967 with great pomp and ceremony, as a prelude to the installation of the new Grand Master, the three remaining founding Lodges would play a big part. Sir Eric Studd had been Secretary for many years in succession to his father Sir Kynaston, and it seemed very appropriate that he should be asked to be Master for 1967, similar gestures being made to senior members in the other two Lodges. Sir Eric accepted the bait, but wished to retain the substance as well as the shadow of power by appointing as Secretary his Grand Secretary General at Duke Street, Sir Donald Makgill, but Donald was a very junior member of the Lodge, had held no office and was an infrequent attender. Alex and I therefore persuaded Kingsley Tubbs the Treasurer to accept the Past Masters' suggestion that he should become Secretary, and that I in turn become Treasurer, an office which (in 1985) I still hold, as my last in any private Lodge. In all this time I have greatly enjoyed the work, which is not hard, but brings me into continual contact with all members.

Although it is a digression I should like to mention the third of the founding Lodges, now Fortitude and Old Cumberland No 12. It had produced Anthony Sayer, the first Grand Master, but, for reasons that have never been made absolutely clear it accepted a warrant in 1722/3 and lost some of its seniority, and much more important, its 'Time Immemorial' status. During the build up to 1967 it occurred to me that if the Lodge would welcome the opportunity, the time was ripe to correct what was probably an injustice in 1722/3, since the story went that the Lodge had accepted a warrant 'though it wanted it not'. The idea appealed to both Grand Lodge and Lord Scarbrough, so No 12 again assumed its Time Immemorial status, and was warmly welcomed by No 2 and No 4, joining in what was then their annual celebration of St John's Day in summer.

Buckinghamshire had a Lodge not unlike the Bard of Avon, namely Methuen No 631: like the Bard which had migrated from Stratford-upon-Avon, Methuen moved eastwards along the Broad gauge of the GWR from Swindon to Taplow, and once in Buckinghamshire wandered about the pleasant meeting places of the Thames Valley. It had maintained close associations with Antiquity, largely through the Inglefield family, so that it was only natural for me to join it in 1964, again under the *aegis* of Alex Frere. It now meets twice at Marlow and once in the winter, in London, when Marlow holds no attraction. In a mild way it has become something of a bone of contention between the Hierarchy of Masonic Buckinghamshire and the older stalwarts from Antiquity and similar London Lodges who tend to regard it as a pleasant summer outing.

QUATUOR CORONATI LODGE

I had never truthfully regarded myself as an erudite Masonic scholar though I was genuinely interested in the material possessions, such as pictures and statuary, of Grand Lodge, and as a one-time historian in the other records of the Craft. I was therefore quite surprised when I was approached by the then Master of Quatuor Coronati Lodge to produce a paper and thereby qualify for consideration as a full member (I was not even a member of the Correspondence Circle at the time). I duly brushed up a paper on the portraits at Freemasons' Hall and subsequently became a member in 1966 and Master two years later. The obligatory inaugural address was on the history of Great Queen Street with special reference to the expansion of Freemasons' Hall along its south side, and a splendid diagram produced by Terry Haunch, the Grand Lodge Librarian, helped me to make it more intelligible. What I found much more difficult was producing votes of thanks from the chair on papers which were sometimes beyond my comprehension and during which I had often dropped off. However the Mastership gave one the *entrée* to the inner councils of the Lodge, and I helped to effect a virtual separation of its organisation and miniscule funds from the big business of the Correspondence Circle which Harry Carr's immense drive and persistence had so greatly increased all over the Masonic world.

Some time later, in 1975, I joined the Old Union Lodge No 46, another of the Red Apron Lodges, which was going through a bad patch, as most Lodges do from time to time, with a lot of members dying—but unfortunately in this case it was the rather important ones who were just reaching or nearing the Chair. I did not take office for some time: indeed I found it difficult for some years to fit its meetings into a crowded calendar, but we kept faith with each other and I duly became Senior Warden in 1982 and Master the following year.

THE GRAND STEWARDS

This brings me to comment and enlarge about the Grand Stewards. They are an absolute enigma to Masons outside London, and even in London, where they are quite often seen, their purpose and status is often misunderstood. If the question is reduced to its simplest terms, 19 Lodges* have acquired the privilege at various times of nominating for the approval of the Grand Master a member, who must be an installed Master and have been a member for five years, to become a Grand Steward at the Annual Investiture and to organise the Grand Festival twelve months later. During that period a Grand Steward is a Grand Officer, but he does not retain the status after his year is over. He does however rank thereafter under Rule 5 of the *Book of Constitutions*, between the Past Grand Tylers and Masters, Past Masters and Wardens of private Lodges who form the main bulk of the membership of Grand Lodge. Past Grand Stewards are therefore senior to any holders of London, Provincial, District or Overseas Grand Rank who are not also Past Grand Officers. They form a very close-knit community, as all alike have served Grand Lodge in a generally active, sometimes onerous but always expensive capacity: they maintain this spirit largely through the Grand Stewards' Lodge which meets

*When I was a Grand Steward for the second time I produced a brief essay on the various Lodge badges which will be found in Appendix II.

The Grand Steward's 1983–84
Back row, left to right: J. G. Newton (1), R. L. Kay (259), I. A. C. Macphersons (99), R. M. Hone (2), A. B. Wilson (28), N. C. R. W. Reid (21), R. O. Linforth (14), F. W. S. Hopton-Scott (23), R. Rowland (26). Front row, left to right: A. J. Matson (91), R. A. Darkin (60), J. R. Owles (58), G. E. Stein (4), Sir Peter Lane, President (8), JWS (46), R. W. B. Scutt (5), D. Thomson (197), R. J. Worsdell (29). The number after each name represents the Lodge of the brother.

immediately before each Quarterly Communication of Grand Lodge, and in January for its annual installation.

Many very distinguished Grand Officers have served also as Grand Stewards, notably the present Deputy Grand Master, and some have reached the Chair of the Grand Stewards' Lodge. This body is 250 years old and as its history *The Grand Stewards and their Lodge* by W Bro Colin Dyer has recently been published I need not here go into detail about it. Over the years I had received much hospitality as well as ready assistance at all times from the Lodge of which I had been an Honorary member almost from my appointment as Grand Secretary, but though I was qualified to become a Grand Steward through Antiquity and later through Old Union as well it had always seemed to me that a conflict of duties and interests might arise if the Grand Secretary became a Grand Steward: I think that Sydney White who was a Past Master of another 'Red Apron' Lodge, Royal Somerset House and Inverness Lodge No 4 probably had felt the same and had refrained from taking this step. However I very much wanted to make amends and as soon as I retired I was put forward by Antiquity. The other 18 Grand Stewards, perhaps predictably, elected me as their President, and we settled down to a happy and contented year in which I was greatly helped by the dynamic secretaryship of Professor Merton Sandler and the financial wizardry of Keith Carmichael who found a good deal more to do with the Board than he did in the otiose function of Grand Treasurer in the Craft and Royal Arch. I duly joined the Grand Stewards' Lodge and was just beginning to attend its meetings, which owing to their duties in the Grand Temple the Grand Stewards of the year cannot, when I was astonished to receive a telephone call saying that I was being recommended by the Lodge Committee for the Mastership. I had also by this time been elected Master of the Royal Alpha Lodge, after all those years as Secretary, and by Old Union after a year as Senior Warden so that I seemed likely to serve a second Grand Stewardship. This time however it was in a private capacity under Sir Peter Lane as President—and none the less enjoyable for not holding office.

So by the end of 1983 I found myself, Masonically speaking, after a gap of nearly twenty years, in the Chairs of three Lodges at the same time: the real crunch came a year later when I installed my successors (two of them devoted Emulationists) as well as Hugh who had reached the Chair of Antiquity, all three of them in eight days.

ROYAL ARCH AND OTHER DEGREES

Life in the Royal Arch had not been so hectic: in May 1947 I was at long last elected to go into the chair of the Apollo University Chapter where I had been holding junior office since 1934. I was installed in all three chairs in November 1947 and in consequence of this qualified for appointment as Assistant Scribe E at the same time as I became Assistant Grand

Secretary. Since then I have joined three other Chapters all closely associated with the Lodges to which they are attached, namely Westminster and Keystone, Carthusian and London First Principals, and have served as First Principal in each. I was fortunate enough to be Third Provincial Grand Principal in the Province of Oxfordshire in a year when there was a consecration and duly took the role of consecrating Third Principal and I was later very glad to have done so as I was thus able to understand, appreciate and sympathise with the difficulties that at times beset a Grand Officer performing that function for the first time.

In general the other degrees in Oxford University Masonry had gone to ground when war broke out, and one of the main preoccupations of a small band of us had been, as I have explained, to get them on their feet again: In the early years Douglas Amery was a tower of strength in Oxford and brought in several dons, such as the redoubtable Maurice Hobby from the Churchill Lodge: but the most consistent and long lasting support came from John Griffith who had settled down as a Classical Tutor at Jesus College and latterly as Public Orator. After a 'palace revolution' had installed him as Secretary of the Apollo he was able to guide the enthusiasms of the undergraduate Masons into the most suitable channels. I served for a number of years as Treasurer of the Mark, Ark Mariners and the Knight Templars, as Director of Ceremonies of the Apollo University Chapter and Recorder of the Oxford University Rose Croix, only giving them up one by one as the new generation came forward, though I still try to get to a Lodge meeting once a term and a visit to all the other degrees annually. I did what I could for the other orders in London and since retirement have been able to enjoy them more freely as will be seen later, various authorities over the years having very kindly appointed me to high rank which I would at least like to justify.

Chapter 12

Celebrating 250 years

Lord Scarbrough used to urge me from time to time to have no hesitation in telling him when I thought he was getting past his job. That need never arose: indeed two days after he had suffered his bad stroke in June 1969 he was writing to me a perfectly well formed and lucid letter on some Masonic subject which was becoming urgent, a letter which, sadly, arrived in the office the day after his death. He had however two other abiding interests, which fortuitously came together in time: one was to bring back the Grand Mastership to the Royal Family after a lapse of some twenty years, the other to celebrate adequately the 250th anniversary of the Premier Grand Lodge.

On one of our earlier journeys together he started to talk about this, and I was able to suggest that midsummer 1967 would be a very suitable time for both ambitions to be achieved, though the exact date was not very material, and that a Royal installation would be the best possible climax to the celebrations. He had, I knew, already discussed the question of Masonry with the Duke of Kent who was understandably anxious to take up the office which his father had held for such a tragically short period. Together we worked out a time schedule, a rather tight but nevertheless practicable one, and the Duke passed through respectively the Chairs of the Royal Alpha Lodge and of the Westminster and Keystone Chapter as his father had done before him, in not dissimilar circumstances: he then became Senior Grand Warden in 1966. At the Annual Investiture in April 1967 Lord Scarbrough announced that he wished in June to propose the election of the Duke of Kent as Grand Master, with the intention of installing him at an Especial Meeting of Grand Lodge later that month, when, as was already known, the 250th Anniversary would be celebrated. Immediately on his election in June, the new Grand Master appointed Lord Scarbrough Pro Grand Master, thus reviving an office that had been in abeyance.

Our preparations for the latter event had of course been going on for months, and it was not unduly difficult to marry up the two functions. What we had done was, first, to make sure that the Royal Albert Hall was available, and to have ready to set in motion the procedures for application forms, ballots and the issue of tickets. Secondly to establish a committee under Sir Allan Adair to decide on the scale of invitations to recognised jurisdictions, and on the general pattern of the entertainment of our guests and in many cases their ladies too. Thirdly to produce suitable mementoes of the occasion.

An official history of Grand Lodge had already been embarked upon under the general direction of Alex Frere, and the more detailed attention of both the Librarian, W Bro Hewitt, and myself. Various Masonic scholars were prevailed upon to write chapters on the period on which each of them seemed to be the most competent authority, and several appendices on special aspects were planned also. I took on the last fifty years (1917-1967) with some part at least of which I had been closely connected, while Reg Hewitt compiled short biographies of the Grand Masters, 'Ancient and Modern' and abbreviated the account he had given a year earlier in Grand Chapter of its own 200 years of history. We had also the rather harder task of adjusting the beginnings and endings of adjacent chapters so that the whole would read smoothly. The contributors were very good and co-operative as also was the University Press at Oxford where a curious jumble of literary conventions was received and amalgamated with the accustomed ease and expertise which one takes for granted from this ancient house, its learned Printer and craftsmen. *Grand Lodge 1717-1867* was ready in time for distribution to our guests, and for sale subsequently to the Masonic public. Supplies were exhausted before I retired, and it is now time for a revised edition to be undertaken.

Another memento of the occasion was produced with a good deal of toil and sweat. When Lord Scarbrough, Frank Douglas and I went to Newfoundland for the Installation of Darroch Macgillivray we had been presented with a Canadian dollar set in a plastic cube, which greatly took Frank's fancy. He agitated for something similar to mark Lord Scarbrough's retirement and the Duke of Kent's installation. The Royal Mint was asked to produce a medallion with a replica of the Grand Lodge Arms on the front and a blank back on which replicas of their respective signatures could be engraved. The Mint did its bit, but Frank then thought that he could save money (and possibly enhance his reputation as a fixer) by getting the plastic work done directly by a small company he knew of instead of handing the medallions over to Messrs Toye, Kenning and Spencer who would gladly, and in fact no more expensively, have handled the whole thing. In the end much valuable energy and time were wasted and the finished articles were only just completed when their distribution was due. Lord Scarbrough's medallion soon became a museum piece, but a few of the Duke's remained over and were in 1980 still available for distribution to Provincial and District Grand Masters on their Installation and to specially distinguished visitors. Incidentally very shortly after the initial issue one was dredged up out of the Serpentine and to the best of my knowledge it was never discovered who the owner might have been.

LOOKING AFTER THE VISITORS

On the administrative side we found that we were going to have to cope with approximately one hundred and fifty visitors, arriving on Sunday 25 June and departing so far as Grand Lodge was concerned on the following Thursday afternoon. Accommodation-wise they were divided up among six leading West End hotels, care being taken so far as was possible to keep like with like. For example the South American contingent were housed at the Waldorf, and the Europeans at the Piccadilly: and a member of Sir Allan Adair's committee was allotted to each hotel where he and his wife generally welcomed and looked after them, but we soon realised that this was going to be more than a whole time job and each was supplied with an assistant. Additionally Ted and Betty Baillieu set up a centre in the Hyde Park Hotel for visiting District Grand Masters and Grand Inspectors, who were not being accommodated but needed a *pied-à-terre* in London, where they could take refuge between events. We had good co-operation with all the hotels, each of which Irene Hainworth and I visited in turn, our only doubt was the adequacy of the bathrooms at Charing Cross, though by then it was too late to do anything about it. Some of the American visitors there murmured but were jollied out of their complaints by the cheerful welcome given them by Billy and Jo Ibberson. Fortunately we had in Ernie Cromack an expert in South American affairs and he looked after our visitors splendidly in the Waldorf: similarly the Europeans who were mainly quartered in the Piccadilly Hotel were looked after by Edgar and Jessie Rutter who knew most of them and were ably assisted by Oscar and Ilde Boehringer who could cope with any language with the exception of modern Greek. The Grand Master of Greece defeated us all, but there was a shrewd suspicion that he understood much more English than he pretended to. In the end having lost him several times Edgar Rutter hired one of the pageboys not to let him out of his sight and to deliver him at the Albert Hall at the exact hour.

Meanwhile we had been planning a programme which would add to the Masonic experience of the visitors over and above the Grand Lodge meeting itself. The Institutions co-operated splendidly and agreed to receive a proportion each of the guests on the following day. We co-opted Sir Donald Wolfit to advise on a suitable variety of shows for the wives to be taken to as unfortunately some of them spoke very little English. This aspect had to cover two evenings, one while we were engaged in dining the Grand Masters and our own Provincial and District Grand Masters at the Savoy while Alex Frere presided over all the other male guests and the various Boards and Committees of Grand Lodge at Grosvenor House, the other while our guests were attending selected Lodge meetings.

Someone, I believe it was Maurice Carpmael, made the inspired suggestion that as most were arriving by air it would be a great boost for their morale if they could be met, however informally, at the airport. I got in touch with the Lodge of Aviation who responded magnificently by keeping a careful watch on arrivals for over 24 hours; to their credit they hardly missed one, welcoming them and even sorting out their transportation into London. On the Sunday morning Richenda and I went round all the hotels with final briefings at each for our 'hosts', and then sat back till the evening when the Committee started the ball rolling with an informal dinner at the Hyde Park Hotel. This went smoothly apart from an attempted gate-crash by two not very important Masons from Utah who had heard of the functions and affected to think that they were free for all. Having speedily seen them off we experienced no further trouble of that sort.

THE INSTALLATION OF THE DUKE OF KENT

On Monday morning the guests were left very much to their own devices and I suspect that most who had wives with them were hauled off on shopping sprees to Harrods. The Grand Master formally welcomed all the guests, and a small number of ourselves at St James's Palace in the early evening before the sexes separated to various dinner parties and theatres. We had completely taken over the Albert Hall early in the day, and most of the staff were there adapting the seating and labelling it for Masonic purposes. Several of us had been through the whole process at least twice before which saved much time and effort. The tickets had of course been despatched a good deal earlier, and I concentrated on the 400 special stewards and their positioning round the auditorium and at the doors as well as organising the dais seating plan. This entailed the Grand Lodge procession which was to enter with Lord Scarbrough as Pro Grand Master, representatives of the three Time Immemorial Lodges, and the offical visitors from 65 Grand Lodges (our Representatives from a similar number of Grand Lodges did not process but were taken to their allotted seats informally). The Masters of the three Lodges as representing the Founders of Grand Lodge had a special function, and they entered before Grand Lodge was opened and presented the Three Great Lights and the historic (? legendary) Wren maul to the Pro Grand Master. At this point a curious incident occurred, as in the excitement of the moment James Young, the Grand Tyler, had omitted to light the Three Lesser Lights. On his omission being noticed he hurried round and rectified it with a cigarette lighter. Very few of the audience queried it, and those who did were told blandly that the Lesser Lights could not take precedence over the Greater and be lit before the latter arrived: instant symbolism!

Seating the acting Grand Officers was complicated by the need for a number of them to be able to leave their seats during the ceremony in order to form a deputation to escort the Grand Master into Grand Lodge. Seating on the dais was cramped and there was no possibility of their stepping past other Grand Officers, so all concerned had to be at the opposite ends of rows in order to come forward simultaneously as they were called out, and then pair off. Some notes had to be taken also of the 'roadworthiness' of some of them: poor Erskine Simes, the Grand Registrar, for example, had managed with pain and effort the incoming procession, and gratefully accepted the suggestion that his deputy, Walter Wigglesworth, should subsequently take his place.

Frank Douglas and I agreed on two minor changes of procedure which have in fact now become standard practice for the installation of Provincial Grand Masters. Sydney White had insisted that whoever it was being installed should have both the apron and chain of his new rank brought in with him, whilst he wore the insignia of his former rank. We argued that the Grand Master became Grand Master at the moment of election and that henceforward his Grand Master's apron was the only correct

HRH the Duke of Kent arriving for his installation as Grand Master at the Royal Albert Hall on 24 June 1967: he is being received by Lord Scarbrough and myself whilst Lt Cmdr (Sir) Richard Buckley is in attendance.

one, which also got over the potentially undignified sight of the Grand Director of Ceremonies struggling to remove one apron and attach another. In the matter of collar and chain Sydney had each time produced his own embroidered collar and lent it, subsequently having a gold stamped notice on the inside saying when and by whom it had been worn. We felt that this was an unnecessary affectation and that it was quite correct, and more dignified, if the Grand Master appeared uncollared, and was then duly invested with his chain.

With a double ceremony such as this there were inevitably a good many speeches. On the 250th anniversary there were three of exemplary brevity, on behalf of the Representatives by the Grand Chancellor of Denmark, and for the visiting Deputations by the Grand Masters of Massachusetts and Belgium, the oldest Grand Lodge in the New World and the newest in the old respectively. Lord Cadogan thanked them with equal, and his customary, brevity.

The Deputation had been introduced in a series of groups as far as possible in reverse order of seniority; each was announced from the far end of the central aisle by Ted Baillieu who made each of them sound as if they were of special interest. (I was much relieved to see in the first group that the Grand Master of Greece had not eluded his escort.) All this took about an hour, and it was at 17.01 exactly that the arrival of the Grand Master was announced: the actual installation was quickly over and at 17.23 another bout of speeches started. Precedent dictates that the Grand Masters of the Sister Jurisdictions of Ireland and Scotland, and of Canada, the senior Grand Lodge in the Commonwealth should offer congratulations, followed by a rather longer address by the Installing Officer. Needless to say Lord Scarbrough's address was a model, while the two Home Grand Masters* were both able to refer to their fathers having been in the same position at previous installations. It was then the moment for the Duke of Kent to reply, and everyone was waiting with the keenest interest to see and hear how he came across on his first public appearance as Grand Master. I had drafted his speech for him some time before and was naturally anxious to hear to what extent he had found it necessary to amend it and also how it would sound through another mouth. Happily it was received with close attention even though the meeting had been going on for almost two hours. It was quite remarkable how many of those present commented on the similarity of his voice, and diction, to his grandfather's which they remembered from Christmas Broadcasts some 30 years earlier.

The Especial Communication of Grand Lodge closed after a few formal announcements and the Hall rapidly emptied. In fact when Alex Frere and I made a tour of it half an hour later to thank the staff and such special Stewards as we could find, it was practically empty and the Grand Lodge paraphernalia, including the three huge thrones, was already being packed up.

Later in the evening a large scale soirée was held in the Connaught Rooms which was attended by the Duke and Duchess who managed to get round the several rooms in which it was held and talk to many of the guests. All attempts however satisfactorily to floodlight the tower of the Hall and, in particular, the clock which had been presented to celebrate the occasion failed: but I doubt if many of our guests as they passed along Great Queen Street on their various ways home took notice of what was really the only non-success of the day.

The following day was devoted to visits to Hove, Rickmansworth,

*Lord Donoughmore and Sir Ronald Orr Ewing.

The Dais in the Royal Albert Hall during the installation of HRH the Duke of Kent as Grand Master in 1967. Lord Donoughmore, Grand Master of Ireland is addressing the Grand Master. Left to right: JWS, Alex Frere, the Grand Director of Ceremonies and his three deputies, Lord Donoughmore, Lord Scarbrough, Lord Cadogan, the Grand Master and Sir Allan Adair.

Bushey and Ravenscourt Park, and later to Lodge meetings and more theatres. Jubilee Masters, Quatuor Coronati, and Canada Lodges were the willing hosts, providing a variety of entertainment and generous hospitality. The guests were by now beginning to slip away, and it was by no means the whole mass of them who turned up for a conducted tour of Freemasons' Hall and a farewell buffet lunch on Thursday. In the course of the celebrations many presentations had been made personally or had arrived by mail, and the Librarian and his staff had managed to mount an exhibition of most of them which was greatly appreciated. A magnificent trophy of Masonic jewels from Pennsylvania arrived just in time to form part of the exhibition having previously had a slow passage through customs.

Finally Richenda and I entertained our magnificent 'hosts and hostesses' from the hotels, the particularly active Grand Officers and others without whom the celebrations could never have succeeded: we were all tired but very content at the happy outcome of our labours.

When life returned to normal, which it did remarkably quickly, arrears of non-urgent business were cleared, and a guard book was composed in which we inserted an example of every circular and instruction, tickets, lists of special stewards and a note of points which were found likely to cause trouble next time. We were helped in this by having had a photographer at the Albert Hall who put on permanent record almost every stage in the proceedings. The bound volume of these photographs and the guard book should in close alliance clear any point of doubt or difficulty in the run-up to the next installation, which may well not occur while any of the main participants in the organisation of 1967 are still current!

Chapter 13

Grand Secretary—Part Two (1967-1980)

In 1967 it was 25 years since there had been a Pro Grand Master and none of us knew from experience what the chain of command should be in theory or was going to be in practice. Fortunately Lord Scarbrough was so well versed in Court procedure and so well known in Royal circles that as long as he lived there was little change in the administration of Grand Lodge, particularly as the new Grand Master was posted to the peace-keeping force in Cyprus. But other changes were in the air; Frank Douglas wished to give up his post of Grand Director of Ceremonies, and as a result was, in April 1968, appointed a Second Assistant Grand Master; but though Alex Frere took more persuasion each year to continue as President of the Board of General Purposes, he went on until 1972. Sir Cullum Welch retired the same year to be succeeded, sadly for only a short time, by his Senior Vice President Bernard Davis. It was however Lord Scarbrough's sudden and unexpected death in 1969 that took us all by surprise, and started a chain reaction of new appointments among the Rulers of the Craft.

So far as I was personally concerned this tragic loss was, palliated only by the immediate appointment of Lord Cadogan to succeed him; readers of *The Four Corners* will realise that he and I, and our wives, had fostered and maintained a very close relationship throughout our various travels. It was going to be easy to work with him, but the question was how fully would he take the place of Lord Scarbrough as adviser to the Grand Master, and also as the *de facto* day-to-day head of the Craft. Lord Scarbrough was commemorated in various ways, and Sir Allan Adair and I attended a service in York Minister, in the preservation of which he had played so prominent a part. He was born in York and had served as Lord Lieutenant of the West Riding for even longer than he had been Grand Master. There had also been the usual Garter Service at Windsor. But the Craft as a whole had not been given the opportunity to express its admiration for a great Mason and Grand Master.

Towards the end of July, that is about a month after his death, we went for our usual holiday to Cyprus without there being any indication of a desire for a more particularly Masonic memorial service. However while we were away the movement began, inspired I think by Ted Baillieu the new Grand Director of Ceremonies, but though a private word was let slip to me in Cyprus I had heard nothing official till I got home. I then learned that St Paul's had been booked for a service on the day of the September Grand Lodge, that it could take place only in the morning so that Grand Lodge had to be postponed till the afternoon, that an order of service was being worked out with the Dean, and best of all that Archbishop Lord Fisher had been persuaded to come out of his Dorset retirement to give the address: it will be recalled that he had given the prayer for the King's restoration to health at Lord Scarbrough's installation. The two of them had been closely associated during the Hannah controversy, and also in the long drawn out debate on the relationship of Religion and Freemasonry, which culminated in the report to Grand Lodge in 1962.* The Cathedral was packed, and the congregation listened with rapt attention to Lord Fisher's address which, lasting a bare eight minutes, said everything that could possibly be said: but to some of us however the high spot in the whole affair was the singing of the closing ode 'Now the evening shadows closing. ...' at the end of the service. Grand Lodge met a few hours later in a sombre mood, fully realising that one of the great men and masons of his generation had been fitly commemorated.

Later I was asked by the editor of *Ars Quatuor Coronatorum* to contribute an obituary note, and I do not think that I can better sum up the feelings of myself and the many thousands of members of the English Constitution than by repeating it here:

In Memoriam

The Rt Hon The Earl of Scarbrough
KG, GCSI, GCIE, GCVO, TD
Pro Grand Master

Lawrence Roger Lumley became a Mason in 1919 while an undergradute at Magdalen College, Oxford, where he had matriculated after war service. Spending only a short time in residence, he held no office in the Apollo University Lodge No 357, in which he was initiated by Rev Thomas Trotter Blockley who later became Provincial Grand Master. He clearly, however, made his mark in the Lodge, as he did in the College, for shortly after going down he was brought into the Westminster and Keystone Lodge No 10, by Sir Colville Smith, who, in addition to being Grand Secretary, was Secretary of both it and the Apollo. He remained a member of this Lodge until his departure for India in 1937 as Governor of Bombay. He had meanwhile become a Founder of the Lodge of St Andrew No 4683, at Hull, in 1925, and a joining member of the Lumley Lodge No 1893 at Skegness in 1928.

Very soon after his arrival in Bombay he joined Lodge St George No 549 and was exalted in the Chapter attached to it. Having served as Master and First Principal respectively, he was appointed District Grand Master in 1940, and Grand Superintendent a year later, in both cases succeding RW Bro W. A. C. Bromham who resigned in his favour and who was reappointed,

* See page 77.

when the Governor's tour of duty came to an end and he resigned his Masonic offices in Bombay. The fact that after his departure from India he became a Founder of two Lodges in Bombay is good evidence of the interest he maintained in Indian Masonic affairs long after his period of active office was over.

The state of Masonry in India always remained one of his major interests. He had little sympathy for the maintenance of a Masonic *status quo* after partition and, not satisfied with creating a District of Northern India and with tidying up the line of demarcation between Bombay and the Punjab, he was the driving force in establishing an Indian Grand Lodge as soon as he was convinced that it was both viable and what a majority of our Indian Brethren really wanted. With infinite patience and the able assistance of RW Bro Sir Harold Williams, he got agreement on all sides and his efforts came to fruition at New Delhi in October 1961 when the Grand Lodge of India was inaugurated.

Following his return to England in the middle of the war and a resumption of his Military and Parliamentary activities (now in the House of Lords for he had succeeded to the Earldom of Scarbrough on the death of his uncle in 1945) there was a lull in his Masonic career. It was however a short one, for when the Duke of Devonshire became Grand Master in 1947, on the death of the Earl of Harewood, he invited Lord Scarbrough to become his Deputy. At that time he was hardly known as a Mason in most parts of England. The stress of war and poor communications abroad had tended to make the Districts still more *terra incognita* than usual, and there were many who did not at once recognise H. E. Sir Roger Lumley in his new style and title as 11th Earl of Scarbrough. Indeed when he announced the appointment in Grand Lodge on 3rd September 1947, the Duke of Devonshire referred to the fact that Lord Scarbrough was not very well known in the Craft in England, but he went on to say how distinguished had been his Masonic services in India, how well he had known him over many years and in many fields, and of what sound commonsense, wisdom in council and ability to get on well with others he was possessed.

The words were indeed prophetic for, when Lord Scarbrough became Grand Master just over three years later, those were to be the qualities which above all distinguished him. While he would never have claimed the Masonic erudition of Lord Harewood, or the width and variety of knowledge of the Duke of Devonshire, he brought to the Grand Mastership those typically English characteristics coupled with a flair for ceremonial and the appearance and indeed the reality of complete equanimity and calm.

When he was elected Grand Master, he said to Grand Lodge,
'I must confess, Brethren, that if at any time in the thirty years in which I have been a Freemason—except for the last three months—anyone had told me that I should one day be Grand Master of the United Grand Lodge of England, I would have thought it a foolish pleasantry—and indeed, nobody in fact ever did make the suggestion to me!'

I told him once of how I first heard of his impending appointment as Deputy Grand Master; it was on a hot summer afternoon when, in the absence of Sydney White, the Duke of Devonshire came through to me on the telephone and said,

'Tell the Grand Secretary, please, when you next see him, that Roger Scarbrough has accepted unconditionally':

he said,
'No, that is not quite what I said; I agreed to do it for five years on condition that there was no possibility of my having to become Grand Master.'

To complete the historic record let it be said that he was Grand Master from March 1951 to June 1967 and Pro Grand Master for the last two years of his life. He died, almost to the day, on the second anniversary of his greatest moment, when he installed as his successor HRH the Duke of Kent, and with over 6,500 Masons drawn from the four quarters of the globe celebrated the 250th anniversary of the original meeting of the premier Grand Lodge.

Such is the rough outline of his Masonic career, though it does not explain that the English Grand Mastership has attached to it the office of First Grand Principal of Supreme Grand Chapter, the Presidency, *ex officio*, of four great Masonic activities, the Royal Masonic Institution for Girls, the Royal Masonic Institution for Boys, the Royal Masonic Benevolent Institution, and the Royal Masonic Hospital, and the indefinable but none the less real responsibility of being the Grand Master of the senior, as well as the largest and most widespread, of all Grand Lodges. He was no figurehead in any of these. Much more often than not (except when the St Leger demanded his attendance in Yorkshire) he presided at Grand Lodge and Grand Chapter. He installed over fifty Provincial and District Grand Masters, and about the same number of Grand Superintendents. He dealt shrewdly and firmly with crises as they arose in the several organisations already referred to. As Lord Chamberlain, as Lord Lieutenant of the West Riding, and as a Director of Lloyds Bank he must have been enormously busy, yet he never seemed to be in a hurry but always to have time to listen to a point of view, and having listened, he either accepted it or gave a ruling that showed clearly that he had seen and considered all sides of the question.

His decisions were clear and definite, and his written word a model of clarity even if, as often happened, it had to be composed in the train from Yorkshire to London.

Beyond this brief reference to the many claims upon his time and energies it is not for me to try to say anything about his activities outside Freemasonry. Within it however, I can speak as one who was very closely associated with him, and can say that Grand Lodge and indeed Freemasonry all over the world has lost by his death a most inspiring leader and wisest of counsellors. We who have been privileged to serve him are not going to forget the ease and dignity with which he conducted Masonic ceremonies, the charm and firmness with which he took the Chair at Meetings where sometimes opinions were very divergent, the official gatherings where he could and did discourse with a maximum of modesty and authority on almost any topic, and his cheerfulness and equability as a travelling companion.

As Grand Secretary I must add that in over 11 years I never had a cross word from him, nor heard an uncharitable one about anyone else.

A NEW GENERATION AND THE BAGNALL REPORT

Lord Scarbrough's death was followed closely by that of Frank Douglas resulting in a new generation beginning to manifest itself in the government of the Craft, and leaving Sir Allan Adair as the only survivor from before my time as Grand Secretary. It has been said that the First World War caused the loss of a whole generation, and therefore the Craft had reason to be very grateful for many survivors returning to control its destinies. Likewise but for other and less obvious reasons there was a similar shortage after the Second World War. Economic changes and the considerable decrease in the numbers of the younger middle aged men who did not have to work unremittingly to earn a living or maintain the standards of previous generations imposed perhaps an even greater difficulty in finding suitable candidates for high office in the Craft. We were however very fortunate in that both Lord Cadogan and Ted Baillieu were available as well as the evergreen Sir Allan: Fiennes Cornwallis also, by outstripping his father and bypassing the Provincial Grand Mastership in Kent, was able to give a great deal towards reorganising the Masonic Institutions in the difficult situation of Chairman of the Committee charged with the implementations of the Bagnall Report. The genesis of the report came about as follows.

Shortly before his death Frank Douglas who was coming to the end of his self imposed task of fund raising for the modernisation of the Royal Masonic Hospital, took up the idea of an ultra high-power committee of enquiry into the more generalised charitable activities. The credit for its original inception must go to Christopher Bathurst (now Lord Bledisloe PSGW) whose influence was strong with Alex Frere and other senior members. With regard to the Chairman my first suggestion was Lord Pearson who perhaps prudently declined, the second, strongly supported by Alex Frere and Christopher Bathurst was Sir Arthur Bagnall, a Chancery Judge: it was an inspired choice. I was instructed to find other members of proven experience and/or of high Masonic standing, and though Frank did not live long enough to see the Bagnall Committee in action he must certainly have thought well of its talented personnel, most of whom he knew personally. I was not directly implicated in its activities, indeed I purposely stood aloof, having rightly surmised that I would be more useful as an 'honest broker' between the various discontented parties when the report finally came out. Its secretarial work, nominally carried out by Dennis Barnard the Deputy Grand Secretary, was actually undertaken by Irene Hainworth my own private secretary, thus depriving me, for well over a year, of much needed support.

I will not comment here in depth about its acceptance in principle and rejections in detail, nor into the tortuous activities of the subsequent committee convoked to put its recommendations into effect. Suffice it to say that many smaller mountains have laboured to produce greater mice, and with less ill will. I felt sorrow for Fiennes Cornwallis, and later Peter Palmer, Provincial Grand Master for Northants and Hunts, who took the chair and also for Alan Jole who acted as secretary. The original report was presented in 1973; the Steering (later Grand Master's) Committee laboured from 1973 to 1983, reporting annually to Grand Lodge. It was dissolved in 1983 with, one hopes, the gratifying testimony of a clear conscience having battled, not unsuccessfully, against many forces of reaction and many entrenched positions. There is however a new and awakening spirit about the whole affair, and there can and must be little doubt that once again following Sir Maurice Bowras' dictum that where there is death there is hope, the spirit, if not the detail, of the Bagnall Report will be achieved.

Sir Arthur Bagnall's own death long before the Steering Committee to which he could have contributed so much had completed its work was a tragedy, from which it is no exaggeration to say that the whole enterprise never recovered: he knew exactly when to ride rough shod over wilful obstinacy, when to persuade, when to cajole and when to give way with grace: regrettably many others did not.

The Masonic Institutions and the Hospital had always maintained their independence of Grand Lodge while in fact depending on the Craft for their very existence. The Board of Benevolence was the only major element of 'Bagnall' with which I was directly concerned: it was not difficult

Talking with HRH the Princess Royal on her last visit to Harewood Court, Hove which was named after her late husband Lord Harewood, Grand Master 1942 to 1947.

to persuade its members to slip into the shape suggested for the General (later Grand) Charity and to get Grand Lodge's approval for the change. I am glad to think that before I retired this, alone of Bagnall's major bodies, was settled in its new form and carrying out the practical spirit if not the whole impractical letter of the Bagnall recommendations.

THE GRAND MASTER

The Duke of Connaught tended to appear in Grand Lodge at its June Quarterly Communications, but his successor before his tragic death had changed this in favour of attending the Annual Investiture in April and himself investing the new Grand Officers. His son has followed this practice with very few exceptions and it has undoubtedly given intense pleasure to those whom he appointed: when one year he was prevented from investing the Craft Grand Officers he made a point of attending Grand Chapter the next day for a similar purpose. Apart from the pleasure afforded to the recipients of Grand Rank, it has afforded an opportunity of addressing Grand Lodge and, through it, the Craft generally on the questions of the hour: for some years these generally concerned the Masonic Charities and the implementation of the Bagnall Report, but more recently he has drawn Grand Lodge's attention to its standing in the world at large and the most practical way of rebutting those attacks on the Order which inevitably and repetitively come up from time to time. These addresses were received with close attention in Grand Lodge, and were in due course widely circulated throughout the Craft: it must be doubted however whether at the level of the Lodge and the individual Mason they made the impression they should have done. Many secretaries cannot read aloud audibly or intelligibly, and they are usually called upon to do so when everyone including thsemselves is tired and thirsty: distribution of copies on a membership basis is not likely to be much more effective. I toyed with the idea of having an instruction issued that the circular version of these addresses should be read at the start rather than at the end of Lodge meetings in the same way that messages from the Grand Master precede any other business in Grand Lodge but came to the conclusion that fewer would hear them and that they would still be read uninterestingly.

While engaged in writing this memoir I have to remind myself of two things. In the first place I am not writing a continuation of the last chapter of *Grand Lodge 1717–1967*, though it is high time that this was taken in hand: secondly my object throughout is to write about matters and people with whom either professionally or domestically I have had close contact. Thus there has been, or will be, a good deal about Lord Scarbrough and Lord Cadogan and about other prominent Masons. On the other hand I seldom felt that I had the same direct access to the Grand Master as I had had to his predecessor (Rule 17 *Book of Constitutions* notwithstanding) though from time to time I accompanied him on visits to private Lodges, it being the accepted protocol that the Grand Master goes nowhere Masonically without his Grand Secretary and the Grand Director of Ceremonies, plus in his case his own Private Secretary. Apart from his visits to Freemasons' Hall when in the short intervals before, between or after functions he was busily engaged in signing the backlog of official documents I doubt if I saw him as much as twice a year, and never felt convinced that my advice was much wanted, or used. Yet he seemed intuitively to move in the right direction; and his dignity and affability have won him a secure place in the respect and affection of the Craft, of which we all must hope that he will continue to be the head for many years.

Dennis Barnard did not long survive his secretaryship of the Bagnall Committee for by late 1976 he was clearly seen to be a very sick man, though he scorned to admit it. I did not realise it myself till I had to take control of some of his work over the Christmas holiday, when it became obvious that he was not himself. He was persuaded to go for tests to the Royal Masonic Hospital, where it was decided that an immediate and very serious operation was necessary. From this he never recovered sufficiently to take up work again, involving as it did the long journey to and from Portsmouth each day: indeed he died only a few months later. Meanwhile the Board had engaged Commander Michael Higham with a view to his ultimately succeeding me as Dennis Barnard was already felt to be not suitable by reason of the age gap, or rather lack of it. However the Ministry of Defence proved tiresomely obstinate in releasing Higham with the result that for some five months I lacked a Deputy and, in addition, was heavily employed in clearing up the Barnard files which, to do him some little justice, he had never had the opportunity of doing himself. His recently appointed secretary, Dora Doctor and I spent many hours, getting very grimy in the process, going through every paper and file in his desk and office and separating his office files from his private and personal papers which seemed to cohabit without rhyme or reason.

Eventually Michael Higham turned up and life at once became more enjoyable and much less exacting: but the delay in his release meant that he now had that much less time to become *au fait* with office procedure and Masonic affairs generally, as the Grand Master was obdurate that I should retire on the stroke of 70!

The sudden removal of Exchange Control served Grand Lodge well, as it put on the labour market a thoroughly experienced Grand Officer in John Ross Guy who had done his three years as a Deputy Grand Director of Ceremonies and had also been a Lodge Secretary for a number of years. While it had always been a moot point whether three men at the top of the Grand Lodge Secretariat was necessary it was generally agreed that a new Grand Secretary needed a second in command at once, preferably *in situ* when he took over. This had proved to be true in the case of Alan Jole and myself, and it was still more so as Michael Higham in fact had a much shorter time with me than I had with Sydney White: but John

Ross Guy had the advantage also of being an expert on ceremonial, as well as banking, and could stand in at the last moment in that context too.

When asked, as I was from time to time, by Lord Cadogan or Jeremy Pemberton how long I was prepared to soldier on my practice was to reply that I would keep going till I was 70 but did not want to go much further (that would also bring Richenda to her retiring age of 65). Having got the two young men settled in I thought that a couple of years more to about 1982 would suit very well from Grand Lodge's, their and my point of view: I was considerably surprised when the Pro Grand Master announced out of the blue that I would finish on my 70th birthday. I am still inclined to think that it was a decision made in a hurry and prematurely from Grand Lodge's point of view, but clearly minds had been made up and there was nothing to be gained by arguing. As usual Lord Cadogan himself showed great consideration for we had been working closely together for over 25 years. When the Grand Master announced my retirement he said some very kind things in Grand Lodge while promoting me to the unheard of rank, so far as Grand Secretaries were concerned, of Past Senior Grand Warden. They were so generous that I cannot forbear to repeat them now.

Extract from the Grand Master's address in April 1980

Retirement of the Grand Secretary

This is the point at which every year I express my thanks to the Grand Secretary and his staff. My gratitude to them on this occasion is no less than it ever is, but it is this time tinged with a certain sadness since in a few months time Right Worshipful Brother Sir James Stubbs will be retiring as Grand Secretary.

He does so at the height of his powers after no less than 22 years as Grand Secretary of the Mother Grand Lodge of the world.

Brother Stubbs' influence and experience have earned him enormous respect in international Masonic circles and far transcend his position as Grand Secretary of the United Grand Lodge of England. Not only has he been a stalwart upholder of the fundamental principles of our Order, but as the Administrative Head of a great organisation, indeed its Senior Professional, his advice and wisdom has been sought by Masons and non-Masons too, throughout the jurisdiction of Grand Lodge and far beyond.

Brother Stubbs will be remembered for his astonishing memory, for his grasp of detail as much as for his breadth of vision and also, just as important, for his light touch and ready wit.

He has travelled all over the world on Masonic business to our many overseas Districts and Lodges, has undertaken the most exhausting programmes and never hesitated to go wherever Masonic duties called him. In these and many other ways his contribution to our Order has been incalculable.

Later this year Sir James will be celebrating the 50th anniversary of his initiation into Freemasonry.

In expressing to him and to Lady Stubbs our warmest good wishes on their retirement, I am happy to think that he will be able to enjoy many more years among his many friends and in devotion to the Craft to which he has given so much of his life.

Brother Grand Director of Ceremonies, I would ask you now please to escort the Grand Secretary to me as I wish to promote him to Past Senior Grand Warden.

Except for a few weeks in the case of Letchworth and Colville Smith, both virtually on their death beds when they gave up, there had not been a Past Grand Secretary since William White junior retired in 1856 after having held office since 1809: he lived for another ten years, and it would be nice to be able to emulate him at least in length of retirement.

This however carries my reminiscences rather too far ahead, and it will be better once again to pick up the threads under the sub-headings of the six Committees of the Board of General Purposes, as the Benevolent side has already been dealt with.

FINANCE COMMITTEE

The finances of Grand Lodge had suffered as much as anybody's from the rapid rise in the rate of inflation, but when Jeremy Pemberton became President of the Board of General Purposes in 1972 having already been a member for several years he was able to put to great advantage the skills he had acquired at Barings. The investments of both Funds were put under more constant surveillance, and he so organised matters that the time lag between a change in annual dues, approved by Grand Lodge and incorporated in the *Book of Constitutions*, and the actual arrival of dues at the new rate was dramatically cut down. Incidentally the Lodges were given a deservedly free hand in fixing their rates of subscription without the need to get the Grand Master's approval (in actual fact mine), for every change. It was felt that in an era of rapid change no Lodge should have to obtain such sanction and that they were unlikely to seek to get their members' approval for changes that were unnecessary.

At one point the Finance Committee and the Library (Arts and Publications) Committee virtually overlapped in the publication of the *Masonic Year Book*. It will be remembered that this cheap but indispensable book had been restarted in 1947; but it had become more and more bulky with the expansion of the Craft, even though each year we looked for possible excisions. Extraneous material including the full lists of Irish and Scottish Lodges was abandoned, and the chronological lists of Grand Officers, Craft and Royal Arch were the next victims. With a great deal of help from Derrick Chanter, from the Librarian, and from various interested Masonic historians a supplement as an entirely separate publication was produced in 1964 with a second edition in 1969 and a further supplement in 1976. It contained full lists of all Grand Officers from 1717 and 1753 respectively, and what purports to be a full record of all Provincial Grand Masters appointed by the Grand Masters of the Premier Grand Lodge, but not of those who held office under the Antients as they tended to be of local election abroad, and non-existent at home. Lodges removed from the Roll since 1863, when the last renumbering took place, were also listed, and in the second edition this was extended to Chapters also.

While such changes undeniably kept the *Year Book* to a convenient size the lists transferred to the supplement were of no great loss to the general Masonic public. Another change was of more general benefit as from the very early days the *Year Book* had contained extracts from Grand Lodge rulings and what were thought to be useful decisions on points of procedure. They however remained virtually unknown, locked up in the Lodge Secretary's papers in spite of yearly admonitions to make them available to the membership generally. In 1968 it was decided to produce annually a booklet incorporating all this material together with the Aims and Relationships and the Basic Principles of Recognition. Annually, but I fear without complete success, Lodges were required to present a copy to every new Mason and to each newly installed Master. *Information for the Guidance of Members of the Craft* is of much more use and interest to members new and old probably than the *Book of Constitutions* which I suspect is both meaningless to, and unread by, the great majority of initiates. However by way of compensation the potted history of the *Year Book* entitled 'Outstanding Masonic Events' was expanded and continues to be kept up to date.

It would be ungracious to leave the Finance Committee without some mention of the Cashiers and their staffs, on whose unremitting efforts much of the efficiency of the whole office depends: Malcolm Grace who had retired shortly before Sydney White's death had been succeeded by John Skinner, whose drive and energy pushed the Board into the scheme for securing greater tax relief, by an internal covenant scheme between the Fund of General Purposes which was liable to tax and the Fund of Benevolence which was charitable. Having decided to take early retirement he was succeeded by the then comparatively unknown Walter Curtis. He was a great success: infinitely industrious and patient he has always produced facts and figures when called upon, and is one of the last of the old timers, recruited by Sydney White. Irrelevantly but affectionately I recall being nursed at the Royal Masonic Hospital by his daughter who treated her father's boss with humour and extreme kindness.

LIBRARY COMMITTEE

Grand Lodge has been fortunate in the variety of its appointed Librarians:

Heron Lepper, and Ivor Grantham, had both kept the links with Quatuor Coronati close. Then followed Reginald Hewitt who was able to apply his high professional skills to reorganising the Library on modern lines, and while doing so did not lose sight of the need to expand the museum as well. My interest in Grand Lodge's portraits, which was my introduction to QC, worked in admirably with his own, and we were able to evolve a hanging plan which with few changes still exists. He was greatly helped by the timely transfer of John Groves from the Secretariat where he was a misfit to the Museum as Assistant Curator in which capacity he has been brilliantly successful. Reg Hewitt retired after sterling contributions to the Bicentenary of Grand Chapter and in the following year to Grand Lodge's 250th celebrations and the production of its history. For the last 14 years I had the great pleasure of the society of Terry Haunch, and it was appropriate that after we had both retired we should be associated in the authorship of the book *Freemasons' Hall, the Home and Heritage of the Craft*. It must not be thought however that the work of the Librarian and Curator is restricted to looking after books and artefacts, or even in acquiring them when they appear. He also concerns himself with a great deal of correspondence on matters of Masonic research and is in a good position to advise students, of whom there are always plenty, where to look for their material. All the Librarians with whom I have been associated together with their assistants have enjoyed a very high reputation for being most helpful in this respect.

PREMISES COMMITTEE

The rest of the building was under the control of the Premises Committee which latterly had the thankless task of being responsible for a building which was beginning to age, like its maintenance staff, most of whom, it will be remembered, had been employed by the builders in the period of construction. It was sad to see them drop off one by one into retirement, or in some cases die whilst still in employment; as one felt that with each loss that a piece of first hand evidence about the building had gone too.

Lines of demarcation between the Library and Premises Committees had never been very clear, but good will between a series of Chairmen on each side prevented any clash, and a series of Grand Superintendents of Works has kept the whole of Freemasons' Hall in a most enviable state.

There were however two long-standing anomalies about the Premises Committee which took many years to remove: the first was ascribable to William Blay's helpfulness towards Sydney White in the war years and his own interest in property acquisition and development. The Committee made itself responsible for the adjacent properties of Grand Lodge, which could not by any stretch of imagination be called Premises and were in fact as clearly investments as any stocks and shares. Eventually it was possible to detach them and establish a Property Sub-Committee of the Finance Committee, parallel to its established Investment Sub-

Committee, a change which fortunately worked well from the start.

The second anomaly was in relation to the maintenance staff and this increased greatly with the opening of the new Freemasons' Hall in 1933 when the wages were under the direct control of the Premises Committee, probably as the 'residuary legatee' of the Building Committee. Its three senior members however had been arbitrarily detached from the rest and their salaries were made matters of discussion for the Officers and Clerks Committee with the rest of us. This system was liable to lead to trouble since the two Committees were open to take quite different views with the result that the differential, between one set of maintenance staff and the other, was constantly varying. It was eventually conceded, not altogether unwillingly, by the Premises Committee that the whole wages structure of the Hall and its staff should be centralised under the Officers and Clerks, which then changed its name to Staff Committee.

STAFF COMMITTEE

I can say with all sincerity that the Staff Committee whether under its present or previous name always showed a breadth of mind and a generosity of outlook on salaries that should have commanded respect; inevitably however there were blind spots—such as the employment of temporary staff for purely routine work. Like Sydney White who had come into the organisation when the clerical staff was a good deal smaller and the maintenance staff practically non-existent I had always tried to run things on what I suppose is now a dirty word, a paternalistic basis. Indeed I thought I had succeeded in securing for all concerned the best possible conditions compatible with efficiency—and one may add, the vagaries of governmental control over wages and holidays. It may well be that I set, in my own working hours, too high a standard and did not realise that it was something a new generation would not accept: I had never really taken too much heed about what seemed to me to be new fangled ideas about job evaluation, since I reckoned to know as well as they did what each and every member of the staff was meant and expected to do. I also felt it was a great part of my duty to them to see that they were properly paid for their effort, and to advise the Board that they in turn were getting value for money. All this was no doubt very old fashioned, and I strongly suspect that discontent had been brewing for some time, and that Dennis Barnard, by then aware that he would in no circumstances have the reversion of my own job, was doing little to allay it. Michael Higham thus came in when change was in the air and was free to introduce new and up to date thinking, with the result that the new regime, if different, is well founded.

This accounts, though very briefly, for the activities of what I would term the spending side of Grand Lodge. Being no financial genius and in fact according to modern jargon very much more literate than numerate, I was particularly relieved to have such experts in their field as Jeremy

Pemberton, Frank Trumper and Arthur Ley in command of their respective Boards and Committees, and to know that they in their turn had confidence in the staff.

PROCEDURE AND EXTERNAL RELATIONS

On the other hand matters of Procedure and Foreign Policy were very much closer to my heart. Successive amendments to the *Book of Constitutions* had stopped many of the loopholes in the rules which led to appeals, but Sir Ralph Hone and Arthur Murphy between them had stirred Grand Lodge to a realisation that when in full session it was not a suitable judge and jury for the hearing of appeals. Not only was it a body incapable as a whole of differentiating between truth and falsehood in appellants, but from its very nature it could not undertake their cross examination: moreover as the majority of cases came from abroad it had to rely solely on the advice, always given with strict impartiality, of the Grand Registrar and his Deputy, and if this advice was against the authority whose decision was being appealed against that authority had no opportunity of explanation. Cases too were not infrequently of a trivial nature, sometimes incomprehensible and occasionally sordid, and the airing of such dirty linen can have done the Craft in England no good particularly among readers of Grand Lodge Proceedings. I have never heard of any regrets over the abolition of the old system nor criticism of the new.

THE GRAND TREASURESHIP

Another procedure matter came up in my later years, the perennial one of Masonic promotion. I do not intend to discuss at any length the questions surrounding Grand Rank, beyond saying that overall it basically remained very much on the same lines throughout my period of office. Such changes as were made and authorised were primarily designed to smooth out proportional inequalities between large and small Provinces and Districts. However within the schedule of Grand Ranks there was one major change, the down grading of the Grand Treasurer, which merits a rather fuller explanation, with the premise that at least from the Union in 1813 Grand Treasurers had done nothing except be the bankers of Grand Lodge while its finances had been, as they still are, in the hands of the Board of General Purposes. In 1877 the last of the banking Grand Treasurers suffered the not unusual disaster of his bank collapsing. He managed to save Grand Lodge's funds which were prudently deposited with the Bank of England, and he then died. There was no Grand Treasurer in the following year, but thereafter the post became a complete *sinecure* though much sought after as a means of getting a very high Grand Rank with the additional cachet of being the elected choice of Grand Lodge. It was not very long before the Provinces started to compete, and it was for the purpose of organising their share in the office that the

Associated Masonic Provinces was established. At first London and the Provinces took equal turns to nominate, but from 1951 it was agreed that the proportion should be two to one in favour of the Provinces. The trouble really came when a Province found itself due for a nomination without anyone suitable to nominate for such a high rank. To put it bluntly it would be too greedy to forego its turn, but then would find itself saddled, perhaps for years with a Past Grand Treasurer much higher in rank than the Deputy Provincial Grand Master and well aware of it. Lord Scarbrough was strongly averse to making Deputies up to Past Grand Wardens on the highly practical grounds that he would have to do it for all or none; the alternative was to down grade the Grand Treasurership, and to find some less violent form of promotion for Deputy Provincial Grand Masters. I put forward as a tentative suggestion that the Grand Sword Bearer and Grand Superintendent of Works, offices dating from 1753 and 1813 respectively (and with few past holders) should become Very Worshipful, and that the two Grand Chaplains, a duality that dated from the Union when each Grand Lodge had one, should be replaced by one Grand Chaplain and a Deputy Grand Chaplain. The scheme was adopted with some additional changes of a minor nature, such as the division between Past Senior and Past Junior in Wardens and Deacons. There were inevitably a few hardship cases where an elderly brother found himself downgraded (it happened to me in Grand Chapter a few years later) but they were mostly capable of being adjusted.

The Grand Treasurership ceased to be worth fighting for in its new seniority; in my view, perhaps unshared by former Grand Treasurers of the older dispensation, it would be much better if the rank was abolished, and the effective and collective treasurership of Grand Lodge's funds was acknowledged to be the Board of General Purposes on the analogy of the Lord High Treasurership of England which was put into commission centuries ago with a First Lord who is *de facto* the Prime Minister. Just as the President of the Board of General Purposes was described by Sir Alfred Robbins speaking about himself as the Prime Minister of the Craft.

LONDON GRAND RANK

It was not altogether surprising that changes in Grand Rank sparked off an agitation for something to be done at the lower levels. It will be remembered that Major Loyd, Alan Jole and I had effected a reorganisation of Provincial ranks, more with a view to making the system comprehensible than to expanding it. If one looks at the matter objectively Provincial rank should be seen as a reward for services rendered to the Province rather than to the individual's own Lodge which has in its own way rewarded him by putting him in the Master's Chair. But what struck everyone was that there were glaring differences between large and small Provinces in the time that it took a Master to obtain Provincial Rank from the moment of leaving the chair: what was more unfair though not so glaringly obvious was that the proportion of appointments to London Grand Rank was considerably lower and that there was no provision, short of Grand Rank, for promoting holders of London Grand Rank. I had earlier attempted to canvass support for the introduction of 'Senior' London Grand Rank but there was a good deal of opposition from some of the older members of the London Grand Rank Association who affected pride in the fact that all holders ranked equally. Thwarted by this attitude I succeeded in enfilading the opposition by getting Senior London Grand *Chapter* Rank introduced: fortunately Masonic memory is often short and within a very few years this rank had ceased to be a novelty and the way was opened (some of the opposition too having died or lapsed into inactivity) for the change to be incorporated into the Craft too.

Alan Ferris was now Grand Director of Ceremonies and Chairman of the Procedure Committee: he was a very willing leader in reform (and extension) of the system being the representative of the largest of all Provinces, the one that was most hardly done by after London, under the existing rules.

Lord Shannon produced some interesting and useful statistics with the aid of which we produced quite new patterns; the essence of it was that each year a Provincial Grand Master was to be entitled to give Provincial Grand Rank to a level of 80% of his total number of Lodges. In fact this almost certainly meant one for one as overall there were certain to be casualties, reappointments and a few refusals. At the same time, though this was not a London battle, we proposed to limit the number of *acting* ranks to that laid down for Grand Rank on the argument that no Province could usefully find scope for more than Grand Lodge, which in fact had slightly reduced its own number of acting ranks on its recent revision and which had, as mentioned earlier, down graded the Grand Treasurer.

There was almost inevitably some opposition, and one Deputy Provincial Grand Master even urged his fellows to be men not mice and oppose the whole scheme, but a few cosmetic alterations, which did not harm anyone were agreed (how glad I was of my experience with War Establishments with Jeremy Pemberton in 1943/4) and the scheme went through Grand Lodge unchanged in any important respect.

So far as London was concerned the increase was only from one in three to one in two, but this and the introduction of Senior London Grand Rank to parallel the facility of promotion in the Provinces was some compensation to London Lodges for still being way behind the Provinces. It did however mean that whoever was due to invest the Londoners was going to have something like 800 instead of 500 hands to shake quite apart from the list of Senior London Grand Rank! Whereas it was possible to combine the two investitures in the Royal Arch, it was clearly going to be too much to do so in the Craft, and the Jubilee Masters Lodge was invited to stage the Senior investiture, leaving the Grand Stewards, as in the past, to cope with the main one: the method is again changing in 1985.

LONDON BOUNDARY

Looking back I can think of only one other re-organisation that I sponsored, and that has not, I fear, been a complete success. It will be generally known that the London Masonic area is a geometrical rather than a political or county entity. It is a ten mile circle drawn round FMH and said to go back to the days when the bills of mortality were recorded within ten miles of our close neighbours, the Metropolitan Magistracy at Bow Street. The circle was liberally interpreted by the adjacent Provinces and it is at least open to argument that Middlesex, Surrey and Essex all have meeting places within the circle, while there is no doubt at all that William Blay had contracted a deal with Sydney White in the days of his Deputy Provincial Grand Mastership of Kent by which quite a slice in the Woolwich area was deemed to be Kentish from the Masonic point of view.

In fact none of these trespasses were doing London much harm, since it was within two miles, not ten, of FMH that the very great proportion of London Lodges met. Between two and five miles there was a smallish number, but beyond that, in the five to ten mile zone, it was practically a Masonic desert. With some 25 years of constantly visiting London Lodges I had come to appreciate how few of their members were actually residents in Central London: they found Central London a convenient meeting place with its bus and underground transport system and the main line termini, and they tended to come to Lodge straight from work (and so needed an evening meal *after* rather than before the meeting). I reckoned that though most of them probably lived outside the ten mile circle, it might be worthwhile trying to get some Masonic activity into the 'Masonic desert', and that the Provinces all round might help, particularly as they had nothing to lose by geographical expansion. Accordingly I produced a large scale map, which incidentally proved useful in other respects and is still preserved by my successor, showing how the desert might be divided between London and the relevant Province. We had a conference, preceded by an excellent lunch, which endorsed the proposals with only minimal adjustments, and the Grand Master readily gave his approval to the adjustment of the boundaries, whilst Grand Lodge passed the necessary legislation; but the effect has proved to be almost negligible. Brethren still prefer to go out to the Provincial centres or come in to the numerous inner-London centres, and I have little doubt that even if the density of population alters considerably they will still continue to do so.

There is a certain amount of complaint not entirely well thought out, that 'West End' Masonry is much more expensive than elsewhere. But those who complain have not always understood how much more convenient it is not only for those who work in London and consequently will get home late, but also for those who have retired or who work in outer London or further away still to be able to get up to central London instead of some other venue which may be convenient to some but inevitably inconvenient to others. With very few exceptions London Lodges do not draw their membership from clearly defined areas as common interests rather than geographical communities prevail.

EXTERNAL AFFAIRS

From time to time I used to prepare, for the External Relations Committee *aides-memoire* on the state of Masonry in various parts of the world. Their aim was two-fold, partly for the general edification of the Committee, and then of the Board if the Committee thought any particular *aide-memoire* was worthy of wider circulation, and partly to bring individual aspects into focus, as there was almost always someone who had a 'bee in his bonnet' for or against some other Grand Lodge. Of course in some respects these documents became dated, but reading them through afterwards perhaps as long as 20 years later, I am surprised how little the overall picture has changed: strangely enough Grand Lodges and areas which were a source of worry in 1950 still continue to be so in 1978.

Edgar Rutter was a splendid chairman; vastly experienced, quick witted and thoroughly imbued with Sir Ernest Cooper's principles he commanded respect both at home and overseas. He handed on much of his experience to Oscar Boehringer who succeeded him as chairman and who had the great advantage of being able to talk to most of European Masonry in its own language: also being of Swiss origin himself he had a clear insight into the problems and weakness of the Grand Lodge Alpina of Switzerland. It is no exaggeration to join in unison with John Wesley and say 'the world is my parish' as between the United Grand Lodge of England and the rest of the Masonic world. Fortunately we are on excellent terms with most of the recognised Grand Lodges, and it is only a small minority that cause a quite disproportionate amount of worry.

It may be useful at this point to mention the late Bro Harry Carr, who was a distinguished Masonic scholar though objected to by Col Rickard one of his predecessors in the Secretaryship of Quatuor Coronati Lodge as 'a scissors-and-paste man': in later years he had travelled widely on his lecture tours, but had listened more attentively than wisely to his hosts. He burned his fingers over the now defunct Grand Lodge of Iran, and was continually 'plugging' the Grand Lodges of Japan and China, in respect of both of which Richard Lee, our District Grand Master for Hong Kong and the Far East had diametrically opposite views. It is difficult to rid oneself of the suspicion that he saw in each of these areas a possible expansion of circulation for *AQC* and that his information, on his own admission second-hand, came from interested parties which had already recognised them rather than from English Masons on the spot in Hong Kong and Kobe.

Alex Frere had carried on the conservative tradition of Sir Ernest Cooper and shown no precipitancy in recognising other Grand Lodges. He had a wide acquaintance with European Masonry the leaders of which quietly recognised him as someone whose eyes wool could not be pulled across. Successive Grand Masters of the Grande Loge Nationale Française were on excellent terms with him and sought his advice. The *de facto* leader of German Masonry, whether he was Grand Master at the time or not was fully prepared to co-operate with him in the attempt to make the United Grand Lodges known all over the world as the international face of German Masonry. In Alex's period of office the Italian question did not become acute and Belgium was to all appearances quietly flourishing; Austria to which we paid a visit together was re-establishing Masonry under a succession of able Grand Masters, and it was only with Switzerland that we were really having difficulty. It was trouble that sprang partly from the Swiss passion for neutrality which could equally well be described as sitting on the fence, partly from their own constitution which is so framed that the Grand Mastership passed in rapid succession from one area to another with no account taken of experience or capability. It was seldom possible to persuade the Grand Lodge to take a firm line as either the Grand Master was so new that he did not know enough to realise what was involved or he had come so near to the end of his period of office that he claimed unwillingness to compromise his successor. Almost invariably the point at issue was Alpina's relations with irregular French Freemasonry and its reluctance to accept regular French Freemasonry (ie, the GLNF). Alpina had theoretically broken off relations with the Grand Orient of France though we had strong suspicions that intervisitation at Lodge level continued in border areas such as Geneva and Basel, which the Swiss authorities were unwilling, or unable, or afraid to stop. With the equally unrecognised and almost equally irregular Grand Lodge of France, Alpina for a long time maintained cordial relations, and it took a formal discontinuance of relations between us and them to achieve a rupture. I thought for some time that it was no more than a face saving formality with private Lodge relations continuing as in the case of the Grand Orient. As I have already maintained there is a good deal of reason to believe that much the same state of affairs prevails between Germany and the irregular French, particularly in the Rhineland where the GLNF is sadly weak.

The recognition of Italy was consummated only when Jeremy Pemberton had become President: attempts had been made spasmodically since the early 1950s to secure our recognition, but these had foundered because the Italians themselves were unable to present a united front: there were two main bodies, and from time to time a succession of splinter groups. The two were centered on the Palazzo Giustiniani and the Palazzo del Gesu and had the distant but strong backing of the two American Supreme Councils, and roughly of the Grand Lodges in whose areas they operated. It was however well known in Italy that we were not prepared to plump for one, leaving the other out, or even to recognise them both: eventually the moment came when at least the cracks were papered over and the Palazzo Giustiniani seemed to be in control. We felt justified in recognising Italy and for some few years there was a constant interchange of visits in the course of which I myself consecrated at the request of their Grand Master an English speaking Lodge in Florence, of which Christopher Pirie Gordon, who had been passed and raised with me in the Apollo was installed as first Master: I also consecrated a Royal Arch Chapter shortly after the Italia Chapter in London had exalted a large group of Italians so as to qualify them as petitioners. Unhappily this honeymoon period soon came to an end, as unity of Italian Masonry broke down with the fall from grace of Lino Salvini. Once more the troubles were exacerbated by the well-intentioned but unsuccessful intervention of an American Supreme Council.

Meanwhile it was becoming obvious that all was not well in Belgium: the restoration of regular Freemasonry which had been achieved by Charles Wagemans was being undermined by dissident elements, largely from Liège. Charles worked hard to keep the Grand Lodge on the right lines but eventually a Grand Master was elected who made no bones about his preference for the irregular elements of European Masonry, and Charles sadly but firmly withdrew from the Grand Lodge of Belgium with a small nucleus and established the Regular Grand Lodge of Belgium. We were in any case about to break off relations with the now avowedly irregular body and were quickly able to come to the aid of the new one. By and large world Masonry seems to have accepted the change with the result that Belgium is now a miniature edition of France with two irregular bodies and one, much smaller, which we are fully satisfied is working regularly.

It will be remembered that shortly before Sydney White's death there was a great Masonic conference in London, called mainly to effect a settlement in Germany, though as usual many other matters were discussed informally. Some of our neighbours were in favour of having such conferences at regular intervals whether or not there was anything of substance to discuss. We ourselves, and by that I mean a succession of Presidents and of Chairmen of the External Relations Committee as well as myself felt that they were rather a waste of time and money, and would lose their impact if held too often without specific objects. We preferred smaller meetings, with Ireland and Scotland, and some interested party to discuss a definite piece of business, and this pattern developed over the years between 1958 and 1980. We were greatly supported in this by successive Grand Masters of Ireland, Raymond Brooke who had disposed of the Dutchman Davidson in 1959 and Lord Donoughmore who had inherited all his father's flair for Masonic politics and added to it his quite remarkable facility for European languages. The succession of Scottish Grand Master Masons were able to contribute considerably in some cases where the three home jurisdictions had Lodges of their own meeting abroad and in close contact.

It was decided in 1976 however to hold a European conference in London at which a number of outstanding matters could be discussed, and by general agreement Lord Donoughmore, who was an English as well as an Irish Mason was invited to take the chair. In spite of his leadership the conference only just missed being a fiasco: its most positive result was to highlight both the Belgian and the Swiss representatives as being very shaky in the matter of relationship with irregular bodies since they practically convicted themselves out of their own mouths: the Germans were rather more discreet. Nothing satisfactory came of asking whether Grand Lodges generally accepted our Aims and Relationships, and the evasiveness of some of those present told its own story. There was on the other hand a useful, though perhaps theoretical discussion as to why Islam had set its face so firmly against Freemasonry, when quite coincidentally as the Germans pointed out there was decreasing hostility from Rome. On the latter point Dr Theodore Vogel had a good deal to say: but sadly, it was the last of many conferences we had with this regenerator of Freemasonry in Germany. I had always got on well with him though there were some who thought him a slippery customer. It is somehow difficult not to like a person who describes you to your face, and with every sign of it being a sincere compliment as 'the Pope of Freemasonry'!

GRAND CHAPTER

It is well known that certain offices in Grand Chapter follow almost automatically equivalent ones in Grand Lodge. Others for the sake of convenience are made to follow suit without being constitutionally bound to do so: hence I had already being successively Assistant Grand Scribe E, and Deputy Grand Scribe E for several years when my appointment as Grand Secretary made me automatically Grand Scribe E. It was, in terms of office duty, not very onerous and I always found it easy to get on with a succession of Presidents of the Grand Chapter Committee (to give that body its shorter and less official title). Sir George Boag, John Wasbrough and finally Sir Leonard Atkinson. Most of what happened between 1946 and 1980 has been told in two short talks to Grand Chapter and is reprinted in Appendix III, but I hope that I may be permitted a short account of what I considered to be the philosophy of administering Royal Arch affairs.

Grand Chapter, like private Chapters and, I suppose, a good many Provincial and District Grand Chapters, had very little in the way of financial reserves: equally it had little in the way of outgoings. It contributed towards the wages of that part of the clerical staff whose work was concerned with the Royal Arch and notionally of some of the rest of us who were partially connected with it. Office space, postage and stationery, rent of the Grand Temple were all free, while travelling expenses were so mixed up with those of the Craft that I arrived at a rule of thumb method by which, if as often happened, a double installation took place, one third of it was charged to Grand Chapter. My object was to minimise the expenses of Royal Arch Masonry at the headquarters level, and with that as an example to encourage Chapters to keep theirs to a bare minimum: there should be no need for a Chapter to do more than just keep its financial head above water, and I was particularly strong in my advice not to become involved in competitive charitable giving—since all the members would have heavy calls on their generosity from their Lodges. At Freemasons' Hall the internal independence of the Royal Arch as a division of the office was gradually eroded, and the idea of a separate department was abandoned: this was made easier by the two innovations in printing that were achieved, namely the cross referencing to the *Book of Constitutions* in the *Royal Arch Regulations* index, and later the binding up of the latter with the former. This I reckoned would bring the Royal Arch to the notice of every new entrant to the Craft, and might encourage a greater proportion towards Exaltation. Whether or not one subscribes to the view that the Royal Arch is the completion of the Third Degree, it cannot be denied by anyone that it carries the lessons of the Craft a long and important step further: in this respect the Mark and the Ark Mariner which are perhaps even more directly linked from this administrative point of view are different as they do not interlock or carry on the story from one to the other.

By a fortunate accident, John Wasbrough was already a member of the Board of General Purposes when he succeeded Sir George Boag as President. Sir George himself as a Past District Grand Master was of too exalted rank to be on the Board of General Purposes where it is an unwritten law that such brethren are not members, or if being already members resign at once when they are installed as Provincial or District Grand Masters. Having the President of the Grand Chapter Committee on the Board was a further unifying influence and I was very glad for that reason as well as for his personal qualities that Sir Leonard Atkinson followed suit.

I have already aired my views on the Grand Treasurership of the Craft, and I will do no more than add that they apply with still greater force in the Royal Arch: I have mentioned that Provinces are unwilling to pass up their turn when it comes to putting forward a nomination, and it is or should be well known that if he is qualified as an Installed First Principal the Grand Treasurer of the Craft automatically assumes the office in the Royal Arch. If by some mischance he is not so qualified, a separate nomination has to be made in November and in due course an election held in Grand Chapter. In 1973 Leicestershire and Rutland put forward an admirable candidate, who unfortunately had no kind of Royal Arch qualification, but did not think to supply a Royal Arch alternative: the flaw was not discovered until too late (Leicestershire and Rutland being a most efficient Province it was blandly assumed that the nomination was in order in both respects). When reference was made to John Bradburn as Grand Registrar, another linked office, he ruled that the dates were mandatory, and that once the nomination was missed in November, nothing could be done. So in 1974 Grand Chapter had no Grand Treasurer for the first time in 96 years, and I am convinced that nobody lost by his absence—or indeed even noticed it.

In the nicest possible way the Royal Arch has been used from time to time as a guinea pig for greater matters in the Craft: its own bi-centenary in 1966 was a prototype for the much greater celebrations in 1967: the unreasoning opposition to Senior London Grand Rank was undermined by its introduction into the Royal Arch some years earlier. So one would like to think that the existence of one type of regalia for Grand Officers might be copied by the Craft.

What I have said hitherto about the administration of Freemasonry has been confined generally to its Boards and Committees, but it should not be lost sight of that the Grand Lodge and Grand Chapter Communications and Convocations have the ultimate responsibility. It must be admitted that the latter are of little interest and are sparsely attended except by Grand Officers who are members of the Grand Chapter Club and have a meal together afterwards: indeed the agenda is so stereotyped that it is thought desirable at least once in the year to eke it out with a short talk on some Royal Arch topic, and my own two are to be found in Appendix III. Apart from Grand Chapter's bi-centenary to which I have already referred I can recall hardly any occasion when a debate has flared up in Grand Chapter. There was however one which showed its futility as a debating ground: the Regulations (no 74) speak of Chapters of Instruction, and the Committee of General Purposes decided to draw attention to this nomenclature being aware that these useful bodies often quite erroneously styled themselves Chapters of Improvement, copying the Emulation Lodge of Improvement. Excellent Companion Shepherd Jones, the doyen of the Aldersgate Chapter of Improvement (*sic*) rose and made an impassioned but irrational speech to the effect that this Chapter's efforts were devoted to improvement. He had clearly not allowed himself to realise that the Committee was doing no more than point out what the Regulations declared to be the correct name: his rational course would have been to organise a change in the Regulations from 'instruction' to 'improvement', or perhaps in a spirit of compromise to allow for both. Sir George Stuart Robertson, like Gallio, cared for none of these things and decided to withdraw the paragraph which gave offence. It is interesting to note that when Companion Shepherd Jones soon afterwards joined the Committee of General Purposes, where incidentally he was a very useful and well liked member, we heard no more about instruction or improvement, and the Regulation and its heading still survive.

My personal view, which is not necessarily correct or shared by others, is that Grand Lodge is itself a Committee of a long since forgotten body of the whole Craft, the sole surviving feature of which is probably the annual Grand Festival. In theory I suppose that any English Masons could apply to the Grand Stewards for a ticket but in practice with the increase in the numbers of those being invested tickets are restricted effectively to those whose attendance is required and to those who administer the affairs of the Craft at Grand Lodge or Provincial/District level. There is however no embargo on Master Masons being invited among the personal guests of the Grand Stewards and perhaps there is a small handful of them each year. So to all practical purposes Grand Lodge in its Quarterly Communications is the Craft as well as its governing body. Many Masters sometimes accompanied by their Wardens, try to attend during their mastership with the result that there is always a strong element of light blue not only in the galleries of the Grand Temple but also on the floor: it is a moot point however what they can contribute to the business of Grand Lodge on such occasional visits, probably not even having seen a paper of business till they arrive. In fact they probably derive more satisfaction visually from the sight of a well filled Grand Temple, and from the ceremonial entrance and departure of the acting Grand Officers.

THE PENALTIES

Just occasionally matters used to come up which excited controversy even after they had been fully explained in the report of the Board of General Purposes, and there would be a larger attendance than usual: an appeal with the possibility of an argument on the floor, especially an appeal from overseas with a touch of the exotic about it, such as references to 'native law and custom' was always a draw. Since the change of procedure spearheaded by Sir Ralph Hone and Arthur Murphy this element has been lost, as recommendations for expulsion are usually so glaringly obvious that there is less interest.

Unquestionably the most exciting debate in my time was about the penalties. This question had been rumbling in the background for many years: it had aroused Sir Ernest Cooper's interest through a Scottish contact, and Harry Carr had taken the matter up too, again probably from his interest in Scottish Masonry. Papers and talks were not infrequently given but Grand Lodge itself had kept aloof in view of the established principle that neither the Board of General Purposes nor Grand Lodge concerned themselves with ritual (it must be remembered that both had burned their fingers in the 1920s over the extended Working of the Installation Ceremony). Soon after the Duke of Kent's initiation both Lord Scarbrough and Bishop Percy Herbert who had taken part in the ceremony mentioned to me that they thought that they had detected revulsion in the candidate's reaction. They were both aware of the growing feeling that physical penalties had never been enforceable and were not even an anachronism, and that the reference to them in the Obligations created an entirely false impression of what Masonry should and does stand for. Bishop Herbert became the champion of reform and following a statement made by him to Grand Lodge in June 1964 a debate was staged six months later.

It produced the largest attendance within living memory at a Quarterly

Communication, and a series of speeches, which even if on the whole rather discursive put the whole question fairly from all points of view. My own part in the affair was restricted to the introduction of the word 'traditional' into the alternative version when for once Harry Carr was at a loss for the *mot juste*, and to organising the speeches into a coherent order: in fact two of the most effective speeches came quite unexpectedly from the floor of Grand Lodge. As is well known Grand Lodge voted overwhelmingly in favour of the adoption by Lodges, should they so desire it, of a formula which brought the physical penalties into their proper perspective as part of Freemasonry's ancient tradition, as providing the basis for certain modes of recognition, and as texts on which sermons of symbolism could be hung. Many Lodges (including as I was glad to see Apollo University Lodge three days later!) proceeded at once to adopt the formula, but in many of them the innate conservatism of members, by no means always the best of them, provided a *vis inertiae* the result of which was a decision to do nothing. After 20 years observation I am more and more persuaded that Preceptors of Lodges of Instruction having learned one script are too lazy or too stupid to learn another.

Grand Chapter followed suit almost immediately by adopting a similar resolution moved by Lord Scarbrough himself, and Grand Lodge adopted the same formula for the Board of Installed Masters which with Wardens present in Grand Lodge could obviously not be detailed in full. The Provinces handled the matter themselves, very much no doubt according to the wishes and prompting of the Provincial Grand Masters. In London I called a meeting of as many representatives as I could find of the large number of various rituals in general use: Emulation was almost the only one that had a definite teaching organisation, and its Committee was most helpful in preparing the alternative version. Inspired by Emulation the leaders of several other rituals adopted something like its system, establishing central bodies to which Lodges could come for advice, and I have noticed that quite a number of eccentricities have disappeared, though here again out of date ritual books and equally out of date Preceptors had the same effect of *inertia*.

When I became Grand Secretary in 1958, I was reminded by Lord Scarbrough that I should never forget that I was dealing with volunteers, many of them not altogether volunteers but impelled by a sense of duty and with jobs to perform. I tried always to remember this and to instil the same idea into the headquarters staff. I remembered too the dictum of Alex Buchan, the brilliant but wayward Grand Secretary of Scotland, that in the last analysis the business of a Grand Secretary was to do what he was told, and also of Hersey Woods that his prime duty was to deal with correspondence, to answer letters promptly and in such terms that without giving offence they finished the subject. To these sentiments I added two minor points of my own: first, if someone wrote to me as Grand Secretary I insisted on signing the reply. It often meant late hours after dinner clearing up my desk so that the results could go out first thing in

Miss Irene Hainworth, private secretary to the Grand Secretary from 1959 to 1981 with the elusive brother Tzazapoulos (Grand Master of the Grand Lodge of Greece) in the background, (see page 120).

the morning, but I sincerely believed then, and still do, that the recipients derived some satisfaction that they were apparently getting personal attention. Secondly I also insisted that letters should be addressed to brethren by name instead of the cold and stilted form of 'Dear Sir and Brother'. Irene Hainworth had an excellent system derived from her years as an MP's secretary of keeping the whole of the pending correspondence and going quickly through it each day before I arrived at the office, so that nothing got completely forgotten by her or myself. Obviously some matters came up many times, but we used to have filing sessions every so often and they too served as useful reminders. She also ensured that details of forthcoming trips to the Provinces were documented stage by stage including the preparation for them. Even so it needed checking from time to time because she never really mastered the difference between Notts, Northants and Northumberland whilst Norfolk was something of a hazard too! It must be admitted though that we never in the end went to the wrong place on the wrong day (the Grand Tyler once turned out the whole of an Installation team at the wrong station) and for that and for so many other things both the Craft and myself are deeply in her debt.

Chapter 14

Provinces and Visits

Having now covered the main facets of work in the office, I should refer to the occasional but many visits made outside London. These were mostly of two kinds, accompanying the (Pro) Grand Master or Deputy Grand Master to install a new Provincial Grand Master or Grand Superintendent, or the presentation of a Bi-Centenary Warrant* The former were often tinged with melancholy as the vacancy that was being filled was caused by the death of an old friend and ally, but the latter were almost always occasions of great celebration and rejoicing. Perhaps the most spectacular was in fact a Royal Arch occasion. The Grand Chapter records in the early days were a trifle sketchy and there were arguments on both sides for the seniority of Cana Chapter at Colne and the Chapter of Nativity at Burnley, so it was decided that they should celebrate and receive their Bi-Centenary Charters as near simultaneously as possible. A suitable venue was found with accommodation for two Chapters to meet in adjacent rooms and for them to be brought together into a larger one where Lord Scarbrough then made the presentation. It was also a nice touch that he and Lord Derby, both Lords Lieutenant, arrived from different directions at the same moment and their cars drew up nose to nose at the entrance to the temporary hall. Others followed a uniform pattern with processional entries, and an oration by a Grand Chaplain after the warrant had been read out and presented. Lord Scarbrough always insisted on remaining to the end as did Lord Cadogan after him, to the dismay of local dignitaries who would normally have retired at a much earlier stage to slake their thirst.

Ten years seems to be about the average tenure of office of a Provincial Grand Master or Grand Superintendent, so that there would normally be about five expeditions into the Provinces each year. These varied much more than the Bi-Centenary meetings, as there is so much difference in the size of Provinces, which is reflected not only in the numbers likely to attend but also in the number of Assistant Provincial Grand Masters to be appointed, or re-appointed, and installed. There are however very few cases where the meeting can take place in a normal Masonic Hall: so this naturally imposes a considerably increased burden on the Provincial Grand Secretary in organising the meeting and any preceding or subsequent meal, and produces many surprises for the Grand Director of Ceremonies and his team when they arrive. I have taken part in instal-

* It has become accepted that Centenaries are handled by the Province.

lations in Zoological Gardens, circus arenas, Chapter Houses, converted Churches, swimming baths, TA drill halls, secondary schools built almost entirely of plate glass, dance halls, assembly rooms and holiday camps: the worst of all was a disused cinema where the steep rake of the floor, the blocks of unmoveable seats and a small stage area made movement extremely difficult. However sending up plenty of instructions and diagrams (for which I had to thank Joe Savill) in very good time made the work before the rehearsal easier, and although the latter looked and sounded quite chaotic, the actual ceremony generally went so well that no one in the audience would be likely to spot anything wrong.

By 1980 there were hardly any Provincial Grand Masters left at whose Installation I had not been present: Lord Stradbroke and Lord Zetland kindly invited me to attend one of their annual meetings, and Colonel Kelway in South Wales, Western Division had found an excuse for getting Lord Cadogan and myself to attend a special meeting at Carmarthen. Michael Higham had taken my place, as I was abroad, at the installation of Dr Temperton in Shropshire, so this was the only Provincial Grand Lodge at which I had not been present: but this deficiency was remedied in 1983 when I was invited to address Provincial Grand Lodge on a subject of my own choosing. I am now very glad I took the opportunity as Dr Temperton who was an old friend and a fellow enthusiast for Masonic history died a few months later.

Photographed at my desk by an American visitor in 1971: much of the furniture of this room dates from the previous Freemasons' Hall.

Chapter 15

Retirement and Prestonian Lectureship

The division of working life between Hammersmith and Great Queen Street had always been pleasantly uneventful, but we had seen what had happened to the previous generation and were anxious not to find ourselves saddled with a house which, even if freehold, was much too big for the two of us and not in very good repair: we also had hankered for years for some place in the mid-centre of London. We had flirted briefly with the idea of the Barbican, and much earlier with Canonbury, though a flat in the Charterhouse had always been in the back of our minds as the perfect answer. The Registrar, Norman Long Brown, had offered one years earlier while Hugh was still at home, but we had to turn it down then as being too small: so it was to our great surprise that it was offered again in 1972 when we were on our own, and we had no hesitation in accepting. The flat needed a lot of work doing to it though structurally it was sound enough. Charles Fry organised the redecorating during a slack time at the Hall and we were putting our minds to schemes of repair and redecoration at Rowan Road when we were besought to let it as it stood to some Australian medicos who were virtually stranded and needed somewhere very quickly. They were followed at once by another Australian family so that there was never a moment when it was unoccupied.

We took as much furniture as we wanted, and which could be fitted into Pensioners Court, but still, unbelievably, left enough at Rowan Road for it to be a real 'furnished let'. Meanwhile Hugh had met Alison Hill in Greece, a not uncommon destiny, and they were married to our great pleasure as we liked both her and her family at sight. They settled in Hugh's Barbican flat until they ultimately decided to take Rowan Road off our hands as being a more suitable milieu for raising a family. Their family doctor, Baker was a former pupil of mine at St Paul's (a quiet and intelligent hard worker*) and I was only sorry that I could not supply a vet as well for their Cavalier Spaniel as Dick Broad, also an ex-pupil (English good: Latin Sentences very weak*!) had decided to abandon household pets in Shepherds Bush for farming stock in Devonshire.

Our own move had taken place in November 1972, and we took a little time to settle down to new journeys to work. For me the move made surprisingly little difference: I missed the certitude of the Piccadilly Tube

* Recollections from my end of term report on them

as against the vagaries of late night buses, but knew that if all else failed it was no more than a twenty minute walk from door to door, and so life went on much as usual after our move from west to east. In Richenda's case I am afraid a much longer one was entailed though she contrived to do a good deal of reading on the train, and she had to accustom herself to a very different shopping area. We both found a set of new and interesting as well as friendly neighbours.

Rev Tom Nevill, Past Deputy Grand Chaplain, was about to retire as Master of Charterhouse, his place being taken by Oliver Van Oss whom I had known since 1923. Apart from the other twelve tenants of flats in Pensioners Court, we gradually got to know several of the Brothers of Sutton's Foundation and found that, all in all, the whole place was a happy and settled community, though Tom had not been particularly encouraging to extra-mural activities and there had been rather an antechamber to death attitude. Oliver however soon brought about a much greater liveliness among the Brothers whom he encouraged to keep up their former activities or take up new ones: apart from his expertise in so many different areas of art he worked wonders with the gardens and by his example encouraged us all to such an extent that even after he had seriously damaged his back and had to restrict his own efforts the good work went on. The change in Registrar from Norman Long Brown to Jock Moss was less happy.

RKTS and JWS with Wendell Walker, Grand Secretary, New York, in Pensioners Court, Charterhouse, 1982.

I have not the slightest doubt that Richenda's and my happiness together over nearly 50 years has been enhanced and strengthened by the fact that we both worked long hours and had no time to get bored with each other's company.

Indeed it was only during holidays that we were able to be constantly together: consequently we made the most of our time generally going abroad and occasionally enjoying some Freemasonry on the way.

In 1967 we started what became a holiday routine: for nearly ten years previously we had hired a car in Europe and driven about in Southern Italy, Sicily, Germany and Austria, France and Belgium with one splendid excursion to Western Canada. A chance meeting with George Meikle who had just become Grand Inspector of Cyprus and his wife Jean prompted another visit for me, Richenda's first, to Cyprus. We both liked it so much that we went back there every year till the division of the island in 1974.

We had to abandon a proposed holiday at short notice, and were warned off Greece by Alexander Bultzo as there was every prospect of a general mobilisation: so we redeployed ourselves to Italy and had been having a splendid time at Ravello and various other places mostly already known to use in the south, when I incurred an acute retention whilst in Tivoli. Fortunately it was almost the end of the holiday, but after some first aid I had to arrange to get myself back poste-haste to London, when I was met on the steps of the Royal Masonic Hospital by both Eddie Tuckwell and Peter Philip as there was some doubt from my telephone calls from Rome Airport which of their services would be the more appropriate. All went well however and, apart from missing the visit to Monte Cassino, I have no lasting regrets over the incident. After Cyprus we had three motoring holidays in Greece which we got to know pretty well, both northern and southern: and we also took two package tours, as already mentioned, to the Seychelles in 1975 and Sri Lanka and the Maldives in 1978. As time went on we began to find the winter season getting to seem increasingly longer and devised a plan whereby we would take a week away after the September Grand Lodge and before the Masonic season set in with its full severity. These autumn holidays included trips to Brittany, Alsace and the Bahamas, which latter was not entirely a holiday as I consecrated four Lodges and Chapters in six days! We also tried to maintain our Scottish connection by paying short visits to Kilravock and elsewhere.

Over the years many kindly and well meaning brethren were wont to say, embarrassingly enough, that it was high time I was knighted, and some even produced far fetched ideas as to how they would effect it. I was however genuinely surprised when I received a letter from Buckingham Palace early in 1979 saying that it was the Queen's wish to confer a KCVO on me in the next Birthday honours: I replied to it using what I hoped were the correct terms and settled down to a period of waiting, which seemed to stretch out to the crack of doom. When the great day

Retirement and Prestonian Lectureship 159

After receiving the KCVO in 1980.

'It will have to be LGR Sir James, we have run out of KCVOs (John Groves, November 1979)

dawned *The Times* was on strike, the *Daily Telegraph* misspelled my name and the *Guardian* omitted the Victorian Order! Enough people however identified the announcement to make the telephone at Charterhouse on that day and at Freemasons' Hall after the week-end fairly hum: by one happy coincidence my sister-in-law Ruth Gervis was celebrating her 85th birthday and we were able to share in the congratulations, by another all of us three KCVO's were connected personally and known to each other, Dean Martin Sullivan of St Paul's, Sir Stephen Miller the Queen's eye specialist and myself.

The actual investiture did not take place till November by which time the flood of congratulations had abated. Leslie Sinclare very kindly provided a car to take us to the Palace and back, after which we had a celebratory lunch in the Connaught Rooms with about a dozen of our closest friends. I was greatly touched by the sincere enthusiasm of the staff at the Hall and by what was clearly demonstrated as genuine pleasure from the Craft as a whole both at home and abroad.

The investiture was hardly over when it became necessary to think seriously of the official handover to Michael Higham. In the circumstances the best I could do was to give him *ad hoc* briefing about things as they turned up and to leave as far as possible to him the long range projects which were unlikely to come to a head till after I had gone. I did however become rather more aware of my innate conservatism, and still more of my unwillingness over the years to spend Grand Lodge's money on what seemed unnecessary frills. I reckoned that Sydney White had laid the foundations of a good office system which I had done little more than carry it on with only minor simplifications: and it was probably time now for someone else to carry the administration into the twenty-first century.

There is always just under the placid surface of English Freemasonry a feeling that everything is centred on London, which is true, and further that it is all being done for the benefit of London, which is not true: so I was anxious, in the last few months, to show myself as much as possible in the Provinces, and I managed to get round to large numbers of Provincial Grand Lodges or to Masonic centres by way of farewell visits. I also dedicated London's then newest venture, the Central London Masonic Centre in the Old Clerkenwell Sessions House: Ted Baillieu had been earmarked for it, but unfortunately could not get out of hospital in time. Except for the Installation of the District Grand Master for Barbados which happened after my retirement and figures in the chapter on our final tour that was the last occasion of many when Alan Ferris and I worked together: I have known five Grand Directors of Ceremonies in my working life and they have all differed in their types of excellence, but I really think that for simple efficiency of execution without fuss and with economy of effort the palm must go to Alan Ferris. Others in that office achieved as much as he did, but not so naturally simply and smoothly: and though others may have made a greater impact on general administration and leadership, none could match him in the strictest sense of the direction of ceremonies: West Lancashire is very lucky to have him.

At the June Quarterly Communication kind things were said by the Pro Grand Master which like those of the Grand Master a few months earlier I do not hesitate to quote together with my reply:

Retirement of Grand Secretary

The MW Pro Grand Master: As you may have worked out for yourselves brethren, today is the last occasion on which RW Bro Sir James Stubbs will be attending Grand Lodge as Grand Secretary. This office he has held with skill, tact and sheer hard work for over 22 years. No words of mine could convey to him how grateful we all are for what he has done for the Craft and the Royal Arch during that long time. In August we shall see the end of the Stubbs era but not the end of James Stubbs himself. I am glad to say that he will still be available as one of the Grand Master's advisers.

I had the great pleasure to know and work with James Stubbs before he became Grand Secretary. Since his appointment he and I have travelled the world on Masonic business, and I can honestly say he and I have never had a single cross word. Probably his proudest achievement was the carrying of the main burden of the 250th Anniversary. That function is still spoken of at home and abroad as the most perfectly organised operation of its kind.

He has two characteristics wherein lies his greatness and success. If he disagrees with a policy that I or anyone else wishes to undertake he will state his opposition clearly and fairly. If we are obstinate and pursue that policy in spite of his warnings, not only does he never mention it again, he does his utmost to make it work. Secondly, he has the most astounding brilliance at remembering names and faces, which no doubt has endeared him to thousands of Masons.

I have received a letter from Lord Donoughmore, Grand Master of Ireland, which he would like me to read to you:

'Dear Pro Grand Master,
 I understand that the Communication of Grand Lodge on 11th June will be the last one in which RW Bro Sir James Stubbs will act in his official capacity. Indeed, he told me of this last year, and I had every intention of attending and of asking your permission to make a suitable tribute. Now, owing to the health troubles which beset me last winter, I am not able to do this. I am therefore writing this letter instead.
 I have now held the office of Grand Master here for just over 15 years, and during this period we have been in constant touch with your Grand Secretary. In all that time we have been treated with the utmost courtesy and have benefited greatly from W Bro Stubbs's wise advice. Both I and my colleagues here are more than grateful for this, and, if you thought it appropriate, would much appreciate if this letter could be read out in Grand Lodge or otherwise added to the Minutes as some token of our gratitude and appreciation.
 Yours sincerely and fraternally,
                    Donoughmore
                    Grand Master'

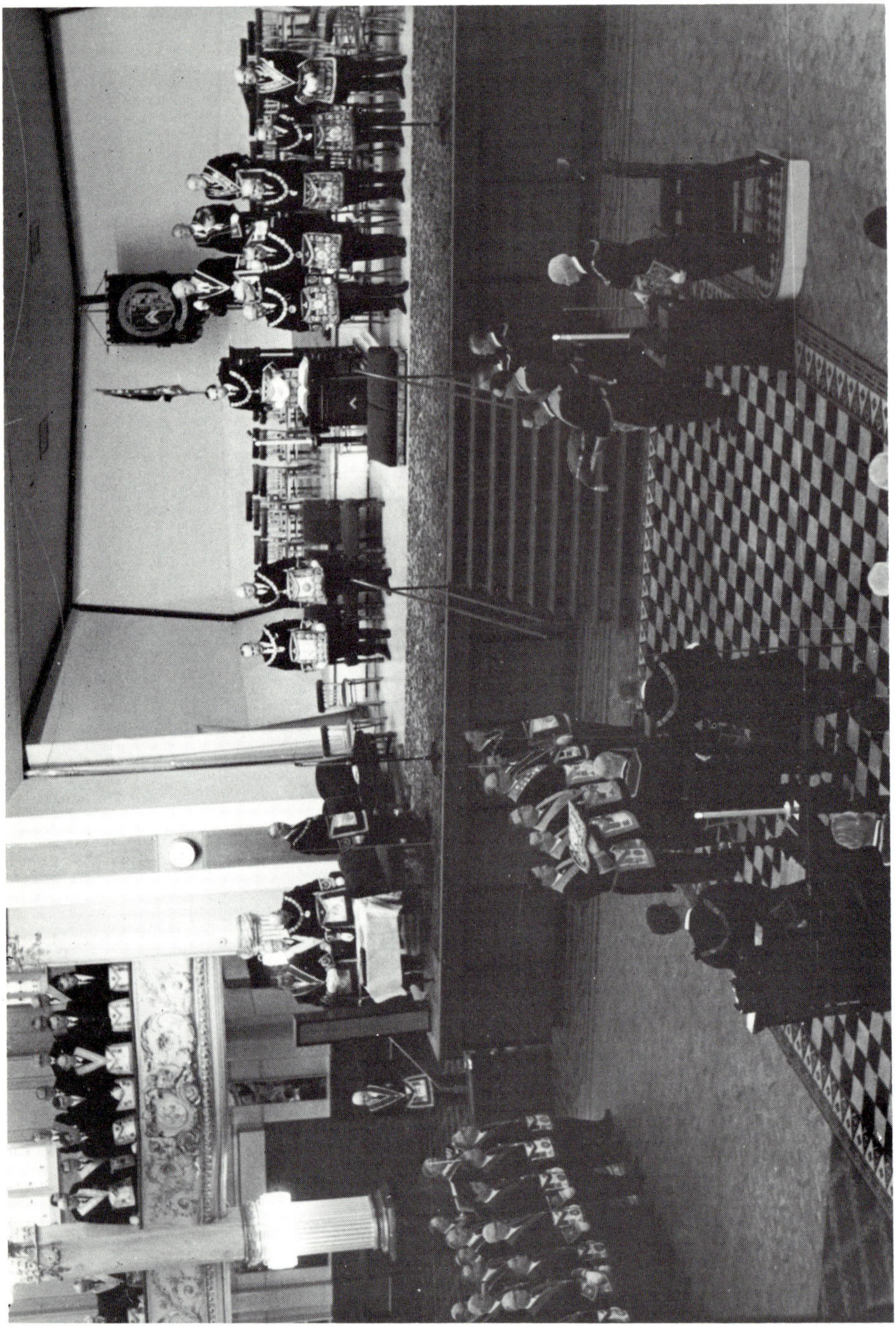

Finally to you James Stubbs, I am not going to say good-bye because I hope you will be with us for many years to come. I just want to say: Thank you for the friendship and wise guidance you have given me. (*Applause.*)

Reply by The Grand Secretary: MW Pro Grand Master and members of Grand Lodge, thank you indeed, MW Pro Grand Master, for the very kind things that you have said about me, not least for communicating the message from Lord Donoughmore, Grand Master of the second senior Grand Lodge to our own and a very present help in all troubles. All that I have done over these years, not only the 22 in question but nearly a decade before that, has owed enormously to the support which I have had from the Rulers of the Craft— Lord Scarbrough perhaps outstandingly so; the Board of General Purposes, which has the virtual management of the Craft and conducts its affairs with such skill and experience; and also some 7,000, and many more than that, in their successive generations, Lodge Secretaries year in year out, to whom we in the Grand Secretary's Office owe a great deal and without whose very great and continuing help, if I may quote from the Prayer that we hear so often, our efforts would be of no avail,

Thank you sincerely, MW Pro Grand Master, and Grand Lodge too.

(*Extract from Quarterly Communication 11 June 1980*)

It became obvious that Irene Hainworth's grim statement that from then onward I was going to have to eat and drink my way out of office was no exaggeration. My diary shows a long succession of what are clearly farewell dates as well as the usual summer functions: but there was one however that gave me particular pleasure, the consecration of the Certa Cito Lodge. Almost every Corps in the Army and a good many regiments too had a Lodge connected with them: yet Royal Signals did not, and efforts over many years seemed to come up against the perpetual brick wall of a minute, many years old, in which a number of long since dead and gone Colonels Commandant had recorded their opposition. Having nothing to lose by incurring the displeasure of the current Corps Committee and feeling pretty certain that Brigadier Fairweather, Dep Prov GM of Yorkshire North and East Riding and Col Dicker, Dep Prov GM of Norfolk were quite a match for the Committee if there was still opposition rather than inertia I pressed on. A meeting was summoned of all the

---

The installation of Sir Knowles Edge as Provincial Grand Master for West Lancashire in 1968 with HRH the Duke of Kent, conducting the ceremony. Left to right, on dais: H. A. Fry (Prov GSec) at table with JWS, Sir J. Newson-Smith (Dep GDC), Lord Cadogan (Dep GM), Lord Scarbrough (Pro GM), HRH the Duke of Kent (GM), Lord Kenyon (Prov GM North Wales), Bishop Claxton of Blackburn (Grand Chaplain) immediately behind Lord Kenyon, A. Johnstone (Prov GM Cheshire), H. K. Potts (Prov GM Cumberland & Westmorland), and R. Gelling Johnson (Prov GM Isle of Man), K. B. Large (PDist GM Bengal). Beneath the dais can be seen Lord Derby (PDep GM and Prov GM East Lancs) as Senior Warden with immediately in front, Sir Knowles Edge (Prov GM designate) and Frank Douglas (GDC). H. Clifford Smith (Prov GM Yorks West Riding) is the Junior Warden and leading the deputation on the left is D. L. Paterson (Dep GDC) and on the right Sir Victor Groom with Alan Ferris on his right. (Photograph by kind permission of A. F. Ferris, Prov GM West Lancashire.)

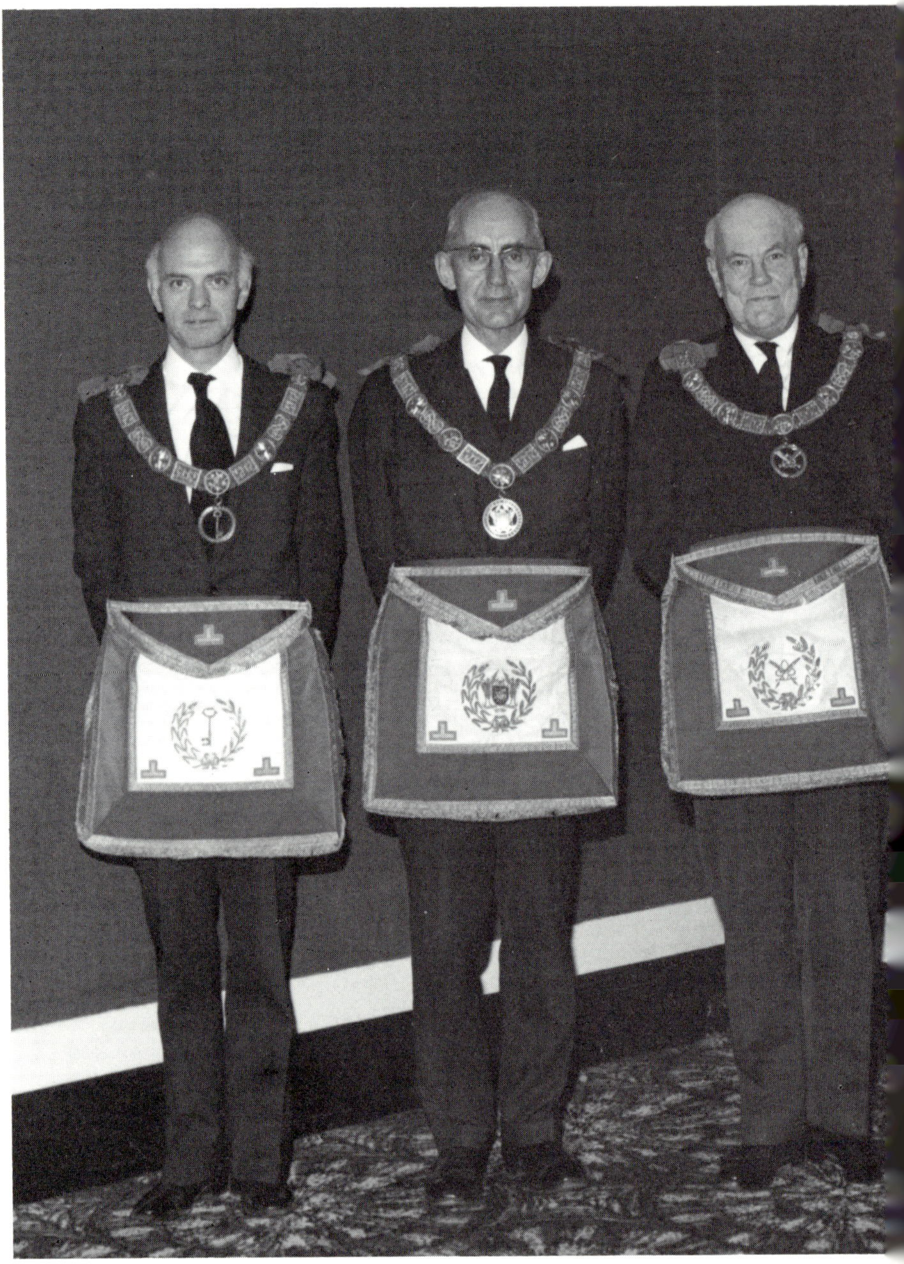

Left to right: Sir John Welch, Jeremy Pemberton, Sir James Stubbs, Cdr M. B. S. Higham and Rev C. E. Leighton Thomson in 1980 when all five were acting Grand Officers and members of Westminster and Keystone Lodge No 10.

Signals personnel that we could get hold of all ranks, present and past. The principle of petitioning the Grand Master for a Lodge was agreed and Brothers Fairweather and Garrett (the latter a prominent clerk in the office) found themselves drafted as Master and Secretary.

When it came to the consecration I was determined to 'keep it in the family', and produced a team everyone of whom had served in the Corps in one capacity or another. I was assisted by RW Bro Earl Kitchener of Khartoum PSGW (1 HQ Signals) as Senior Warden, W Bro J. E. Bullen, Assistant PGM Hants and Isle of White (once my invaluable orderly room sergeant in 43 Div Signals) as Junior Warden, W Bro Rev James Reeves PAG Chaplain (who had done his national service in the Corps) as Chaplain, RM Bro Jeremy Pemberton President B of GP (who had been with me at Prestatyn and in Signals 5 in the War Office and with Jimmy Bullen before my time in 43 Div Signals) coming back into office as DC, and W Bro (Sir) John Welch PG Treasurer (once commanding a Line Construction Section in the Canal Zone). It was a great evening and the Lodge has continued to flourish ever since holding successful meetings at Catterick or Richmond and Blandford in addition to its regular ones in London.

Another most enjoyable function was when George Richardson, Secretary of the Delegates of the Oxford University Press and Vivian Ridler, Printer to the University assembled some close friends and gave a dinner in my honour at St Edmund Hall. The Press and I had had many satisfactory encounters over the annual printing and publishing of the *Masonic Year Book*, the *Book of Constitutions*, which we had rationalised together, and *Grand Lodge 1717-1967*. In 1982 the Press kindly undertook to print *The Four Corners* for me, and by general consent made an excellent job of it in the usual Press tradition.

In July the Boards of General Purposes and Benevolence and Grand Chapter's Committee of General Purposes combined together to organise a farewell lunch at which I was presented with a token of several cases of admirable wine and the reality of the 'microscopic' Oxford English Dictionary. I made a speech of which I remember very little except a comparison with Elijah going up to heaven in a fiery chariot and leaving his cloak (apron) to Elisha (Michael Higham), nor indeed do I remember how we disentangled the three parties and got them all settled to their afternoon meetings. I had in the meantime already accompanied the Grand Master on one of his unofficial visits to a Lodge (in Buckinghamshire) and been able to bow myself out ceremonially.

This was followed by an office party and one for the maintenance staff earlier in the day before the cleaners departed. I was much touched by the office's additional gift of a photograph album in which they all figured. Rather sadly we had to break away from the office party in order to attend the funeral of Miss Haig, who between 1917 and 1959 had been Private Secretary to two of my predecessors as well as myself: she would not have wished to be the cause of such disruption.

Three days later after signing the last Salary and Wages cheque of a long career, and having spent a dreadful Sunday evacuating ourselves from 22 years partial residence in Freemasons' Hall, we set off on the long farewell trip which is described in a later chapter. We returned from the last leg of it which we spent in Portugal to take up a rather more private mode of life. Richenda had retired from Charing Cross Hospital a few months before me and so we both had to readjust and remould ourselves to the new way of life. Richenda found herself well occupied with the affairs of the Charing Cross Hospital Holiday Trust for Kidney Patients, which she had helped Professor Hugh de Wardener to establish some years earlier. It had grown considerably and even though the patients made use of the home at Emsworth and the Caravan at Great Yarmouth for only part of the year, the Trust's fund raising and other activities were never ending. Meanwhile her second sister Noel Streatfeild had ceased to be able to look after herself in consequence of a number of strokes with the result that finding nursing homes and visiting her in them was a major preoccupation. Although Noel had become somewhat confused she was quite well enough to know that she was awarded an OBE in January 1982, and to attend the investiture which greatly gratified her. She had a wide fan mail mostly from child readers in the USA and Canada, and for a long time this was dealt with by her devoted ex-secretary 'Con' (Mrs Boret), but when she died this burden too fell on Richenda.

THE PRESTONIAN LECTURE

I naturally found very little to do actively in Craft Masonry, apart from visits to Lodges of which I was either a subscribing or an honorary member, and it was clear that my advice ought not to be given unasked.

So I will freely admit that at first I found it irksome to hear odd bits of news about Masonic activities instead of being in most cases either the originator or the first to hear about them: but membership of the Grand Master's Council, to which the Grand Master had very kindly appointed me was an alleviating help. Very much to my surprise I was approached by Jeremy Pemberton to undertake the Prestonian Lectureship in 1982 as although I had given a few papers to Quatuor Coronati Lodge over the years I had never had the time, nor indeed the capacity, to become a profound Masonic scholar. I had always however been convinced that the Prestonian Lecture should be something which any Masonic audience should be able to appreciate, and I made sure that mine on *The Government of the Craft* kept its feet and mine firmly on the ground. In addition to delivering the Lecture nearly 50 times in England, Wales and the Channel Islands to audiences totalling about 7,000 I was privileged also to go to Hong Kong, to deliver one of three official ones and took the opportunity to deliver it on the way home in both Kuala Lumpur and Singapore. Dick Lee added to his very many kindnesses by taking us for a week's tour in China as guests of the Chinese Government: this was undoubtedly the highlight of the Lectureship.

There were good audiences in all three places, but it was sheer bad luck that the meeting in Hong Kong was sadly diminished in numbers by the arrival of Prime Minister Margaret Thatcher and her entourage and the consequent offical functions. We had not taken a summer holiday earlier in the year and had therefore arranged to break our flight from Singapore in Thailand, where we spent a pleasantly idle week in the sun.

When I was Grand Secretary I often had the uneasy feeling that it was only lip service when we used to refer each year in the Board's report to Grand Lodge on the official nature of the Lecture—and after that paid only scant attention. So having become one of them I tried to induce some corporate spirit among Past Lecturers and I therefore arranged a luncheon in the Connaught Rooms with the three trustees. Many of the Lecturers had not met their predecessors or successors, and few indeed had any acquaintance with the trustees, and vice versa. The function was, I believe, a success, and I hope that within the next few years it will be repeated. I felt also that as the Lectureship was an official appointment it was appropriate that its holders, present and past should be distinguished by a collarette and jewel. Here, though they were in favour of it and the Grand Master on the recommendation of his Council had approved it, it took over two years to produce. The first jewels were presented to seven former lecturers at the December Quarterly Communication of Grand Lodge in 1984.

The Grand Secretary's office kindly organised the business side of the publication of the lecture from which the Grand Secretary's fund, the Royal Masonic Benevolent Institution and the Trinity Hospice (formerly Hostel of God) derived some benefit. The evident eagerness with which copies were snapped up encouraged me to try to market the collected reports of various travels abroad that I had undertaken from 1958 onwards. All but one had already appeared in Grand Lodge Proceedings, and it was little more than a matter of producing a coherent and logical link up between each: but the long trip had to be written up from memory and from Richenda's invaluable diaries. I had found it very difficult to get a straight answer from the authorities as to whether any such publication would be approved. Eventually the approval came and I went to work with help from John Skelly of the Oxford University Press and Jim Davis of Matthews, Drew and Shelbourne. The former organised the printing and the latter the publication, order forms and despatch. There was a good initial response to the order forms, which were circulated by courtesy of the Board of General Purposes and the Grand Chapter Committee with their respective papers of business, and a little later by the London Grand Rank Association and Quatuor Coronati Lodge. But sales slowed down very much and it looked as if there were going to be very many copies left on my hands. At this point I took a decision to be my own salesman rather than rely on the order forms, almost thousands of which were still lying about if they had not found their way into wastepaper baskets. I took to carrying a packet with me whenever I visited a Lodge or Chapter with the result that in about six months the whole stock was cleared. In fact the labour was evenly divided between the order forms which were dealt with by Matthews Drew and my own activity. It was fun while it lasted but I do not think that I should want to do it again, and must look to more orthodox methods for this present venture. Here again however as in the case of the printed lectures there was tangible proof that members of the Craft are half starved for lack of reading material, not only at the research level, but about things that have interested them in their Masonic lives, and a publication such as Harry Mendoza's own Prestonian Lecture on *Getting and Giving Masonic Knowledge* has much to commend it.

MARK DEGREE AND SUPREME COUNCIL

The *lacuna* in Masonic activity that seemed likely to follow the end of the Prestonian Lectures in June 1983 had in fact already been filled up. Although I had been a Past Grand Junior Warden in the Mark since 1959 and, without playing a very active part in the affairs, had always tried to keep the two bodies of Craft and Mark in close conjunction and patiently undo the latent jealousies that had never been far below the surface ever since the unfortunate Lumley Smith – Sydney White affair, I was very pleasantly surprised in the spring of 1983 to be offered the appointment of Grand Senior Warden in succession to Ted Baillieu. This involved a year as a member of the General Board which I greatly enjoyed among a lot of old friends as well as making several visits outside London for the installation of Provincial Grand Masters and two consecrations, all of which were ceremonies which I was now looking at from the other side. Just as I was beginning to think regretfully that like all good things my Board Membership was coming to an end, I was delighted to receive an offer of nomination for a place among the elected members.

Shortly before I retired Sir Ralph Hone came to see me and asked whether I would co-operate in a scheme which was being worked out, to provide Inspectors General under the Supreme Council, of which he was then Grand Commander, to look after the 70 odd London Chapters. The plan was for five to be appointed and installed, each with 14 Chapters under his jurisdiction. I had certain qualms about it, both for London and for my own prospective part, as I had always been strongly opposed (and still am) to what I regard as the impracticable, extravagant and useless idea of splitting London's 1,600 Lodges into Provinces like the rest of the country. I regard it as impracticable because the greater part of the Lodges do not have a basic membership of Londoners and I see no prospect of finding an adequate succession of brethren in London with the qualities needed in a Provincial Grand Master and his senior officers:

extravagant because each such Province would call for an expensive Provincial organisation and office: useless because Freemasons' Hall ie, the Grand Secretary's Office, can look after them all just as well as a Provincial Office or offices.

Under the Supreme Council there was no Provincial organisation anywhere: it delegates some of its functions to local Inspectors General who have, in most cases, a District Recorder to help them clerically: to extend this system (less the Recorder) to London did not in any way give a lead to the 'Provincialisation' of London, which I could still logically oppose even after becoming a London Inspector General. So I accepted the offer and soon after our return to England in 1981 was installed as Inspector General of the St John Group. This has provided me with a new interest within an order of which I had always been fond since I entered it over 50 years ago.

I discovered in due course that the other four were Malcolm Dunlop, son-in-law of Bobbie Loyd who has already figured in these pages, Patrick Pirie Gordon whom I had helped to initiate into the Apollo and whose elder brother, Christopher, had been a close friend at Oxford. Then Sir John Stebbings also of the Apollo and currently President of the Grand Charity, with whom and his wife Patricia we are on terms of close friendship and affection, and last but not least there was also Watkin Williams who had been a year or two senior to me at Summer Fields. The scheme came to fruition while we were abroad, and I was the last of the five to be installed soon after our return. Rather ironically I had already, on behalf of the Supreme Council, installed the first Inspector General in Jamaica—and I soon realised when my turn came what a long time I had kept my victim standing in Kingston while I addressed him on his duties and responsibilities: I rather think that Sir Ralph let me off some of it. I started almost at once to visit my 14 Chapters and have now come to know them quite well.

If I am accused of insincerity or double-thinking, in as much as I am thought to be taking the opposite stance in respect of the Rose Croix Chapters, I am fully prepared to defend myself on the basis that like is not being compared to like. There is no real comparison between the organisation of a Craft or Royal Arch Province, and an Inspectorate under the Supreme Council, even if fortuitously they cover the same or nearly the same, geographical area. A Grand Inspector is neither a Provincial Grand Master nor a one-man Provincial Grand Lodge. Equally the five Inspectors General are not to be considered as models or prototypes for the Provincialisation of London. If they had been I could certainly never have accepted the office in the first place: and if they showed any sign of becoming such my resignation would be immediate. It has almost certainly been forgotten by now that about the time of World War II, some very distinguished brethren were advanced to the 33rd degree with the vague idea that they would 'look after' London Chapters generally: nothing very much happened and as they died they were not replaced.

The new (1980) deal was better founded, and the five were given our responsibilities for the Chapters placed under them in much the same way as are the Inspectors General everywhere else, except that the Supreme Council office (where incidentally all the Chapters meet) carries some of our burdens.

Quatuor Coronati Lodge No 2076 luncheon at the Connaught Rooms to commemorate my retirement as Grand Secretary. Left to right: Harry Mendoza, Terence Haunch, Roy Wells, John Hamill, JWS, George Draffen, Frederick Smyth, Will Read, Cyril Batham, Ellic Howe and John Cooper.

Chapter 16

Farewell Tour

(This chapter was first published in *The Four Corners* but is reproduced here for completeness and for those who have not read this former publication. It will be apparent that it is composed in a rather different style, bearing some similarity to the formal reports to Grand Lodge of other tours. I have not attempted to rewrite it as I felt that it was more comparable to such reports than to the general style and matter of the rest of the book.)

When retirement was pronounced for me on reaching 70 it was suggested by the Assistant Grand Master that we might like to revisit and say 'Goodbye' to some of the old friends and places of our previous tours: I had already made up my mind so far as was possible in the time to get round the Provinces and do just that. In fact I was able one way or another to visit well over half of them in the early months of 1980: it seemed still more important to visit the Districts. Apart from this I felt it was desirable to get out from under my successor's feet, feeling convinced that if I continued about the place there would be a good deal of playing one off against the other. Both my wife and I felt also that we needed a change of scene on reaching retirement at approximately the same time.

As plans developed it became clear to us that it was going to be very difficult, not to say invidious to leave any of the Districts out, and a short trip gradually expanded into a world tour: the Board of General Purposes and the Grand Chapter Committee most generously subsidised it, and we were able to finalize our plans with the comfortable feeling that apart from Malta and Gibraltar which could be visited on other occasions, Pakistan which was virtually closed down, and the Inspectorate of Bermuda, but including a number of 'unattached' Lodges no one was left out. Moreover the Supreme Council asked me whether I would be willing to visit some of their isolated chapters and for good measure to form their Jamaican chapters into a District by installing the new Inspector General. As will be seen things did not quite work out as planned, and South America and Fiji fell casualties to my illness, and Nigeria to the aggravation of the authorities there that we had recently been to South Africa.

STAGE ONE: THE AMERICAS

23 July   On the way to London Airport I discharged my last official duty at Freemasons' Hall, appropriately enough by signing the July salary and wages cheque. We went straight on to Heathrow where we were met by W Bro Ivor Gregory and entertained till it was time to emplane for Newfoundland. After what seemed a very short flight we landed at St John's where RW Bro Gordon Barnes, *24 July* the District Grand Master, and Mrs Barnes met us and took us to the Newfoundland Hotel. The following morning we paid, with them, official calls on the Mayor, Mrs Dorothy Wyatt, and then the Lieutenant Governor, the Hon R. G. Winter: this was followed by an official lunch where we were particularly pleased to see Mrs Doris Macgillivray the widow of a previous District Grand Master. In the evening there was a gathering of the Masons of St John's and its neighbourhood at the Masonic Hall with their ladies, a highly enjoyable function marred only by an accident to the District Grand Master. The next morning W Bro and Mrs Bromley drove us round some of the Avalon Peninsula before *25 July* taking us to the Airport for our short flight to Halifax.

The Newfoundland welcome was as warm and hearty as ever, but it was sad that the season of the year here as in the rest of Canada militated against the holding of any Lodge meeting: however I will say at this point, as I have about previous trips, that informal gatherings such as we were invited to attend afforded an excellent opportunity of meeting the local Masons and their ladies—and probably did more to bring home the unity of English Freemasonry than the more formal atmosphere of the Lodge Room.

We were met at Halifax Airport by W Bro Kimber, an old friend: a similar party to that at St John's occurred the next day, organized by the Royal Standard Lodge No 398, at which it was very pleasant also to meet *27 July* representatives of the Grand Lodge of Nova Scotia. Our short stay in this attractive city ended with a train journey to St Andrews, New Brunswick, where we were the guests of Mrs Hope the widow of the former Grand Inspector VW Bro Charles Hope, OSM: it was nice to meet four generations of that delightful family.

29 July   The next morning we just caught our flight to Montreal after a drive through appalling weather and were met by W Bro Angus Murray who looked after us with the greatest care throughout our stay. The Masons of our Lodges combined to meet and entertain us in the St Paul's Lodge Masonic Hall, which has unhappily since been very seriously damaged by fire. Between the two Lodges I met a number of old friends and but for the height of the holiday season would undoubtedly have met many more: there were numerous enquiries after the Pro Grand Master and W Bro R. G. Read, P. Dep, GDC, who had handled St Paul's Bicentenary in 1970.

31 July We next flew to Toronto, where we were hospitably entertained by the Grand Lodge of Canada in the Province of Ontario with which we have had particularly close relations over many years. The new Grand Secretary RW Bro Robert Davies and Mrs Davies kindly drove us to Hamilton to call on MW Bro Ewart Dixon, one of his predecessors and probably the doyen of us all. We found him a little immobile but in no way short of his usual incisiveness.

At this point we had a completely non-Masonic day with friends in and around Toronto before leaving for *3 August* the West.

In the course of a summer holiday in 1966 we had driven through the Rocky Mountains from and to Vancouver, and had long wished to do it again in a more leisurely way by train: this we now proceeded to do using Winnipeg as our railhead. We were greatly helped by the Deputy Grand Master of Manitoba, RW Bro Iles, a former Londoner, and in Vancouver by the Grand Secretary RW Bro Lorimer and Mrs Lorimer who entertained us at their home on our one night 'stop off' between trains and took us sightseeing the next morning. It was a picturesque and restful journey each way, but unfortunately most of the really exciting scenery such as the Kicking Horse Pass and the Great Divide are passed during the hours of darkness. Two pleasant surprises befell us: we were met at Vancouver by RW Bro Sir John and Lady Stebbings and two of their family who took charge of our luggage, and at Calgary by RW Bro Ned Rivers, for many years my contemporary Grand Secretary, and a strong supporter of the English tradition of *8 August* Freemasonry. Bro Iles again met us at Winnipeg and after giving us breakfast showed us round the Park and Zoo area before dropping us off at the Airport. A complicated series of flights brought us late in the evening to Nassau where we were met by VW Bro Sid Larkin and W Bros McKinney and Hall. It is worthy of mention here that only once in seven months did any of our baggage go astray, and that was only one out of seven pieces and for only twelve hours! Our stay in the Bahamas was mainly a matter of saying Goodbye to old friends whom I had met on my various visits to Nassau and Freeport on consecration trips.

11 August

Our next port of call was Jamaica: we landed at Montego Bay where we were met by W Bro Hugh Brown, the Assistant District Grand Master, who later entertained us at his beautiful house on the high ground behind the Bay. It was there that we first met W Bro Maj-Gen Rudolf Green, the Deputy District Grand Master, one of the most quietly efficient and charming Masons with whom I have ever worked. He looked after us most assiduously till we left the island four days later. On the 12th I laid the foundation stone of a new Masonic Hall at Lucea, the ceremony being unexpectedly (so far as I was concerned) graced with the presence of RW Bro Aubrey Jacobs, the District Grand Master. We celebrated my seventieth birthday with the beautiful drive from Montego Bay by way of Ocho Rivas and Spanish Town to Kingston where I later installed V Ill Bro George Finsen as Inspector-General 33° of the newly formed District. A District Grand Lodge meeting was held on the following day, and finally on the 15th a day of social visits and sightseeing included Bro Jacob's orchids and a quiet dinner with Maj-Gen Green who saw us off early the next morning. Here again it was a mixture of old and new friends whom it would be impracticable to mention individually: we can only say how grateful we both are for the arrangements for us separately or together.

13 August

16 August

The less said about the journey from Jamaica to St Thomas (US Virgin Islands), by way of Haiti and Puerto Rico, the better: it started badly by the hotel failing to call us, and it was only thanks to Maj-Gen Green's punctual arrival and swift driving that we reached the airport in time.

We eventually got to St Thomas and were delighted to find RW Bro Alan Ferris waiting for us with Bros Vialet and Henné: we were the guests of the brethren in Bluebeard's Castle, a delightful hotel with dramatic views and excellent facilities. The reason for the visit was to consecrate a new Lodge to work at Tortola (British Virgin Islands): the idea was that with all the equipment and furniture to hand in St Thomas it would be simpler

18 August

to bring the petitioners there than to transfer everything to Tortola. So, indeed, it would have been but for a disastrous fire, probably arson, that had gutted the St Thomas Hall. In spite of this the ceremony proceeded in traditional form (though I doubt if Alan Ferris or I have ever been so inadequately tiled). We were greatly assisted by, indeed could not have done without, the help of a contingent from the Bahamas. The Harmonic Lodge No 356, St Thomas, is in an almost unique position, English Constitution on American soil, and with what is basically a strong Scandinavian membership. It is very much on its own and it is to be hoped that the new Lodge, St Ursula's No 8952, and Harmonic Lodge, will be a mutual source of strength. St Ursula of Cologne is reputed to have had 11,000 Virgins with her: looking at the group of island from the high ground one appreciates how appropriately the Lodge is named.

Together with Bro Ferris we moved on to Antigua where we spent an outstandingly happy two days, meeting many of the Leeward Islands Masons and their wives in formal or informal surroundings, sightseeing at Clarence House and English Harbour, lunching at Government House with HE Sir Wilfred (Ebenezer) Jacobs and Lady Jacobs. (By special request the GDC was shown one of the local golf courses and I found myself sitting on a sofa between two middle aged Antiguan ladies having an erudite argument on the decline and fall of slow bowling.) He and I attended a joint meeting of the two Antiguan Lodges with the backing too of the Monserrat Brethren, during which my wife was most hospitably entertained by Mrs Christians and a score of ladies.

21 August

At this point we parted temporarily with Bro Ferris who went direct to Barbados: we made a twenty-four hour stop at St Lucia which was still showing signs of the terrible damage caused by a recent hurricane the edge of which had also caught the north coast of Jamaica. In spite of this a Lodge meeting was held as previously fixed, and makeshift but exceedingly competent arrangements were made for a gathering and dinner at the Green Parrot restaurant where it was a privilege to meet the ex-Governor-General W Bro Sir Alan Lewis, PSGD. We had some difficulty in getting away from the island as the Air Company denied all knowledge of us: they were brought to heel however by Bro Michael Daniel who took control and had lunch with us before we took off.

23 August

It was a short flight to Barbados where we were met by the outgoing Deputy District Grand Master and taken to Coral Reef Club: in the evening the District Grand Master designate, Dr Cooper and Mrs Cooper entertained us and a large gathering, which was an excellent introduction to the next day's ceremony. RW Bro Cooper's installation (the fourth major ceremony I had undertaken in ten days) passed off with nothing more untoward than a complete electrical blackout during it. The following day was spent in sightseeing and relaxation, and a quiet evening with Bro Ferris.

The short evening flight on 25 August to Guyana was uneventful but the entry into the Co-operative People's Republic was chaotic: however we got through customs in the end, helped by the District Grand Master's son, Nicholas Taylor, and reached our hotel shortly before 1 a.m. There were two meetings arranged in Georgetown, both of which were enjoyable and well attended, to a large extent by the same people. Between them we were shown the various sights including the quite unforgettable Kaieteur falls, known to me hitherto only by views on British Guiana postage stamps.

28 August

In the course of the second night I developed acute gastroenteritis and though a little better by breakfast time was in a shaky state throughout the preparations for departure and the actual flight to Trinidad. We arrived very late and I was due almost at once at a meeting of Royal Philanthropic Lodge No 405, of which my recollections are very vague. The next morning after a brighter start I collapsed at the house of Bro McEachrane on the University Campus with the result that after a visit to Dr Whatley, the island's best cardiologist I was consigned to a nursing home for a week. We had been hitherto looked after with the greatest kindness and sympathy and it came as an unpleasant shock, to people not accustomed to transatlantic methods, to find not even a chair provided at the nursing home till actual *cash* had been handed over for the whole recommended length of the stay (it is the only time too that I have known American Express Travellers Cheques refused): let English visitors beware! In itself the nursing home was not too bad and the nursing care was as good as the food was deplorable.

29 August-
5ˢᵗ September

My wife had the task of unscrambling the next month's arrangements and planning what to do when we were on the road again: it meant scrapping Curacao,

South America, and Fiji, and finding a route from Trinidad to New Zealand. While I was incarcerated she was looked after most kindly by the Deputy District Grand Master W Bro Frank Drayton (the District Grand Master was in England) and other Brethren and their ladies who vied with each other in kindness: it would be wrong not to mention the High Commissioner's Office too, where Mr Cruickshank organised reading material and his own very comfortable presence.

6–24 September

The Normandie Hotel, where the Pro Grand Master and I had previously stayed was an ideal place for convalescence. All the rooms looked on to the pool which became, much more than the actual reception rooms, its social centre. It was there that for the first ten days or so a constant stream of visitors turned up: Bro Drayton in particular, the Gumbrells, the Innises, the Roses, the Grahams, the McEachranes, the Knaggses, the Frasers, the Farrells, with on their return from Europe W Bro Burnett, District Grand Secretary, and his wife and in due course RW Bro Nicol and Mrs Nicol. The final week found me able to get about a good deal, and we were taken to other parts of the island for highly enjoyable day trips. Dr Whatley cleared me for flying on 24 September and by the efforts of the Air Canada office we just got our travelling details, which included night stops at Los Angeles and Honolulu *en route* for New Zealand, in time.

It is not easy to put into words our gratitude for the kindness shown us over a long period by the Trinidadian Brethren and their ladies: it must sometimes have seemed to them that they were going to have us and our travelling problems on their hands for ever. Our apologies are due also to those whom we had to miss out and who have shown a most forebearing spirit in asking us to come again two years later. In the event we arrived at Auckland within a few hours of our original schedule.

The flights and the intermediate stops were alike comfortable; but it was a long haul and we were very glad to touch down and find RW Bro Ivan and Mrs Whale and VW Bro Wilfred and Mrs Fortune awaiting us with the new District Grand Secretary and Mrs Gibbs.

STAGE TWO: NEW ZEALAND

28 September After settling in to the White Heron Hotel which was to be our centre while in and around Auckland, we were entertained by Bro and Mrs Whale at their home. On the following day after some administrative details we visited the Mount Roskill Home, greatly extended and developed since our visit in 1960—like the oaktree which I had planted on that occasion. Later in the day we were able to entertain W Bro Gerald Rutter and his wife, son and daughter in law of the redoubtable Deputy Provincial Grand Master of South Wales Eastern Division (we saw his eldest son too on one of our return visits). The District had arranged a road tour of North Island, on which we set out next morning with the Whales, the Millers, and the Gibbses. The climax was a trip up the 90 mile beach to the most northerly point of the Dominion, Cape Reinga. This road tour, which most unfortunately I had to miss was followed by a boat trip round the Bay of Islands which I was able to enjoy to the full: the evening was occupied by a reception for the Masons of North Island and their wives, many of whom we recognized quite easily from 1960.

1 October

4 October When we returned the next day to Auckland, I attended the 125th anniversary of Waitemata Lodge, No 689, which developed from a formal Lodge meeting into a great gathering of nearly 200 for reception, dinner, and speeches. Our next visit was to Gisborne after a morning, cold and blowy, on the harbour, though not too cold and blowy to prevent us enjoying an excellent picnic lunch on board, all of it fixed up for us by W Bro Vernon Avery with his sailing friends. We flew in the evening to Gisborne. After a morning's sightseeing with W Bro da Costa which his expert knowledge of the area made all the more interesting, I attended the Installation meeting of Turanganui Lodge, No 1480, where W Bro Ovenden was most admirably installed. W Bro and Mrs Wilson took us by road by way of Opotiki where we were met and shown the old wooden Lodge premises by W Bro Parkinson who entertained us to lunch in his home. Thence we went to Rotorua where the Wilsons handed us over to the Fortunes who did the honours of the thermal area and showed us the Old People's Homes before they in their turn handed us over to W Bro Ross Collins. With him we drove to New Plymouth a delightful meandering route through rich farming country and finally down to the coast where we got out and stretched our legs on a beach of coal-black sand. On arrival at an excellent hotel in New Plymouth I got ready for a visit to Mount Egmont Lodge No 670, which was attended by brethren from considerable distances. W Bro Tony Smale, now OSM, was very much in charge: Bro Collins' stint was now finished and we said Goodbye to him with regret as he was a friend of many years standing. Bro Smale took us to Wanganui where W Bro and Mrs Hodder met us, and subsequently spent a happy evening with us. It came as a terrible shock to be rung up by Bro Whale from Auckland with the news that Bro Hodder had died in the night. In spite of this it was decided so far as possible to carry on with the programme which included a visit to another old people's home, to an old Maori Church, and to Wanganui's look out station from which we got a splendid view of the city. After lunch with W Bro Smith and Mrs Smith we were shown round Wanganui Collegiate and might well have been in the grounds of an English Public School (this is intended as a compliment!). The evening was spent with the brethren and ladies of the Tongariro Lodge No 705.

12 October

We moved on by way of Palmerston North and the farm of one of the numerous Rowlands where there was a large and extended family lunch, to Wellington with W Bro R. R. Reeves and Mrs Reeves. Here we spent four nights, an unusually long stop every moment of which seemed full of Masonic, family, and social engagements. (The weather had been pretty unkind to us since Rotorua as we never saw Mount Egmont at all and Wellington lived up to its name of 'windy'.)

16 October

We said Goodbye to the Reeves with real regret, and to the North Island too where we had been looked after with a superb mixture of kindness and efficiency, and flew to Christchurch where we were met by RW Bro F. B. Price, the District Grand Master for South Island, and Mrs Price. Our original intention had been to have a few days private sight seeing in parts of the South Island where we had not been in 1960, but it was taken out of our hands in the most kindly way by another succession of guides and companions, providentially so as I do not think I could have managed the long drives.

After a lunch party with the leading lights of the Craft and Royal Arch Districts a major topic was the objection taken by the Grand Lodge of New Zealand to the removal of a Lodge from the West Coast to Amberley and its rather fatuous pronouncement that the Lodge so became 'clandestine'. Meanwhile my wife was being entertained at Bishop's Court by Mrs Pagatt and a number of other ladies. The District had organized a big party at the Town Hall, where we must have met a great proportion of the English Masons as well as my, then, opposite number as Representative. The following morning we set off on the first stage of our tour with W Bro and Mrs Williams who took us via a lunch party at Timaru organized by the St John's Lodge No 1137, to Dunedin where we were entertained by the Deputy District Grand Master and Mrs Gray, and had the pleasure of meeting again Mrs Lord, the widow of RW Bro Leslie Lord who had been District Grand Master at the time of our last visit.

18 October Real Scottish weather (not intended as a compliment!) now settled in and a visit to the Park Gardens and later to Port Chalmers could well have been to the shores of the Minch. However, a meeting of Port Chalmers Marine Lodge passed off very pleasantly, as a vehicle for a reception by the Dunedin Lodges, as well. On our way to Wanaka we stopped at Lawrence where the Lodge premises had been most beautifully redecorated, and we were given the same lavish welcome as in 1960. Our car journey was later interrupted by a boat trip between Roxburgh and Alexandra which was spectacular even by the high standards of Otago. It being early spring the countryside was a mass of fruit blossom with a backdrop of snowy mountains. We stopped for lunch at Alexandra and for tea with Bro and Mrs Smith at Lydgate and reached Wanaka in good time. After an early night we woke to an almost cloudless day which we spent by the lake and later on a sheep station on the slopes of Mount Aspiring. RW Bro Price and Mrs Price arrived in the evening to be our companions back to Christchurch and we said Goodbye to the Grays and Bro Kelly with many thanks for their escort from Dunedin.

21 October We started early from Wanaka in case the Haast Pass road was closed but got through without difficulty and reached the coast where we enjoyed a picnic lunch thoughtfully provided by W Bro King who had also been responsible for our visit to the sheep station. On our way through to Franz Josef we stopped at the remains of the Fox Glacier which is retreating quite rapidly. The weather had changed by now and views were intermittent but we were lucky enough to see Mount Cook from the west as well as we had seen it in the dawn from the Hermitage 20 years earlier.

We were now coming back to Masonic surroundings: after quite a long drive from Franz Josef we reached Hokitika and had a meal with some of the surviving brethren and their ladies (it will be remembered that it was this Lodge No 1229, that had removed itself to Amberley) and then attended a civic reception followed by a Lodge meeting at Greymouth. I was very sorry to miss the after-proceedings but my wife held the fort for me and having received two presents made a popular speech recalling that we had now been to every English Masonic centre in the South Island.

24 October

We were now on the last lap, the magnificent road back to Christchurch over Arthur's Pass with the railway in constant attendance. All too soon we were back on the Canterbury Plain and in what seemed a very short time unpacking in the Clarendon Hotel which we had left just a week before. Our time was running out and after a delightful dinner at the home of W Bro and Mrs Chamberlain we repacked for what was in effect the long haul to Hong Kong, punctuated by a night in Auckland.

We said Goodbye first to W Bro and Mrs Price who had organized the South Island as skilfully as the Whales had done the North, and some twenty-four hours later to the Whales themselves and the Grays. It may seem a commonplace to say that we had been treated like part of the New Zealand family, but it was undoubtedly the case.

STAGE THREE: THE FAR EAST

It *was* a long day to Hong Kong, but we knew that we were going to meet old friends in accustomed surroundings, and it was a pleasure and no surprise to find Mrs Richard Lee awaiting us at the airport (the District Grand Master was at an official function) with the Deputy District Grand Master, W Bro Christopher Haffner, and the District Grand Secretary W Bro Norman Gillanders.

27 October

The earlier part of the day was spent in organizing ourselves for the next stages and in sorting out the immediate past: it should be remembered that since leaving Trinidad we had only twice been more than two nights in one place. Our three evenings were fully occupied, for myself with an immaculate third degree ceremony in the

University Lodge of Hong Kong, No 3666, and an equally good ceremony in the St Mary Magdalene RC Chapter carried out by Bro Gillanders: during both these functions my wife was entertained by ladies connected with the Lodge and Chapter. A superb Chinese dinner with Bro and Mrs Lee rounded off three happy days where the generosity of the District vied with the welcome of its individual members. We had also two more personal interludes where we were entertained to lunch at the Club by W Bro Gilbert Rodway, PM of Westminster and Keystone Lodge No 10, one of twenty-five successive Masters who had made me their Secretary, and we entertained Major and Mrs Cawthorne and her mother, having known Richard since his schooldays and having last met him, overseas, in 1968 at Malacca.

30 October

Bro and Mrs Haffner gave us a farewell lunch high above the city of Hong Kong in a revolving restaurant, and we moved on comfortably and well rested to the hitherto unknown island of Penang, where we were met at the Airport by the Assistant District Grand Master W Bro Dr Goh and Mrs Goh and representatives of the Royal Prince of Wales Lodge, No 1555. Our hotel was some way out of the city but our hosts looked after us most assiduously and we were shown all the sights including a tour round the island—and still had some time for relaxation in the hotel garden and beach. On 1 November I attended the Lodge where there was a second degree and the elections, all carried out most efficiently. The Lodge Secretary W Bro Ho added to his kindnesses by getting our suit cases which were succumbing to constant air travel made safe, and we travelled thereafter with greater confidence. A short flight brought us to Singapore where the rest of the District Grand Lodge executive, or so it seemed, met us. We had a quiet Sunday night dinner with the District Grand Master and Mrs Eu, the Deputy District Grand Master and Mrs Buckeridge, W Bros Yeo and Caulfield.

2 November

In Singapore I again had two Masonic meetings as well as a pleasant succession of less formal ones, while my wife was ceaselessly entertained also. Lodge Singapore, No 7178, did an excellent initiation and Mount Calvary in the East RC Chapter enthroned their new sovereign impeccably but spoilt things so far as a very weary visitor was concerned by an unconscionable delay between chapter and dinner having photographs taken by the only incompetent photographer I met in seven months. Finally I retired, undined and probably unregretted by the Chapter, and was very kindly taken back to the hotel by W Bro Parker, a former District Grand Secretary.

5 November

Anyone who has attended Charity Festivals assiduously for over thirty years will know how consistently generous the Hong Kong and the Far East and the Eastern Archipelago have been since their resurrection in 1946, and doubtless pre-war too: their generosity is surpassed only by their hospitality and the efficiency of their organization and of the work in their Lodges and Chapters; we were very sorry to see the last of them. A short flight took us to Rangoon, where I was the first visitor of any great standing since the 1930s. Consequently both sides tended to be surprise packets.

The Ambassador and Lady Booth had most kindly offered to put us up, and we were delightfully entertained: not only that, but they also entertained two parties of Burmese Masons, to drinks and two nights later to dinner. I am sure that this must have made a deep and lasting impression on the District. For us it was sheer delight to be away from the hotel existence for a few days after three months and more of it.

We were shown the Shwedaung Pagoda one day, and taken to the Peace Centre and the Malami Pagoda on the next. I had a long and useful conference at the Masonic Hall with W Bro Htoon the District Grand Secretary: in spite of, or perhaps because of, the isolation in which it has been for so long the District has preserved its individuality and has been much less permeated by change and the influence of other Constitutions than is generally the case abroad. A succession of strong and able District Grand Masters, well supported lower down, has obviously won for the Craft the appreciation of the government in spite of its contacts with an outside body, the Grand Lodge in London, and it has continued quite unabashed when most foreign-oriented bodies have had to close down. The Craft should be grateful to RW Bros Lao Htin Si, Louk Choon Foung, Chan Cheng Hock, and now Saw William Paw.

8 November

We left the Embassy, Rangoon, and Burma of which we had been able to see so little in three days, with deep regret. A short flight via Calcutta took us to Kathmandu where the Lodge, though in an independent country, is under the jurisdiction of the District Grand Lodge of Bengal.

STAGE FOUR: NEPAL, INDIA, AND SRI LANKA

In the original planning stage when corresponding with the various Districts I had tried to make it clear that it would be nice to visit not only the main centres but also Lodges on the periphery. In 1968 we had been with RW Bro Forwood up into Assam where he held a District Grand Lodge: on this occasion I suggested Kathmandu and Kanpur (formerly Cawnpore) for the same reason.

Accordingly we arrived in Nepal where we were met at the Airport by W Bro Maj Binks, a serving officer attached to the Gurkha Depot and Bro Manekshaw: Bro Binks was Master and Bro Manekshaw it transpired, was about to be elected to that office. The Lodge owes much to the efforts of W Bro Qualtrough, one of the few 'permanents' in Kathmandu, and it is easy to see that it might have foundered without him. Anyhow a very adequate second degree ceremony was put on in unusual surroundings which we all had a hand in turning into a Lodge Room. On the social side the meeting was followed by an even more than usually multi-racial gathering with every kind of dietary complication: but it was a thoroughly enjoyable function, typical of a location far out in the Masonic wilds and with little chance of welcoming visitors. The next day, being Sunday, we were shown round the Capital by Maj Binks and were able to appreciate the variety of cultures, and later taken with his family to a picnic in the country from which we enjoyed glorious views of the Himalayas. We were subsequently very kindly entertained by the British Ambassador and Mrs Dawson.

After two nights of mountain air and a certain amount of worry between the various airlines we emplaned for Calcutta. Here we lived up at once to our reputation for causing power cuts, though I think the Calcutta supply has no need of adventitious aids to break down. W Bro Banks and Mrs Banks gave us the kindest possible hospitality throughout our stay. The following evening, after an enjoyable lunch at the Bengal Club where the District Grand Master, RW Bro A. M. Adams was the host, we were guests of honour at an open air party in the Banks' house and garden at which speeches and presentations were made.

12 November A District Grand Lodge meeting of a formal nature was held in conjunction with a regular meeting of Star in the East Lodge No 67, which can honourably share with the Dorsetshire Regiment the title 'Primus in Indis': Brother Barnes presided, and there was a very competently performed initiation ceremony. I attended Unity RA Chapter the following evening for an exaltation, again well done. I had previously spent some time at the District Grand Lodge office while my wife was escorted by Mrs Banks to the Salvation Army, where very similar work to that of Mother Theresa but without the same degree of publicity is carried on, and to St Mary's Old People's Home for old Anglo-Indian ladies: we joined up for a lunch at a Restaurant where W Bro Poladian, the Deputy District Grand Master, was our host on a dry and meatless day, which notwithstanding allowed us a tasty meal.

We left Calcutta where the creature discomforts of intermittent light and ventilation were far outweighed by the warmth of welcome from our oldest District Grand Lodge headquarters and the members of the fraternity generally. Our next port of call was reached by night train in company with the District Authorities (it was not a dry day, or perhaps trains do not count as in the good old days of the bona fide traveller in Scotland). We reached Kanpur after a short night (5 am) where we were met by W Bro and Mrs Trickler who took us to their home and firmly sent us back to bed. There was a convocation of Harmony and Fidelity Chapter, No 438 at midday followed by lunch al fresco at the Tricklers' home. After this it was almost at once time to prepare for the Lodge meeting and the inevitable photograph where the photographer had to compete against a setting sun (no Joshua he!) and only just won. The Lodge Building in its compound is one of the oldest in the city and the only European one to escape destruction in 1857: it has preserved numerous treasures and is altogether one of the most interesting I visited. The afterproceedings consisted of a mixed gathering under a *shalimar* in the compound and in the refectory, so everyone had a good opportunity of seeing a most interesting Masonic survival. We were due to leave Bengal District for Northern India the following day, but not till late, and so had a tour round Kanpur (instead of the usual power failure the Stubbs's were greeted here with an outbreak of communal violence and a curfew) seeing a magnificent modern Hindu Temple and views of the Ganges from the Clubhouse of the local Golf Club. It was again a short and easy flight, saddened by having to say Goodbye to our hosts from the District and on a shorter term of hospitality the Tricklers who had put themselves to an infinity of trouble on our behalf.

We were met at New Delhi Airport by His Highness of Faridkot, the District Grand Master and his Deputy W Bro Sehgal, and taken to very comfortable quarters in his palace and to an evening party in his private appartments where we met an interesting cross-section of the District and others. The following day, after sightseeing with His Highness and a pleasant lunch with the Regional Grand Master, Indian Constitution RW Bro Saitaram Jaipuria, I went to a meeting of Kitchener Lodge, No 2998, which had been moved by dispensation to coincide with my visit. W Bro Mukundan was very competently installed as the 78th Master. I had hoped it might be possible to attend a Lodge Meeting outside Delhi (eg at Simla) having been to Amritsar in 1968, but this was ruled out as impracticable: instead His Highness arranged for us to go by road first to Agra which we enjoyed just as much on a second visit, particularly as we stayed the night, and to Gwalior with which I have family associations. It is quite unnecessary to dilate on Agra, but at Gwalior where we were shown round by Brigadier Sant Singh; the city was very much *en fête* as the day was astrologically propitious for weddings. We were shown the vast fort with its seven miles of fortifications and a remarkable statue of the Ranee of Jhansi who had perished during the fighting of 1857/8. Although it is a small District it was an active one, and His Highness takes much care and trouble over it. He was more than kind in his hospitality and when he said Goodbye to us in Delhi we felt that we were leaving an old friend. We were now due to fly into Bombay District where RW Bro Shroff had organized a District Grand Lodge meeting at Jabalpur, a place well known to me by name over the years as the Indian Signal Training Centre.

20 November

We were met at the Airport by a large deputation of the District, garlanded, and taken off to an Army guest house where we were to unpack and catch up with our mail. There followed a half yearly District Grand Lodge, such as RW Bro Shroff usually holds outside Bombay in order to give the more distant brethren a chance of attending. Our train to Bombay was not due the next day till the evening so we were taken to see the gorge and marble cliffs which are quite as remarkable as the Roxburgh gorge in the Clutha River to which I have referred earlier.

After another comfortable night in a train we reached Bombay, rather late, about midday and were taken to the Yacht Club which was to be our home for the next few days. Several functions had been arranged including a cocktail party at the Masonic Hall on Sunday evening which was enjoyable and interesting as there was such a variation of guests from those we had been meeting in Eastern and Northern India. On Monday the District Grand Master himself installed W Bro H.J. Ranina as Master of the Lions Lodge, No 7713, and I gave the address to the Master. We both took full advantage of a relatively long stay (three nights) in Bombay to get ourselves organized again and to do some Christmas shopping, and were greatly assisted in this by Mrs Jaggor and by the generous loan of his car by W Bro Gilbert the Deputy District Grand Master. Without it and the very helpful driver we would have done much less in much longer time. Bro Gilbert entertained us to a dinner on the one free evening and saw us off to Madras at the end of our stay. It was certainly no fault of his that we both caught colds on the way—indeed he told us that the next time he flew in an airbus the same happened to him owing to a quirk in the ventilation system.

25 November

An old friend W Bro Krishna Rav, PAGDC, then District Grand Secretary, met us at the airport and took us to the Connemara Hotel: the District Grand Master, RW Bro G. S. Gill, also an old friend was in hospital and not well enough to see visitors, but Mrs Gill had arranged a family breakfast party at the Madras Club which we enjoyed very much. I next addressed the Acacia Study Circle on the progress of Royal Arch Masonry since 1947, almost inaudibly as I had lost my voice. After lunch with the Study Circle there was a brief period of rest before a regular meeting of the Archibald Campbell Lodge, No 4998, which had an ambitious programme of first and second degrees. Masons and ladies alike then foregathered in the Lodge Refectory, and we were delighted to find among them Mrs Tara Cherian who had been our hostess at Raj Bhavan in Bombay in 1968. The ladies were for the first time ever allowed to see the Lodge Room, and though their interest in it considerably delayed the serving of dinner I am sure that it was very well worthwhile.

We made an early start from Madras for Cochin on the west coast with Bro Rav and Bro Chelappa who succeeded him as District Grand Secretary. Met on our arrival by W Bro S. S. Koder the Deputy District Grand Master, and a dozen of both the Masonic and Jewish communities, the latter sadly shrunk in numbers after some 1,500 years. We were shown over Old Cochin with its temples, palace, synagogue, and Church of St Francis. The Cochin Lodge, No 4359, met in the evening for an initiation, followed by a mixed gathering from which we excused ourselves after an eighteen hour day. This was followed the next morning by a tour on water of the extensive and complicated (and largely man-made) harbour and island system; in the evening W Bro and Mrs Koder entertained a large and interesting party to meet us. It was a very good cross section of the Cochin community and we were very pleased to meet what was to us again a completely different set of people, even though by then the airbus colds were at their worst.

29 November   Our last complete day in India was occupied with a flight to Trivandrum, still accompanied by Bros Rav and Chelappa: we said Goodbye to Cochin with deep regret as it had proved to be a beautiful as well as a welcoming place of which Bro and Mrs Koder were for us the brightest lights. Trivandrum, just as friendly, was a very different place but we had little time to enjoy it as I had to prepare almost at once for a meeting of Minchin Lodge, No 2710, preceded by the usual race with darkness for a group photograph. The other Lodges in the neighbourhood had been invited to attend, so it was a large gathering that I addressed, a little less inaudibly than on the previous day, after an eloquent speech of welcome from the Master, W Bro Manomohan. My wife also addressed the large number who remained to dine with their ladies.

The flight to Sri Lanka did not leave till the afternoon, so we were taken to the beach at Coralam where we enjoyed a delightful tropical bathe with Bro Chelappa. It was a pleasant ending to a short three weeks in the subcontinent, during which we had travelled extensively, attended a variety of meetings in widely differing surroundings, and always met with friendly companionship and a wealth of Masonic feeling.

The flight to Colombo Airport was short and uneventful when with the help of Bro Chelappa and some of the Trivandrum brethren who were on duty at the

2 December

airport we had managed to get ourselves through the exit formalities—less exacting there than at Delhi twelve years earlier.

The District Grand Master RW Bro C. M. F. Jennings was at the airport and drove us into Colombo where W Bro Jilla was waiting at our hotel. We all had a pleasant and relaxed dinner at the Mount Lavinia Hotel. The District had very kindly arranged a tour of the island's antiquities by road under the escorting care of the District Grand Master. So after a day in Colombo in the course of which I attended Adams Peak, the one Rose Croix Chapter in the island, we set out for Anuradhapura and Polonnaruwa where we spent a night, thence to Sigiriya, Dambula, and Kandy where on the following day we visited the Masonic Hall which is in excellent condition. Unfortunately I saw nothing more in a formal way of Masonry in the island, rather less indeed than during a summer holiday spent there a couple of years earlier, but travelling with the District Grand Master was a liberal education in itself about the state of Masonry and its problems. On our return to Colombo after a thoroughly enjoyable trip, made much more interesting by Bro Jennings expert knowledge, we went to a farewell party at the Victoria Masonic Hall prior to catching the midnight plane to Africa: this was rather an anticlimax as the British Airways aircraft was having hydraulic trouble with the result that after being on board for some hours we were removed to an excellent local hotel for what little remained of the night. That afternoon we got off and after some hesitation in the Seychelles we eventually made Johannesburg soon after midnight on the 6/7 December instead of at first light on the 6th: it was virtually the only flight in seven months that did not go according to plan. Our stop at Johannesburg had never been meant to be anything more than a staging point, and our real sojourn in South Africa was still a month away. However the District had already begun to take care of us, and I am afraid that Bro Dixon had had many weary hours of waiting for us. When we did eventually arrive he got us in double quick time to our hotel near the airport for a few hours rest. Later that morning the District Grand Master RW Bro E. T. Ablett came to collect us for the flight to Salisbury.

STAGE FIVE: CENTRAL AFRICA

We were greeted on arrival by two members of the High Commissioner's Staff and, later, outside the customs area by the District Grand Master, RW Bro Dr Wright and Mrs Wright, and by the Deputy District Grand Master W Bro E. K. Hutchings and Mrs Hutchings, who took us to Meikles Hotel. Dr Wright produced, almost like a conjurer, a much needed bottle of cough mixture.

7 December

We got ourselves organized in the course of the morning, and I paid a call on the High Commissioner before we both went to a lunch party of the leading Masons of Salisbury with their ladies. In the evening an emergency meeting of Federation Lodge, No 7363, had been called for my benefit, and a candidate for passing had been borrowed from Ellis Robins Lodge, No 8136: meanwhile my wife was being entertained by the local ladies at a performance of Alice in Wonderland and Through the Looking Glass.

The next day was very agreeably spent in Salisbury, in the course of which a lunch party had been arranged for me to meet the senior Rose Croix Masons and the Sovereigns of the three Chapters one of whom had made the long journey from Bulawayo. In the evening there was a delightful party given in a private house and garden by the two members of the High Commission. We were now beginning to realize that Christmas was approaching as the shops were decorated and there was a general air of festivity. The District had arranged matters so well that I had a chance of meeting almost all the active Masons in and around Salisbury and many from much further away. A change in flight timing meant that

10 December

we had virtually the whole of the next day in Zimbabwe, during which Dr and Mrs Wright took us out to Lake MacIlwaine by way of a snake farm and a bird sanctuary. We were seen off as we had been met on arrival by Bros Cox and Broadfoot as well as by the District authorities.

The flight to Lusaka was a short one, but in spite of the failure of the postal service to deliver our programme some months earlier (in Zimbabwe too as we found out later, though it had not transpired at the time) the District turned out in force to meet us. The hotel arrangements had collapsed—if indeed they had ever existed— and W Bro Peter Radford and Mrs Radford very kindly put us up overnight before we proceeded to Livingstone, on the border between Zambia and Zimbabwe. I was very glad to be able to attend Victoria Falls Lodge, No 5327, in the evening as I knew what a rough time it had been having during the virtual closure of the frontier: it was an excellent meeting, and I was left in no doubt that the Lodge had weathered the storm. We were both very pleased to be able to see the Victoria Falls (from both sides) as we had been foiled on two previous visits to Central Africa: as it was we had two distinct views, from Livingstone where our hotel was within sound of the Falls, and by dint of passing the frontier from the rain forest too. The District Grand Master, RW Bro MacDonald and Mrs MacDonald and W Bro and Mrs Thornberry looked after us most admirably both there and in Lusaka, to which we returned in the evening just in time for a party given by W Bro Scher and Mrs Scher: we were again housed by the Radfords and had rather more time to appreciate their house and garden. Our

13 December

departure for Nairobi was a little delayed (lunch at 6 pm on the plane) but it was a comfortable flight and we found many old friends awaiting us at the new airport. Sunday was in every sense a day of rest and by Monday we were quite ready to face, as it turned out, a complete change of programme caused by the Nigerian High Commission refusing visas on the ground that when wanting to enter Nigeria we would have been in South Africa: Ghana and Sierra Leone made no objection except that the latter could find no room to stamp my passport and I had to get a new one which our own High Commission produced in 45 minutes. In fact the next two days were mostly spent in trying to organize a new set of dates from one side of Africa to another and we were exceptionally lucky in having W Bro and Mrs Hollister's beautiful and peaceful home as a base for

18 December

operations. We had been invited also to stay with RW Nevill and Mrs Nevill and later on with W Bro Mauladad, the Deputy District Grand Master and Mrs Mauladad. While with the Nevills I went in twice to Nairobi to attend a meeting of Lodge Harmony, No 3084, which was doing a second degree and on the next evening the Namirembe RC Chapter which too had a ceremony: the latter is a refugee from Uganda but has settled down. In both of them I encountered several old friends as members or visitors.

22 December

The District realizing that we were going to be in

Kenya over Christmas had made us a very generous present of a week at the Mount Kenya Safari Club which is on the equator and 7,000 feet above sea level. We reached it by car on the 22nd and had a delightful relaxed holiday from which the trouble and toil of getting to West Africa seemed very distant. Our sole engagement during the week was an al fresco lunch party organized in our honour by the Mount Kenya Lodge, No 5638, at W Bro Halstead's farm quite a bit higher than the Club: W Bro Wright from Nanyuki drove us there and back pointing out many objects of interest on the way.

30 December   At the end of our rest at the Club the Hollisters collected us to take us to the Samburu Game Park where we spent two nights and the intervening day and saw a wide variety of game. We spent New Year's Eve there but the jollification was sadly diminished by the news of the bomb attack on the Norfolk Hotel in Nairobi, about which the wildest rumours began to circulate.

We returned to Nairobi on New Year's Day by way of Outspan Lodge and a visit to Lord and Lady Baden-Powell's grave, and left early the next morning for the
2 January   Republic of South Africa being seen off by W Bro Alex Smith the District Grand Secretary, who had already borne the brunt of our earlier search for visas. We had spent almost a month between the three Districts and though because of the Christmas break I had not been able to attend very many meetings we had met a considerable number of Masons and their families, and had enjoyed a great deal of kindness and hospitality in each of the three.

STAGE SIX: SOUTH AFRICA

Though we visited all seven Districts in South Africa (in the geographical sense) we did not take them in direct sequence and on several occasions retraced our steps: it will be simpler to recount our month's visit in date order, making it clear in which District we were at any particular time. Suffice is to say that both Johannesburg and Cape Town, particularly the former, were the centres from which we set out on several occasions. It will be no surprise to any Mason who has travelled in those Districts to know that we were overwhelmed with attention wherever we went and treated with outstanding generosity. We were met at the Airport again by Bro Dixon and in the VIP Lounge by the District Grand Master and Mrs Ablett and several others. Our headquarters in the Transvaal was the Sunnyside Park Hotel at Johannesburg already well known from our stay there two years previously: we returned to it several times and always found it comfortable and welcoming—and conveniently sited for the Masonic Hall. We spent a happy and reminiscent evening with W Bro Lief Egeland, PJGD, and Mrs Egeland (he had been a law don at Brasenose in my early days, and present at my initiation). We were taken there by W Bro John Garvey and Mrs Garvey. Bro Garvey was the author of an important report on Transvaal Charitable Funds, and had played a large part in the Secretariat of the Conference of District Grand Masters held by the Pro Grand Master in Pretoria in 1978. The following day saw us driving with the Abletts to Swaziland to attend the St George's Lodge, No 8322 at Mbabane. The Lodge which was then just over ten years old was flourishing and produced a good initiation ceremony: it is much indebted for its success to W Bro Treadway, who kindly brought us up to date the next day with our gamma globulin injections before showing us an outstandingly well equipped clinic and taking us for a drive in the countryside. After a late lunch we drove back to Johannesburg (150 miles each way) for a quiet evening in preparation for our next journey: this was by courtesy of the District and took us on the Blue Train down to Cape Town. Much has been written of this famous route and I will only say that it quite lived up to our expectations. We had as fellow travellers RW Bro McIntyre, Past District Grand Master for South Africa, Western Division, and Mrs McIntyre, and were greeted at Kimberley by the District Grand Master for South Africa, Central Division, and Mrs Evans of whom we saw a lot later on. It was a superb journey, the last and probably the best part of it in beautiful weather.

6 January   We were met at Cape Town by members of the District of South Africa, Western Division, and taken to our hotel to the west of the City: for the evening a reception had been arranged to include representatives of all the Cape Town and neighbouring Lodges at the new, and very impressive, Masonic Hall. We were greeted formally by the Deputy District Grand Master W Bro Gordon Allerton (the District Grand Master lives over 200 miles away and we were going to meet him nearer his home ground): we tried not altogether successfully to have a word with everybody, and hope that they enjoyed the party as much as we did. After a morning of administrative details we were taken over to Simonstown for the Centenary of Phoenix Lodge, No 1860, where I presented what must have been about the last last centenary warrant to bear my signature. Bro Price took us there and back, and varied the route on our return so that we got an excellent view of Cape Town by night from the high ground.

8 January

We interrupted our stay in South Africa, Western Division, to fly to South West Africa: we were met at the new airport (very different from 1964) at Windhoek by RW Bro Glen Smith the District Grand Master and Mrs Smith: we were shown the Masonic Hall, victim of a recent bomb attack, and then taken to the Ex-Servicemens' Club where a number of Masons and their wives had gathered. The next day afforded us a journey of outstanding interest across the mountains and desert to Swakopmund: space will not permit recounting it in full details, but we saw a great variety of wild life, had a splendid *braii*, lost one of the five cars for some time, while another punctured its petrol tank and had it repaired with soap! The following day I attended the Welwitschia Lodge, No 8768, named after a remarkable desert plant which has managed to survive in inhospitable desert conditions for centuries: the meeting was some distance away at Walvis Bay, though the subsequent dinner was held rather closer to Swakopmund at the Social Club of the local mines. (I persuaded my wife to make the speech of thanks.) Our two days in South West Africa

11 January

came to an end when the District Grand Master saw us, not without difficulty, on to a plane for Cape Town: it had been a delightful and all too short visit, but we were able to tell ourselves that with our visit in 1964 to the north of the country we had been to every place where an English Lodge met. RW Bro Herbert Cowburn and Mrs Cowburn met us at the airport together with the District Grand Secretary and Mrs Purcell and dropped us at our hotel. The evening was occupied with a very interesting dinner party of the senior Masons of the District. Bro Cowburn was our escort along the garden route where we broke off for a meeting of St Blaize Lodge, No 1938, at Mossel Bay: during the meeting my wife was entertained at the Rectory (the Master W Bro Charlesworth being the Rector) and we all gathered there after-

14 January

wards. We moved on early to complete our journey to Port Elizabeth, leaving Western and entering Eastern

Division: soon after our arrival RW Bro Anderson and a party from the District Grand Lodge called to cement arrangements for our stay in his District: these involved a formal lunch party at the Port Elizabeth Club, a visit to the Livingstone Hospital (native) where Bro Anderson is in charge of a comprehensive rebuilding operation, and which we both found extremely interesting, a meeting of the Lodge of Good Hope, No 863, whose agenda seemed to consist almost solely of an address by myself: it was a real pleasure to meet RW Bros Leo Simmons, OSM, and Owen Eaton and their wives again after the meeting. Outside of Port Elizabeth a day trip to Grahamstown and Port Alfred was scheduled: this made a long but pleasant day through beautiful scenery quite apart from visiting two old and interesting Masonic centres. A farewell dinner for over thirty at the St George's Club was a relaxed ending to a happy visit.

17 January

We next flew to Bloemfontein, to go thence by road to Ladybrand, Orange Free State where the District Grand Master, RW Bro A. L. du Plooy was to install W Bro Burkill as Master of Sir John Brand Lodge, No 3035: it was a hot meeting, well conducted but with every possible complication and frill. The Lodge had been in low water, but was reviving very largely with the help of the Maseru Lodge, No 2835, which had temporarily moved out of Lesotho to Ladybrand. The next day before going to Bloemfontein, we went into Lesotho to see and informally declare open the admirable premises which the Masonic brethren had built themselves after losing the temple I had visited in 1964. Following the opening there was an excellent hot lunch put together by the local ladies. Bros Moore and Burkill saw us back through immigration and drove us to Bloemfontein for a short night's stop before being driven by Bro Swart to Kimberley in South Africa, Central Division. I attended a crowded meeting of the Richard Giddy Lodge, No 1574, where a third degree was well done: the rest of our time in Kimberley was mostly spent with R. W. Bro and Mrs Evans, both experts in the history of the place: we were shown the De Beers diamond sorting department, the Mine Museum, and the following morning the Bantu Museum.

The flight to Durban was a rough one but improved after changing planes very hurriedly at Johannesburg. We were met on arrival by W Bro N. C. Pooke the Deputy District Grand Master, and Bro James Dow who drove us in state to our hotel. We spent the evening with old army friends, and the next morning after a tour of Durban with a former pupil and his family. The Addington Lodge, No 1937, had a second degree on its agenda which was admirably and simply done.

23 January

The Pookes took us by a long and interesting drive through the mountains and the Natal Lion Park to Pietermaritzburg: by this time we had picked up with RW Bro Bernard Armitage District Grand Master for Natal and with W Bro Harris and his wife. A large gathering of over 200 was held at the Agricultural Ground's hall in the evening, the entertainment being provided by some local nurses who sang beautifully and a mass of Zulu dancers from the Dunlop Factory. We got back late to Durban through bad weather which persisted through the next day which I spent visiting the Old People's Home at Park Rynie and a meeting of the Kokstad RC Chapter, on the edge of the Transkei where we were joined by Bro Armitage: on the way back late at night we passed through a spectacular series of thunder and rain storms. My wife meanwhile had remained in Durban where she was hospitably entertained by the Pookes and W Bro Gray, Master of Addington Lodge, and Mrs Gray.

25 January

We left Durban for Johannesburg where we were met by W Bro Douglas Vieler and later taken to a Sunday evening party at the Abletts to meet the Executive Officers of the District and members of the Ablett family in cheerful and informal surroundings. In 1964 I had consecrated Alchemy Lodge, No 7956, with the help as Director of Ceremonies of RW Bro Leslie Hinett, till recently District Grand Master: a third degree was done quite admirably, and I was pleased to see not only what progress had been made but also a number of the founders. The next day we again left the Transvaal for a short time to spend twenty-four hours in Botswana: there are two English Lodges in that vast and rapidly developing area, one at Selebi Pikwe, No 8715, under the District Grand Lodge of Zambia and the other at Gaborone, No 8781, directly under Freemasons' Hall. It was this one that I visited and saw Bro J. D. Wragge initiated. We flew over in a chartered Cessna with W Bro Merton Freeman, now the Deputy District Grand Master and himself an experienced pilot. We were most hospitably entertained by W Bro and Mrs Hampshire in their home which got more and more full of guests as the evening

29 January

wore on. Gaborone is rapidly becoming a centre of the diamond industry and it was most interesting to us, having seen the processing in Kimberley, to see the differences of personnel and techniques. We returned, just dodging some very bad weather, the next morning in time for me to address the Lyceum Lodge of Research, No 8682, on 'The formation and operation of Grand Lodges' with special reference to those that I had been in contact with during the previous six months. The meeting was followed by a formal dinner complete with toastmaster. Once more we were able to enjoy Sunnyside Park Hotel for one night before being driven 250 miles to the extreme north of the District to attend Pietersburg United Lodge, No 2485, our last meeting in South Africa and one of the best attended. It was particularly pleasant to find RW Bro Vic Peterson, Past District Grand Master for Zambia, at the meeting and to hear about his family whom we had met in Zambia when the District Grand Lodge was inaugurated in 1967. The installation went with a swing and so did the afterproceedings. We started back early the next morning, reached Johannesburg in time for lunch, packed, said Goodbye at the Hall, and emplaned for Nairobi, as a step in the direction of West Africa.

It will be seen that we spent just four weeks in South Africa: it was a busy and most enjoyable period. The Districts in South Africa probably suffer less than those in other parts of the world from a constantly changing membership and this is reflected in the administration which is almost always immaculate and in the Lodge work, which is much less pervaded with 'foreign' customs. Though the distances are vast and there are fuel restrictions which make weekend meetings a matter of careful logistics, the Lodges manage to get good numbers of official and private visitors.

STAGE SEVEN: WEST AFRICA

An undue proportion of our time both in Nairobi in December and intermittently in South Africa had been taken up with, first and uselessly, trying to keep out tryst with Nigeria, and secondly trying to superimpose an alternative plan that would upset as little as possible the arrangements made with the other two Districts. It was cardinal in any case that we should enter West Africa

Farewell Tour

from East and not South: eventually Ethiopian Airlines produced a flight on the right day to Ghana, and we decided to throw ourselves on the mercy and goodwill of the District, hoping that we would more easily sort out our plans for Sierra Leone from there. RW Bro Sackey who met us at the airport took the change of plan with complete calm: he had arranged for us to say in the first instance with W Bro Gordon Hyde, and later with W Bro Hans Roth-Kwafo and Mrs Roth-Kwafo who were old friends from 1975.

1 February

This Sunday was a real day of rest: we went to matins at the United Church with the Sackeys, but were virtually non-persons as we were not expected to be in Accra at all and Dr Sackey insisted, very kindly, in keeping everything unofficial: much the same applied to Monday when it transpired that no plane was leaving for Freetown. We were most kindly entertained by VW Bro Barnes and Mrs Barnes as well as Bro Hyde and had an early night in the expectation of an early start for

3 February

Sierra Leone. This actually happened and we reached our destination as we, if no one else, expected. We were

JWS and RKTS being welcomed by RW Bro Dr Sackey, District Grand Master for Ghana, in the official flat in State House, Accra, November 1975.

met by the District Grand Secretary W Bro A. Z. Beckley at the airport and by the District Grand Master RW Bro Cole at the ferry: the rest of the day passed in a flash. After a late lunch I was already late for the District Grand Lodge meeting which preceded a well attended Foundation Stone laying in the open air as dusk fell. It had been well prepared beforehand and in spite of, or possibly because of, the encircling gloom it went well and after the formal closing of Grand Lodge was followed by an enjoyable dinner. Reveille 5.45 am in Accra, lights out 11.30 pm in Freetown had made it a long day, particularly as it was far from clear how and when we would get back on course for our official visit to Ghana. W Bro Solomon Pratt, PAGDC took a great deal of time which he could ill spare from his ministerial duties, and all his ingenuity to find a method. It meant that unfortunately we had to leave Freetown a day earlier and go by way of Dakar—rather like going from London to Cornwall by way of Inverness! However, by great efforts all round our tickets were changed and we even had time for a very pleasant and restful lunch with the High Commissioner and Mrs Morgan in their beautiful house on the high ground behind the city.

Our stay in Dakar was interesting for being so unlike anything else we had seen of West Africa. However, we were very glad to arrive back in Accra late, but ready for what had originally been arranged. This entailed going by road the next day to Kumasi to attend the installation meeting of the Asanteman Lodge, No 8351. It was a long journey pleasantly interrupted by calls on Eastern Lodge, No 8930, at Koforidua for 'elevenses' and Okwawuman Lodge, No 8754, at Abetifi where Bro Dr Quinus Aldo entertained the party to lunch. We thus arrived at Kumasi, where we were kindly put up at the Brewery Guest House by W Bro and Mrs Beasley, in time for the meeting which went well enough though lasting longer than a similar one would at home: the afterproceedings though long also were well conducted.

7 February

The Asantahene had kindly bidden us call upon him the next morning and we spent half an hour with him, the more interesting because he was about to fly to England in connection with the Ashanti Exhibition which we visited ourselves in London soon after our return. The journey to Accra was direct and we were welcomed back by the Roths with an excellent lunch and a much needed siesta. A special meeting of the District Grand Lodge was held in the evening culminating in a dinner at the Ambassador Hotel: this was in the strict Masonic sense the finale of our tour, and a very suitable one as we had made so many good friends in Ghana.

8 February   Four days however remained before we left the country and they were fully occupied with sightseeing and unofficial meetings which included on Sunday a lunch party given by the Circle Lodge, No 8964, which was televised and subsequently played back to us. On Monday we visited the Castle and met the Vice President W Bro Graft-Johnson who subsequently entertained us to a magnificent lunch party. Then to tea with the Deputy High Commissioner and Mrs James; thence to an evening party at the Sackey's home with several members of the family and a number of senior Masons. On our previous visit we had been taken to see the Volta Dam and we were now shown the next stage, nearly completed, which will double the electric output.

11 February   Our final day was spent in a little sightseeing, a round of farewells, packing, and enjoying the company of the Roth-Kwafos. Our second visit to Ghana will remain a happy memory of well attended Lodges with excellent ritual but even more of good fellowship and friendliness: it was a very nice way of bringing a long tour to a close.

Not without some difficulty we had transferred ourselves to Lufthansa in order to get to our next port of call which was a few days acclimatization in Portugal: had we been able to go to Nigeria we were safely booked in for a flight via Madrid, but in fact went rather more comfortably and just as quickly via Frankfurt. After nearly a week at Cascais we were quite ready to take the

17 February   final flight home and after an uneventful journey found W Bro Ivor Gregory waiting for us—I almost added as usual—just as he had seen us off on 23 July.

It would be difficult to sum up on paper or to say what we or I had found best or worst in those seven months, and I have often been asked that question. There were so many and so greatly different aspects that it would be unfair to particularize: what I can say, however, without fear of contradiction is that the English Craft overseas is flourishing and in good heart. With the improvement of conditions and in speed of travel there can now be much better interrelations between Districts and between Grand Lodge and its Districts. I am inclined to think that though it may be desirable to attach an official visit to the celebration of some great occasion such as an Installation of a District Grand Master, the Dedication of a Temple, or even a Lodge Bicentenary a more useful purpose is generally served by touring the outling areas and visits to private Lodges in their normal circumstances. I was very fortunate that both these different types came my way, as well as the prime object which was to sign off as Grand Secretary and to say goodbye to old friends and allies of some twenty years.

Chapter 17

Conclusion

Having started with a Chapter on my forebears it seems logical to end with the current generation, who are my contemporaries, and briefly with the next one. On the Stubbs side I must start with a statement by my grandfather Bishop Stubbs (I do not quote it exactly) that it is a curious dispensation of providence that we tend to dislike our relatives more than anyone else, and a piece of kindly advice inherited from my youngest uncle Sir Edward. 'If you have nothing pleasant to say about someone say nothing': his three children are sadly all dead but we are in touch with the offspring and are always glad to see them: Laurence my father's elder brother had four children, of whom the three boys are alive and well, whilst his daughter, who as so often happens was the real expert on family affairs which she was always able to expound with a mixture of charity and malice, died recently, leaving a son whom I have not seen since his schooldays: Bill, the eldest, is living beside his daughter in Dorset, and last Christmas I was delighted to meet his great grandchildren for the first time. His grandson, Julian Brazier followed me to Brasenose and now has his walls covered with the college prints I had collected over many years. John with his wife Kay settled in County Waterford when the Indian Civil Service packed up on partition: but she died after some years of ill health though we do see John on our rare visits to Ireland, and his sons on various family occasions. Miles, the youngest, who was contemporary with me at Oxford, also settled for Ireland when the Sudan Civil Service similarly packed up; and his son Patrick, when I last saw him, was Master of his Lodge in Cork.

My brother Tom remained a bachelor, spending his working life as a master at Clifton apart from war service as a government chemist. He was a universal godfather, one of his godchildren paying him the unusual compliment of asking him to be godfather to her daughter. He died quite recently leaving an irreplaceable gap, for there being only some 16 months between us we had almost identical memories of the past. My younger brother Hugh who was already featured as having been born at Kilravock became a classics don after the war at Exeter University. He married Ljubiça Dzodan a delightful Jugoslav whom we all welcomed into the family, particularly my mother: and they have a son and daughter, named respectively Thomas and Kitty. Thomas has shown a great flair for computers (one cannot but wonder whether like most Stubbses that is the only way he can add and subtract) and works for London University:

Kitty has trained as a multi-lingual secretary—Serbian being an innate extra—and should be able to and make good use of the languages. We often see two of the Feaver children and their families, the eldest of whom, though female had followed family footsteps to Keble, while the rest are still growing up in South London. We are particularly attached to the younger girl Liz and her family, and I try to time my visits to the Apollo so as to go first to see them at Woodstock.

Hugh and Alison have practically rebuilt the old home in Rowan Road, and their two children, George and Phoebe went straight to it from the maternity ward as their father had done in 1946.

Bishop Stubbs's 11 children, of whom admittedly only three ever married, have currently six in the next generation still surviving. Richenda's family was as large, her father being the eldest of ten, all but two of whom married: Their survivors, our generation that is to say, number 16. So when one gets down to the next generation there is a widespread cousinhood, and even that does not take into account the Popes, the Roses and the Bigges with whom this book began.

It is generally accepted that nature abhors a vacuum, and I have already explained how I personally found much to do in the Masonic sphere in the five years since I retired: these activities did to a limited extent keep me informed at a gossip level with what was going on in the wider field of Masonry both at home and overseas. I was often talked and written to by the Provincial and District Grand Masters with whom I had so to speak grown up in Masonry, but their numbers diminished by death and, increasingly, by resignation as the accent on youth was maintained. I was able by other means also to remain a ringside observer of what was going on: the effects were occasionally irritating, more often stimulating and frequently a reminder that if Masonry does not move forward it will inevitably slide backward: I found that I needed to put out of my mind the undergraduate apothegm of my Oxford contemporary, Christopher Pirie Gordon, who with his brother Patrick, has already figured in these pages—'all progress however salutary is undesirable'. When I was in office I compelled myself to think of the disadvantages as well as the advantages of any proposal: after I retired I could take a broader view as I would not be responsible for the outcome, and like a subaltern in an old fashioned Mess was expected not to speak unless spoken to.

Thus I have been able to watch the gradual unfolding of the new deal about the Masonic Charities: the increased accent on age care as exemplified by the proliferation of RMBI and other homes and the tentative approaches towards shelter and housing. Both of these fall logically into place when one realises that we, unlike so much of the Third World, are an ageing population: but that they fall logically into place does also mean that they will have to be paid for heavily and increasingly so, and that there can never hope to be enough of them to satisfy the growing need.

It needs to be constantly borne in mind that though founding enthusiasm will often produce a new establishment, paying for its running costs even with contributions from the residents will be a continuing tax upon Masonic resources: I am in a good position too from my experience of the ageing Freemasons' Hall to realise that however carefully one plans yearly schemes of renovation and replacement the time suddenly comes—and the best and wisest of us knows not how soon—when there will be a sudden and unforeseen call for capital expenditure.

The difficulties which confront those responsible for old people's homes pall into insignificance when compared to those of the Royal Masonic Hospital. Homes can be, and are, spread fairly widely over the country: they are less subject to the constant changes of technical equipment, and far less dependent on highly qualified staff: it is not too much to say that this very success as they have grown from one block of flats at Hove is largely due to the aged finding accommodation not too far away from their old surroundings, their relations and friends. In this respect too the Hospital is at a real disadvantage: no one has ever seriously suggested (to my knowledge at least) that there should be a proliferation of Hospitals similar to that of the Homes; indeed the very idea verges on the absurd. Thence it follows that the Hospital is of much more use to that part of the Masonic population that is within easy reach of it or, and this is a minor but not unimportant consideration, has no good hospitals within easy reach. This means easy reach not only for patients but also for visitors who make life for the patients so much less tedious, and who for themselves will like to know at first hand how the patients are getting on.

On the other hand I think that the comparative emptiness of the Hospital now compared with 15 years ago, of which a good deal is made is at least partially accounted for by shorter stays: it is no more than simple arithmetic that if patients stay half as long as they did, one needs twice as many to achieve the same bed occupancy. It is however equally simple economics that a half empty hospital costs nearly as much to run as a full one.

I have attended a number of Hospital meetings, but have yet to hear any convincing argument as to how the Hospital can be preserved without placing an intolerable financial burden on the Craft on behalf of a small section of its membership. I hope that the good sense of the Board will be maintained against the factious and in many cases self-centred opposition to its proposals, and that the mass of subscribers will in due course realise that financial help to prospective patients throughout the whole jurisdiction for treatment in or near their home areas is not only equitable but sensible too.

Over the years I have seen, though I have only indirectly been concerned with, the closure of three out of four of our Schools. I have also in other spheres seen how Schools designed just for one section of the community have opened their doors: I have seen the growth of coeducation culminating in male rowing blues from women's colleges and many sixth forms leavened by a proportion of girls, though I have it in my heart to be sorry for the girl's schools which they have left prematurely: the School at Rickmansworth is a good example of the door-opening process, and I doubt if there can be anyone who can sincerely say that it would be better to have the School half full with only 'petition' girls, or indeed that the two streams of entry are not mutually advantageous. I would indeed go further and be glad to see a policy not only adopted in theory but carried out in practice of reversing the general trend through the country by encouraging annual intakes of boys to use the outstanding facilities at Rickmansworth: if the school has a headmaster why not a headboy too?

I am not altogether sorry that the Charity festival system has taken on a new lease of life; if it is not overdone the competitive spirit it engenders between Province and Province keeps interest from flagging. I am not so happy however about bringing the Grand Charity into its orbit: the tangible attraction of the Homes and the School, and the personal quality of Annuitants and Out educated pupils is a great draw, but the Grand Charity has its own captive income under the *Book of Constitutions*, which Grand Lodge can raise at its discretion like any other amending action. With this sure source, because it is unthinkable that Grand Lodge would ever reduce the amount payable under its rules it is hard to see how any case could be made that would arouse the same kind of enthusiasm as the other two 'new' Charities can so readily evoke. My own hope is that this particular type of festival will be allowed gradually to lapse, and that the Grand Charity will act with its statutory income as a reservoir of funds on which the other two can call with every hope of success when an emergency arises.

Freemasonry has been through periods of stress at various times in its history: the Revolutionary Wars at the end of the eighteenth century, the Napoleonic bogy and fears of Jacobinism might well have had a fatally depressing effect; the Morgan affair in the USA nearly killed it: the antagonisms of the Papacy drove it underground and into highly undesirable courses in countries where the Papal word was law. But it has always, survived, and outlived its persecutors. Till very recently those responsible for the conduct of the affairs of the Craft, at least in the English Constitution, have taken no notice of the gibes of their enemies, thus eventually putting to 'silence the ignorance of foolish men'. The time has probably now come to fight back and to tell the world the truth about ourselves: it can certainly do no harm, though I doubt if it will produce changes of heart. It would be over optimistic to expect dramatic changes of attitude in our opponents, but as elsewhere there is a good body of 'don't knows', benevolent neutrals for whom any explanation of what Freemasonry is about can only be interesting and helpful. We should all be grateful to the Grand Master for setting this new course, and indeed the Grand Secretary for his successful debut as our radio champion.

On the other hand it must not be thought either that this present time is our first ever period of persecution, or that whatever steps are now taken it will be the last: much more notoriety and cash may be gathered from abusing the Craft, or from pretending to disclose its secrets, than by defending it. Truth tends to be dull but it has a way of prevailing in the end, and our leaders are going about it.

Finally I admit to disappointment that the penalties debate in 1964 which came down so heavily in favour of Bishop Herbert's thesis did not bear more fruit: I have already commented on this, but feel that as the whole matter is being aired again (in 1985) it will do no harm to revert to it. One of those who spoke against the Herbert resolutions was my old friend and fellow Grand Secretary (in Grand Mark Lodge) Jack Chitty: possibly under his influence there seems to have been no parallel action in the degrees controlled from Mark Masons' Hall. This too may have had some inhibiting influence on the putting into effect of the resolutions in the Craft and Royal Arch: however it is the more surprising in that 'Duke Street' with which the Mark and various other degrees are generally closely interwound on the personal if not the constitutional level gets on very well without any penalties at all.

My hope in 1964 had been that what was in effect a compromise situation based on a voluntary choice would be satisfactory to all concerned, not least to our critics outside the Craft; perhaps this was always over sanguine: possibly if the resolutions had been completely taken into use it would still have been over sanguine. Now following a suggestion (March 1985) from the Grand Master it seems likely that a new and more radical approach will be made to the problem: it will not be difficult to find precedents (for those who want them) for removing penalties completely from our obligations—though it strikes me as odd that the Mother Grand Lodge should need to find precedents from its descendants! Nor will it be difficult to devise a few paragraphs that will fit into the ceremonies and explain the reasons for their existence. What worries me, particularly in the light of 1964, is that the Craft will find itself on the horns of a dilemma if and when a meeting of Grand Lodge agrees, as it did so whole-heartedly in 1964, to a new formula. I fear that if its implementation is left to the free choice of Lodges no more will happen than did last time round: it will not only be the *vis inertiae* of the preceptors, but the retired schoolmaster remembers that those who have been fags are the keenest to retain fagging, those who have been beaten to retain corporal punishment. On the other hand a direct order to all Lodges to make the change, in whatever form it ultimately emerges, will indeed be a revolutionary step compared with which the changes leading up to the Union of 1813 would be very small beer. A law that cannot be enforced is almost by definition a bad law; but would it ever be possible to secure enforcement without an intolerable degree of supervision?

Indeed the last and greatest trial for our Grand Master, and for his immediate associates is likely to be whether they will be able to exert such powers of leadership that the whole Craft will follow them unreservedly whether a voluntary or compulsory change comes to be the decision of Grand Lodge: it is hardly conceivable that a well prepared and well thought scheme would fail to commend itself to Grand Lodge, but its implementation could be quite another matter.

At this moment the Craft seems to have run into one of those periods when every man's hand is raised against it. Perhaps this is one of the penalties of success: perhaps a little chastisement will do it no harm: in a rather different context Horace Walpole expressed his belief that nothing but a persecution will bring the Freemasons into vogue again. He was writing about a temporary eclipse, which is certainly not the case in 1985, but the principle is still the same.

APPENDICES

Appendix I

PRESTONIAN LECTURE 1982

The Government of the Craft

CONTENTS

Introduction	*page*	215
The First Tier		
The Private Lodges		216
The Second Tier		
The Provincial and District Grand Lodges		218
Lodges directly administered from Freemasons' Hall		222
The Third Tier		
The Grand Lodge		223
The Board of General Purposes		223
The Board of Benevolence		232
The Grand Lodge and the Craft		232
The Grand Mastership		233
The Pro Grand Mastership		235
The Deputy and Assistant Grand Mastership		236
The Masonic Civil Service		236
Conclusion		237
Notes		238

INTRODUCTION

Many Prestonian Lectures have started with a description of William Preston's life and works and a well-deserved eulogy: as however, with four exceptions, the first twenty-seven have been collected and reprinted—and I would here urge that the series be brought up to date with a second volume of reprints—there is little point in doing this once more. As an alternative, I am going at once to acknowledge my indebtedness to Plato's *Republic* and to two other equally non-Masonic works written by eminent historians of the last century: the *English Constitution* by Walter Bagehot which I first read as a schoolboy, and the *Constitutional History of England* by my grandfather, Bishop Stubbs of Oxford *CG, DD*, under the shadow of which I grew up.

My grandfather drew out the long thread of continuity in the development of our political institutions from the Dark Ages to the Wars of the Roses: it was an exposition of government as it developed rather than of the governed, and little would be gained by bringing his views to bear upon our private Lodges or even the higher organisations, but I would commend to close attention Bagehot's classic demonstration of the various elements of government, and in particular, his essay on checks and balances of power. I owe a debt, incurred unwillingly at the time, to Plato whose *Republic* Books 8 and 9, contain what is still the best and clearest analysis of the different types of government and leaders, of his own time and indeed of ours. But we should ask ourselves scrupulously whether Plato's classic definitions of aristocracy, oligarchy, democracy and tyranny can still be fruitfully applied: I think that they can, provided that we clear our minds of the cant definitions in vogue nowadays of these forms and relate to any consideration of Masonic Government only their original senses within the city state of the Greeks.

It would have been tempting to entitle this lecture 'The Constitution of Freemasonry at home and abroad', but I was deterred on two grounds: first, I can speak only at secondhand—good secondhand having been corresponding with other Grand Lodges consistently over the last thirty years and more—of their theory and practice; secondly 'Constitution' and its derivatives are terms of art in the Craft not bearing the same connotations as in the works I have quoted: out rules, the act of establishment associated with the ceremony of consecration of the Lodges and, in the more distant past, the actual physical authority by which power was conveyed to an individual Freemason or to a group desirous of working corporately, as a Lodge, have all pre-empted that title. However the 'Government of the Craft' is one that all should be able to understand even if, as I suspect, it does not rate very high in terms of popular interest.

Looked at from the constitutional or governmental point of view Freemasonry consists of three tiers in England, Ireland and Scotland, and in a few other parts of the world which have copied the grand originals:— these tiers are the private Lodges, the Provinces or Districts, and the

Grand Lodge. I propose as far as circumstances permit to deal with them in that order.

THE PRIVATE LODGES

The Lodge is the basic, as indeed it is the oldest, organisation in Freemasonry, and it should not be forgotten when we come to consider the power and authority of the higher bodies that at least up to 1717, and probably in remoter areas till a good deal later, Lodges were entirely self-governing. We can have no certainty (and mere speculation is of little use) how the pre-1717 Lodges governed themselves: it will be rather more profitable to move on to the mid-18th century and to consider briefly the differences between those holding from the Premier Grand Lodge and those from the Antients. The latter tended to be at least on the surface more democratic bodies as all officers instead of only Master, Treasurer and Tyler were elected. This is something which has substantially been handed down to us in our Royal Arch Chapters, and preserved in many bodies overseas that derive from the Antients. On the other hand, in the Premier Grand Lodge's constituent bodies the appointment of officers lay for the much greater part in the hands of the Master, a practice which prevailed at the Union in 1813.

The election of Master by the members is, I believe, universal practice: once elected and installed, he is responsible for his Lodge's behaviour and still more for its good name. But how does he stand in actual power? He still has the last word in the appointment of officers other than the Treasurer and the Tyler: it would however be a foolhardy Master Elect who did not go through some process of consultation with senior members, particularly if changes of consequence are envisaged. The surest route to an unhappy, and generally an unproductive year, is to disregard, and to show that this is being done intentionally, the advice of the Lodge's elder statesmen. But this said, we must ask ourselves what power and authority these elders have. It is not obligatory[1] to have a Lodge Committee: its primary function, if authorised and appointed at all, is to consider and report on proposals for membership. Other matters may be specifically referred to it for consideration and report and, within defined limits, action: but no Committees can be invested with any general executive powers. Even however with this shaky basis, we all know that the Lodge Committee almost invariably guides the Lodge, and does it very well: from time to time one hears of agitation from less senior and probably less experienced members, more often than not members of the Lodge of Instruction who meet, particularly in London, very much more often than the Lodge or the Lodge Committee.[2]

Having doubts as to these two being absolute sources of constitutional power, and being aware that votes in open Lodge are infrequently split down the middle of the membership, we should examine the powers of the Master in the light of the limitations imposed on him: we have already seen that his power of appointment of officers, though theoretically absolute, is in fact limited by the need to carry the Past Masters and the Lodge Committee with him: it may well be, as some rituals announce, that all offices are declared vacant when the installation begins, but in practice some officers will remain where they are and others almost automatically take a step forward. Through the Secretary the Master summons Lodge regular meetings but he is not a free agent as there is no power to cancel a meeting,[3] nor is he any longer permitted to summon an emergency meeting without authority from above. (This limitation was imposed soon after World War II when it was clear that if they were not controlled in some way Lodges would take in far more candidates than they could absorb.) Rule 180 *Book of Constitutions* lays upon the Master the requirement to admonish unharmonious behaviour in the Lodge, and if persisted in, to censure it, or even exclude the brother causing the disharmony for the remainder of the meeting, but only if the majority of the members agree. It is undoubtedly his prerogative to decide what is to be the business transacted at each Lodge meeting, but much of this is governed by the by-laws of the Lodge and the *Book of Constitutions*. As regards degree work as often as not a pattern has evolved over the years, and he will do well to fall in with this: he has, however, more freedom in seeking assistance or in deciding to 'go it alone' with the actual ceremonies. Here too, there is a good deal of variation of established practice: to generalise, it would seem that the further one goes from London the less ritual work is undertaken by the Master and the more is usurped by Past Masters. So it would appear that the Master's absolute power is strictly limited both in extent and in the way it can usefully be practised—in extent because the *Book of Constitutions* generally and the Lodge bylaws in particular hedge him round, and in practice because he will have seen on his way up the Lodge that there is a considerable brake put upon his own impulses—if indeed he has any—by the elder statesmen of the Lodge.

From the point of view of legislation, neither Master nor Lodge has any absolute authority, since no by-law or amendment can be effective until it has been approved by a higher authority: in any case the Grand Master's approval would not be given to any by-law or amendment which was repugnant to the *Book of Constitutions*.

In the matter of internal discipline, a Lodge is free to exclude one of its members 'for sufficient cause', provided that it goes the right constitutional way about it; and I cannot recall a case where an appeal against such action on the grounds that the cause was insufficient has succeeded. Indeed, unless the cause is thoroughly frivolous the members are held to be in much the best position to decide if they would sooner be without someone's company. Still it must be borne in mind that one Lodge's meat may be another Lodge's poison: I well remember a case where a previous Grand Master refused to exercise his powers under Rule 182(a) *Book of*

Constitutions as it now is and order the reinstatement of a member in a Lodge that had excluded him, precisely when he was appointing him to London Grand Rank following another Lodge's recommendation.

Queries often arise, generally from disgruntled members who have lost an argument, as to the full meaning of Rule 155 *Book of Constitutions* which states that the members *present at any Lodge duly summoned* have an undoubted right to regulate their own proceedings. ... In many cases the words are taken out of their context and used in a far wider sense to claim that Lodge affairs generally, and not just their handling in Lodge itself, are the business of the members only, and that no interference from outside is permissible.

A Lodge has indeed much of the semblance of a democracy with one man one vote on all matters of domestic concern, but it is the shadow rather than the substance, since it is governed not only by its by-laws, which as we have seen are subject to outside control, but also by the *Book of Constitutions* and by the abundance of case law arising from decisions of Grand Lodge itself.

THE PROVINCIAL AND DISTRICT GRAND LODGES

What has been expressed so far may be taken as applying with but little variation to all Lodges, but when we pass on to the second tier of government, that of Provincial and District Grand Lodges, it would be rash to treat them all as if cast in one mould (For the sake of brevity it is proposed to use 'Provincial' only.) Provincial Grand Masters have been appointed from the earliest days of organised English Masonry, often indeed before there was anything for them to be Masters of: we can also pass quickly by those early stages when a Provincial Grand Lodge may have consisted of little more than the Provincial Grand Master's own private Lodge, and arrive at the point where there was really something to guide and control—in the words of a Grand Superintendent's patent 'advise, instruct and where necessary admonish'. It is obvious that with strengths varying from over five hundred to single figures there must be great varieties in the methods of internal administration and government, but there are some basic principles which apply to both great and small. The Provincial Grand Master is appointed by the Grand Master, like all other Grand Officers except for the anachronistic Grand Treasurer, and he has his prescribed place in the Grand Officer's table of precedence.[4] After his installation (for till then as Provincial Grand Master designate he has no power except to summon a Provincial Grand Lodge meeting for his installation) he is in full control: he will have been asked to appoint or confirm the existing appointment of officers to the scale laid down in Rule 68 *Book of Constitutions* and to confirm with his approval the by-laws of his Province. Henceforward he is in a position of great power and responsibility: he is the fountain of honour within his Province, and to a numerically lesser, but practically more important extent, it will be only by his recommendation that members of his Province as such have their names submitted to the Grand Master for the ultimate honour of Grand Rank. He has very considerable powers of Masonic discipline subject only to the right of appeal from his decision to the Grand Lodge: his effective power however lies in his largely unwritten '*auctoritas*': this Latin word is not quite the same as 'authority' and has no precise equivalent in English: it means that, because they trust him, his brethren will do what they believe that he wants them to do, will follow his lead, and take his personal advice much as if it had constitutional force.

In the great majority of cases Provincial Grand Officers are appointed for a year only, and their ranks are honours conferred for work done or to be expected. Some offices, however, varying from Province to Province, are semi-permanent, and it is on the holders of such offices that the Provincial Grand Master will rely for the day-to-day government of his Province. Such government has, as elsewhere, increased greatly in complexity, and a full-time Provincial Grand Secretary is no longer the rarity he was in 1930. It was recognised by the Grand Master, as long ago as 1919, that a Provincial Grand Master needed more than a Deputy to help him discharge his duties, and the introduction of Assistant Provincial Grand Masters has done much to bring a closer relationship between the private Lodges and the government of the Province: indeed so useful have they proved that the scale permitting their appointment has been adjusted twice in the last thirty years till there may now be one for every forty Lodges. How they are actually deployed varies from Province to Province: the most comprehensive, and probably the most efficient, method is geographical. Although this is not always possible, it is desirable somehow to give some kind of group responsibility, not only to ease the burden on the Provincial Grand Master and his Deputy but also to give the Assistant(s) additional experience by taking charge of a number of Lodges.

Generations ago when many Provincial Grand Masters were local magnates, or absentees, or both, it was not unusual for a Province to be effectually ruled by the Deputy in the name of his Provincial Grand Master, and many Provinces were none the worse for an oligarchy of the Deputy and the Provincial Grand Secretary acting for their rather nominal Master. Such a Deputy would probably have had little or no thought of succeeding in due time to the Provincial Grand Mastership, nor inclination either, and when a vacancy arose and a new appointment was made he was there to supply valuable continuity: the position also gave him a great deal more authority than was strictly his, and there is a well attested story of a Deputy Provincial Grand Master of not so long ago who declined the offer of appointment to Provincial Grand Master with the comment 'If I accepted I would lose all my power'.

Inevitably, however, where a Province has increased beyond the size where it is the case that everybody knows everybody of any masonic consequence some form of representative body, or bodies, will need to be set up. What form they take varies a good deal, as also do the frequency of their meetings and the degree to which they are brought into lively discussion of the Province's affairs. In general it may be said that there will be a Committee for charitable purposes, itself two headed, for the relief of distress within the Province and for the organisation of major collections for the Central Charities when that Province's turn comes round: the other will have to deal with such routine matters of administration as are referred to it by the Provincial Grand Master and the Provincial Grand Secretary. It should be emphasised that its function is mainly consultative, and, if it does recommend some course of action to the Provincial Grand Lodge, it is more than likely that it is echoing the views of others.

It will be well to be clear as to the composition of a Provincial Grand Lodge: it is essentially a body of qualified individuals, who are not in the strict sense representatives or delegates of their Lodges: the ordinary Master Mason, though encouraged to be present, is there as a courtesy and has neither voice nor vote in its proceedings. The membership is clearly defined by the *Book of Constitutions*[5] and is virtually the same as that of Grand Lodge localised to the Province. Each Lodge may have some of its members attending such meetings, but there is in no sense an equality of voting strength between one Lodge and another, and one can easily visualise a meeting packed by determined members of a Lodge, or group of Lodges, pushing through or blocking resolutions where feelings run strongly; the rest of the Province would have no remedy—except to try again next time.

We should next ask ourselves what then is the function of Provincial Grand Lodge: in most cases it meets annually and the main, or at any rate the longest, item of business is the appointment and investiture of officers.[6] The actual form of the meeting is based, from start to finish, on the procedure at the Annual Investiture and Quarterly Communications of Grand Lodge: the formal entry and recession, the ritual opening and closing, the presentation of reports are all to be found at both levels. Provincial Grand Lodge no doubt has the power to refuse to accept a report downright, or to ask its proponents to think again: it alone can pass resolutions to amend its own by-laws, and this includes the rate of annual dues and fees generally. In respect of conferment of honours the power of the Provincial Grand Master is limited, but in this case by a comprehensive set of Rules in the *Book of Constitutions*, designed to apply with the least possible inequity to Provinces both large and small.

It would appear, therefore, that of the powers which exist at this intermediate level there lie with the Provincial Grand Master discipline with which Provincial Grand Lodge has nothing to do, conferment of honours, and presiding over meetings which he alone summons.[7] The Provincial Grand Lodge decides what taxation to impose, and what by-laws to lay down. Neither of them can establish a new Lodge or bring to final conclusion the activities of an existing one. Neither, therefore, can claim absolute or unfettered power: the *Book of Constitutions* controls the actions of both, while within the meetings of the Provincial Grand Lodge those present as members could, if feelings were sufficiently aroused or predilections antagonised, vote down any recommendations put to it.

A Provincial Grand Lodge can hardly be described as a democratic organisation since it consists of perhaps only a fifth (ie Past Masters, Master and Wardens) of the whole body which it taxes, and for which it legislates, while the other four fifths can only in a vague and farfetched sense be said to be represented by them, and are certainly not for the much greater part chosen by them. On the other hand, it is by no means an oligarchy in the accepted sense of the word, and it would be unjust so to describe it; nor by any stretch of the imagination can a Provincial Grand Master be equated with Plato's typical tyrant. Plato's concept of aristocracy, as government by those best qualified by nature and improved by training, could without overstraining the truth be applied to the membership of such a body as we have been considering. For it should be an absolute article of faith of Masons that the members of the Craft are good men, and it is at least to be hoped that in the years between initiation and wardenship they will have acquired something of the principles of Masonry as well as is ritual.

It remains briefly to consider such differences as there still are between Provinces at home and Districts overseas, a distinction in name dating from 1865: in the era of slower and even more unreliable mails it was desirable to give Masonic authorities (of whom it should be remembered that there were proportionately far more than now)[8] a greater degree of independence. This took various forms. First, there is the power of the District Grand Master to issue provisional warrants for new Lodges[9]: it should be noted that this provision is a time-saver pure and simple, and does not in any real sense enhance the District Grand Masters' powers. Secondly, where a Province has one or more Committees, a small District may, and a larger one must, have a District Board of General Purposes, which is a small edition of Grand Lodge's Board of General Purposes and has wide but defined functions:[10] there may also be a District Board of Benevolence, something of an anomaly now that the Board of Benevolence has put an end to itself. Thirdly, the Rules governing changes of dues are made more easy for isolated Lodges whose members would find it difficult to get to a District Grand Lodge meeting to express their views. Fourthly, District Grand Secretaries are sent blank Grand Lodge certificates of a very slightly different pattern which they issue to the members of their Lodges and account for quarter by quarter to the Grand Secretary: this is a matter of two way convenience as also is the practice in Districts of collecting all annual returns and sending them in bulk to London.[11]

It will be seen that, as indicated earlier, there are no basic differences in the powers of Province and Districts and their respective rulers: such differences as exist were created for convenience, speed and ease of administration.

LODGES DIRECTLY ADMINISTERED FROM FREEMASONS' HALL

No specific reference has been made to the Masonic government of 31 scattered Lodges, some of which are loosely put together under 4 Grand Inspectors[12] whose patent from the Grand Master quotes in detail the powers delegated to them: these make them each almost a one-man District Grand Lodge. A similar number is controlled directly from Freemasons' Hall. Last but in no way least, nearly one-fifth of Lodges in England and Wales are directly under the jurisdiction of Grand Lodge: these include three out of the four that formed the premier Grand Lodge in 1717 (the fourth has perished) and a very high proportion of Lodges already in their second and third centuries of existence. Their honours derive from the Grand Master directly, their problems and discipline are dealt with by the Board of General Purposes through the Grand Secretary and his office, and about one third of them recognise Freemasons' Hall as their Masonic home. While they are described as London Lodges for purposes of jurisdiction it would be as unrealistic to state that they are composed of Londoners as to claim that every Freeman of the City of London lives within the 'square mile'. They are, in fact, composed of brethren who find central London the most convenient gathering place from all parts of the country: there is no homogeneity about them like 'friends around the Wrekin', 'Red Rose', 'White Rose' or 'Men of Kent', but there is great pride in one and all being London Masons, the descendants of those who formed Grand Lodge and gave the pattern to Freemasonry all over the world. Attempts are made from time to time to diffuse this pride by inserting arbitrarily the same kind of Masonic government as has sprung up naturally in the geographical limits of the Provinces: an attempt by Lord Ampthill so to do was frustrated by the outbreak of war in 1914, from which he returned a wiser, if no less longwinded, man.

The carrot hopefully dangled before the Masonic donkey includes the likelihood of a larger proportion of Masonic honours and more supervision by Masonic visitations: however to continue the homely metaphor, the ass is an intelligent animal and can see the disadvantages too—higher dues because somehow such visitations and general administration will have to be paid for, less liberty of action than they present enjoy, loss of direct contact with the central government of the Craft and the straitjacket of charitable activities, into which Provinces[13] are fitted every ten years or so, instead of their own methods which, even if haphazard, are less forced and therefore more truly charitable.

It is at least arguable that London Lodges are more independent than those in the Provinces, and have therefore a greater aptitude for inculcating their own lessons of character building—indeed a wider experience of self government which the authorities at Freemasons' Hall do nothing to diminish.

THE GRAND LODGE

Having now considered the Private Lodges and various forms of intermediate control we proceed logically to the heart of government: but before doing so must again look back in the history of English Masonry and recall that two bodies came together in 1813 in an act of reconciliation which had been none the easier to achieve for its being common sense.[14] Their differences at Lodge level have already been outlined: when we come to the two sovereign bodies, it is not too much of an oversimplification to state that the strength of the Premier Grand Lodge was rather theoretical administrative machinery, and of the Antients' its enthusiasms for Masonic ritual and 'tradition'. At home the Antients had neither a headquarters nor a Provincial organisation (nor one would suspect any more control over their Provinces abroad than the Premier Grand Lodge). Their rivals had had for generations a well tried, if laxly administered, system deriving from the Committee of Charity, as well as a long established headquarters. This system was expanded after the Union into a complex organisation, the details of which are as follows.

THE DEVELOPMENT OF THE BOARD OF GENERAL PURPOSES AND ITS COMMITTEES

1. Prior to the union of the two Grand Lodges in 1813 there had been no Boards as such, but administration was carried out by the Committee of Charity for the Premier Grand Lodge and its Stewards' Lodge for the Antients. No useful purpose seems likely to be served by going into the details of pre-Union administration, and it will be best to start with the new situation as it emerged on 27th December, 1813.
2. Resolutions by the Grand Assembly for the Union established five separate Boards, all of whose functions were prescribed in the 1815 Book of Constitutions: they were:—
   General Purposes
   Finance
   Works
   Schools
   Benevolence

   In addition it should be mentioned that there was to be a 'General Committee' and an 'Audit Committee'. With this plethora of administration (and two Grand Secretaries) the re-united Craft proceeded to business.
3. It is however only fair to mention that the Board of Benevolence, which is referred to from time to time as the Committee or Lodge of Benevolence, was restricted from the start to charitable activities and

never impinged upon administration as its predecessor in the Premier Grand Lodge had done. It does not appear ever to have had any control even over the administration of the Fund of Benevolence, except in the matter of distribution to those qualified to be relieved. Its activities and constitution are therefore irrelevant to this review.

4. As the Boards of Works and Schools disappeared with the 1818 revision of the Book of Constitutions, it is tempting to suppose that they had never been intended to go on longer than was needed to sort out the problem of the two Schools, one a Premier and the other an Antient foundation, and to organize something agreeable to both parties in the matter of Freemasons' Hall, which was a purely Premier Grand Lodge building. This however would be an over-simplification. The Schools Board's function was to certify to Grand Lodge whether the money Grand Lodge voted was being applied to its object, and to report generally on the needs of the Institutions and on the sums of money required for their support or expansion: it was not however 'in any way to interfere with the privileges of the governors and subscribers thereto in the management and control of such establishment'. It had no regular dates of meeting.

Similarly the Board of Works was to have the direction of everything relating to the building and furniture of Grand Lodge, to suggest improvements, to make preparations for meetings in Freemasons' Hall, and to see that the Master of the Tavern made adequate arrangements for meetings held there. The Board was to control normal expenditure but to obtain the sanction of Grand Lodge for extraordinary expenses.

5. The Board of Finance was designed to see that no unnecessary or improvident expenditure took place: it was to check bills and order the Grand Treasurer to pay them—the order then as now being signed by the President and Grand Secretary, the Grand Treasurer being simply Grand Lodge's banker. Before each Quarterly Communication a balance was to be struck and reported to Grand Lodge, and the list of Lodge Contributions printed and published (this went on till 1940). Annually the Board was to prepare the accounts for the audit committee and circulate the accounts for the past year. At first it met monthly, but by 1819 had reverted to quarterly meetings: it disappeared in 1838 by a mutually agreed amalgamation with the Board of General Purposes, when Grand Secretary Harper (formerly of the Antients) retired and a general reorganization ensued.

Reference has been made to the Audit Committee which consisted of the Grand Officers of the year and twenty-four Masters of London Lodges. Its function seems to have been identical with that of the Grand Lodge Auditor, who does not appear till 1859, when he is appointed by the Grand Master: by 1881 the Auditor is elected by Grand Lodge as he now is. The Committee fades out of existence between 1859 and 1881, having indeed been found, as large Audit

Committees generally are, quite unsuited to its task.
6. The functions of the early casualties have now been dealt with, but it may be useful to look at their pattern of membership: each of the four had a President and Vice-President. In the case of the Board of Works, it was automatically the Grand Superintendent of Works (for many years Sir John Soane). The Grand Master, Deputy Grand Master and Grand Wardens were *ex officio* members together with 12 others (20 in the case of General Purposes). Half were appointed by the Grand Master, and half were elected by Grand Lodge from among the actual Masters: at least one third of the members went out of office each year. This must have ensured a regular turnover, accentuated by the fact that among the elected members it would be unlikely that an 'actual Master' would be so for more than two years at the most. Meetings were mostly monthly (but see Finance and Schools above).
7. Apart from the Board of General Purposes and what has sprung from it, only the General Committee now remains to be considered. This body had a long existence though it must be admitted that with the increase in the Craft, the introduction of penny postage and the better circulation of Papers of Business, its usefulness diminished: it served a useful purpose at first, but when it was finally abolished in 1918 it died almost unnoticed. Its function was to go through the Paper of Business a few weeks before Grand Lodge and 'vet' any motions that might be proposed from the floor, so that those attending Grand Lodge might not be caught unawares. Its membership consisted of all Grand Officers and all Masters of Lodges or their accredited representatives: as in this respect it was at the time practically identical with the Board of Benevolence and met on the same date, that Board seems in effect to have run the Committee. When it was laid down in 1858 and 1871 that the Paper of Business was to be circulated to all Lodges (and to Grand Officers) before Quarterly Communications, the Craft obtained prior cognizance of all official business, and it was felt by the Board of General Purposes that it was itself the body which should be made aware formally, and not by the accident of the General Committee's review, of any other motions. In December, 1918, after a long debate this view prevailed and to all intents and purposes the Board took over the functions of the General Committee.
8. During the long Grand Mastership of Lord Zetland (1844-1870) we find the first stirring of Masonic independence overseas: it started with Canada and there is little doubt that money was at the back of it: the Lodges thought they were being overcharged for registration and certificates (no dues were payable for administration or benevolence). When Grand Lodge at last tried to assuage their resentment by reducing the fee it was too late, and there was no hope of persuading them to remain under Grand Lodge. Correspondence with Lodges overseas had always been fraught with difficulty: both sides com-

plained justly of lack of attention, and even if a letter arrived safely at either end and was answered, the time lag was so long that it had probably lost its relevance. Besides there was no particular body in Grand Lodge that was directly responsible for supervising such correspondence. It is significant that in 1857, very soon after the Grand Lodge of Canada (now restricted geographically to Ontario), had won its independence, the Colonial Board started work. (This was the year too when Grand Secretary White at last resigned: he had served since 1809, his father having first come on the scene in 1781, no less than 76 years earlier: before the end of such a long tenure was in sight it may well have been difficult to introduce such an innovation.) The Board was established to review all overseas correspondence, whatever its nature. It met monthly though not infrequently failing to produce a quorum, with a Chairman, a Vice-Chairman, and eight other members. Much of its work was concerned with quarrels in and between overseas Lodges, especially those that were not under any local organization, but it was also concerned with problems arising from the establishment of other Grand Lodges in the Colonies. Eventually the Board was wound up and its functions were absorbed by the Board of General Purposes, which produced a further Committee with the full title of the Colonial, Indian and Foreign Committee. A good deal of argument occurred as to its membership, since it was felt that it should have adequate representation from overseas: it was eventually decided that as far as possible it should be composed of members of the Board who were Past Masters of Lodges abroad, but no provision was made to ensure that such qualified Brethren were elected to the Board. The Rule was thus anomalous, and must have remained something of a dead letter till authority was given a good many years later to the Committee to invite to its deliberations Brethren who had overseas experience: the last of them was RW Bro Sir Henry McMahon, since whose death no further advantage has been taken of the permission.

After the establishment of the Committee under this cumbersome title its work embraced all the relations of Grand Lodge with other Masonic powers including even Ireland and Scotland. Colonial however soon became an opprobrious word (particularly to a Canadian President) and general satisfaction ensued when in 1954 its name was changed to External Relations, without any alteration of its function.

9. The dissolution of the Board of Finance, to which reference has been made, was followed at once by the establishment of the *Finance Committee*. It is not clear that this change was the direct result of Harper's resignation, but there seems to be little doubt that there was a good deal of financial confusion brought about by his unbusinesslike methods: one item in the consequent reorganization lasted unchanged until 1960, as Grand Lodge's contribution to the educational Institutions of £150 a year in lieu of a percentage of the Registration Fees

remained unaffected by either the growth of the Craft or the fall in the purchasing power of the pound.

While in many organisations the equivalent to the Finance Committee has gradually accumulated additional powers and control, this has never been the case in the government of the Craft, since the Board has consistently refused to delegate its authority in any general sense to any of its Committees; all six stand in an equal relationship to the Board. Similarly the Board has never granted powers of general application to a Committee specially brought into existence for that purpose. From time to time this type of predominance has been suggested, but no evidence is forthcoming that it has been more than a suggestion, the nearest to actuality being a Committee of Chairmen of the 'Spending Committees' (presumably Finance, Premises, Officers and Clerks and Library, Art and Publications). This body, which met a few times in 1917-1918, was mainly concerned with estimating the future expenditure of its various Committees in order to obtain a forecast of the General Purposes bank balance with a view to advising on investments, a far cry from real control. In very recent times the investments of the two funds of Grand Lodge ceased to be solely gilt edged, and under the exhilarating influence of RW Bros Sir Frank Newson-Smith and F. W. R. Douglas an attack was made on equities. It became obvious that it was not practicable for the best effects of such a policy to be achieved through the monthly meetings of the Finance Committee, and an Investment Sub-Committee was formed in 1951: its work was so conspicuously successful that it is surprising that it took two decades to realise that Grand Lodge's real estate was just as much an investment as its stocks and shares, and needed to be similarly treated. Eventually, however, in 1971 the two sources of revenue were put on a comparable basis, and the Finance Committee established a Property Sub-Committee which took over the functions hitherto exercised by the Premises Committee in respect of properties other than Freemasons' Hall.

10. While these two Committees have existed without interruption since their establishment, even if the name and scope of one of them has altered, the same is not quite the case with the *Premises Committee* which first came into being in 1845. It is reasonable to assume that the Board assigned to it functions similar to those with which the old Board of Works had been invested in 1813, but when the almost complete rebuilding of Freemasons' Hall was contemplated in 1862 a special Building Committee was set up, not by the Board but by Grand Lodge itself, with full authority to pay bills in connection with the rebuilding without even reference to the Board. A similar procedure followed sixty years later with the Masonic Peace Memorial, whose Special Committee operated from 1919 to 1938.

When the 19th century rebuilding was completed in 1869 the Building Committee was wound up. It appears that the Premises Committee came back into activity: it has continued uninterrupted ever since and, by a curious chain of circumstance, assumed, or was assigned, a responsibility for Grand Lodge's other properties too. There is no need to go in detail into the gradual acquisition of properties which were not directly used by the Craft, as were Freemasons' Hall, the Tavern (now the Connaught Rooms), and Bacon's Hotel (later Mark Masons' Hall now part of the Connaught Rooms). What happened however was that at the peak of the purchasing movement the Chairman of the Premises Committee (RW Bro Blay), a builder himself and a dabbler in the property market, came to the rescue of the Grand Secretary, who at that time had no Deputy or Assistant and was moreover heavily committed in running the basement of Freemasons' Hall as an air-raid shelter. Bro Blay virtually took control of that part of the Board's affairs and the system continued till 1971, when as indicated above it was recognised that property as much as investments were income producing, and should be under the control of the Finance Committee.

11. A *Library Committee* appears in 1837 very soon after the decision to establish a Library. Over the next generation the Board Minutes refer on several occasions to the Library: there were rules for its use in 1848: in the next year evening opening was terminated as insufficient use was made of the facility. By 1860 at the latest it had become the Calendar Committee, and the Calendar or *Year Book* in fact seems to have been its principal function for many years: this is hardly surprising when one considers how little there was by way of Library or Museum, for only in 1898 did a new phase of building produce them a permanent home. In 1881 the double title Calendar and Library appears for the first time and persisted till 1911 when Publications took the place of Calendar: two years later the existing title appears in the *Masonic Year Book*.

In this title Library, it need hardly be said, includes the Museum: Publications over and above the *Year Book* now includes ordering and price-fixing for the *Book of Constitutions*, other printed matter, and latterly the very popular transparencies of the building and its contents. Art as part of the title is almost inexplicable, since outside the Library and Museum Grand Lodge's art treasures amount to forty portraits of dead and living Masons, half a dozen busts and the massive statue of the Duke of Sussex.

12. The first reference to the *Officers' and Clerks' Committee* is in 1894. By 1911, when the earliest extant Committee Book begins, the Committee interested itself in matters so diverse as typewriters and addressographs on the one hand, and on the other the selection of a Chief Clerk (*alias* Assistant Grand Secretary) and the wages of the stoker. In 1913, at the same time as negotiations were going on with the Commerical Union to effect a pension scheme, the Committee turned down a recommendation from the Chairman of the Finance Com-

mittee that the Cashier's salary should be increased (ie without reference to those enjoyed by the other clerks). During the first war the Committee, rather surprisingly, dealt with the preparation of a Library Catalogue. Appointments were put forward to the Board from time to time for the Library on the recommendation of the Library, Art and Publications Committee, and for the Porters' Staff at the Committee's own initiative. In general it has throughout its existence been primarily concerned with salaries and pensions, and only comparatively seldom have other matters, eg holidays and the five day week, come its way. In 1975 it was more appropriately renamed the *Staff Committee*, as by then it covered the whole workforce of Freemasons' Hall.

13. The *Procedure Committee* as such came into existence only in 1917, but on various occasions before then special committees had been formed to deal with the subjects which thereafter fell naturally within its scope: the Committee almost at once found itself dealing with such thorny subjects as music in Lodges, full dress regalia, proposal forms, and women Masons. A great deal of what the Committee considered and recommended to the Board was included in the revisions of the *Book of Constitutions* of 1926 and 1940, while other points of procedure were printed in the *Masonic Year Book*, and more recently in the booklet *Information for the Guidance of Members of the Craft*. Hence it follows that at the present time meetings are less frequent and agendas shorter than in its early days. In the main the Committee took care to avoid involvement in ritual matters, particularly after the episode of the extended installation ceremony.

14. All six of the 'statutory' committees have now been touched upon, but the Board from early times has had the power, and used it, to appoint committees for specific purposes: though sometimes wrongly referred to as Sub-Committees, a title which belongs to bodies appointed by one or other of the six committees, they are in fact in the same relationship to the Board as those Committees, ie they make recommendations which the Board proceeds to consider.

    The most frequent is the Committee on Committees, which started in 1914. It is set up each year and normally consists of all six Chairmen, the Vice-President and two other members, representing the Provinces and London: the President takes the Chair. Its sole function is to allocate membership of the six Committees equitably among the Board Members.

    Perhaps the longest lived and best known of such Committees was the one formed to deal with the question of the Loyal Order of Moose: it did so in such masterly fashion that subsequent questions about para-Masonic bodies have been dealt with in the light of its findings.

    Special Committees have from time to time considered appeals procedure, vocal music, precedence of Grand Officers, and have reported their findings in due course to the Board which has taken such action as it has thought fit.

15. From time to time a Judicial Committee was suggested, but nothing came of it following doubts expressed by the Grand Registrar of the time as to its constitutional propriety. Eventually however, and in stages, sufficiently recent to need no recapitulation, the judicial aspect of Grand Lodge was put on to an effective basis without involving the Board as such or any Committee emerging from it: this preserved the tradition of Grand Lodge as the ultimate Court of Appeal, while doing away with the ineffectual method of hearing appeals in circumstances where the weighing of evidence by an informed jury of 1500 was impossible and an appellant could, if he tried, win the sympathy of Grand Lodge by calling upon their compassion at the expense of their comprehension.

Looked at purely as a matter of political theory, the solution finally reached was much sounder than it would have been to have had a Committee of the Board acting as judge, jury and prosecutor.

16. The Board has never fettered itself with standing orders, or if it has outlined them they have quickly passed into oblivion. The nearest equivalent is perhaps the three or four line descriptions issued each year about the duties of the six Committees for the benefit of new members, which might very unofficially be described as their charters.

It does not appear that the absence of standing orders has in anyway impaired the efficiency of the Board's machinery. For the most part, the Board respects the judgment of the various Committees which tend to remain much the same from year to year, and to gain thereby considerable experience in the matters that come before them.

It may be seen from this that over the generations since 1813 the Board of General Purposes has gradually absorbed administrative control over the affairs of Grand Lodge, and, while doing so, has at the same time become a less unrepresentative body: the most notable step in this direction was taken in 1917, when it became possible for the Provincial members of Grand Lodge to have some positive say in the choice of Board membership. The complicated procedure[15] is eased by the arbitrary but self imposed division of the forty seven Provinces into twelve groups, each of which by courtesy supplies one member: it must be emphasised, however, that these twelve are primarily members of the Board and only very secondarily delegates from, or representatives of, the Provinces which have nominated them and organised their election. Other constituent elements of the Board are (*i*) twelve elected members from London Lodges, who often are coincidentally members of Provincial Lodges also, (*ii*) eight nominated each year by the Grand Master and more often than not reappointed from year to year, (*iii*) the occupants of certain defined offices in the Grand Lodge, at present fourteen in all: the Grand Secretary is very properly not a member of the Board, but is the channel of communication to and from it. He may come to be considered its guide, philospher and friend.

In much greater detail than for Provincial Grand Lodge Committees or those of Private Lodges the functions of the Board are laid down in the *Book of Constitutions:* it has the administration and control of the property and finances of the Grand Lodge and the regulation of all its affairs. 'Generally the Board shall take cognizance of all matters in any way relating to the Craft'.[16] Thus it conducts correspondence with other Grand Lodges and with Private Lodges, and, most important, may recommend or report to the Grand Lodge or to the Craft (an interesting distinction to which we will return) whatever it may deem conducive to the welfare and good government of the Craft. Any such references when adopted by the Grand Lodge are treated as its edicts, that is to say become part of the Masonic case law. Case law used to derive also from decisions by Grand Lodge when deciding appeals or expulsion, but there is little now of new principle to be found from this source, and the much more practical method of conducting such business through Appeals Court has virtually brought it to an end. As a Court of First Instance the Board also acts as a kind of corporate Provincial Grand Master in judicial matters affecting London Lodges or members, or elsewhere where there are no Provincial or District Grand Masters: it has just the same powers as they do, and there is a similar right of appeal from its decisions.

With all these powers and duties and with a wealth of experience at its disposal, it might be thought that the Board would indeed be supreme: this however is not the case, for numerous examples could be turned up where the Grand Lodge has not been in agreement with the Board, and its proposals have had to be amended or abandoned. Much will depend on the care with which its reports are drafted, and still more on the tact with which they are submitted by its President: but most of all it is vital that the Board should have the confidence of the Craft that it is working for the benefit of the Craft as a whole and not for itself or any single section of the Craft. Fortunately this is much more the case now than it was at the beginning of the century, when rows and arguments in Quarterly Communications proliferated. Sir Alfred Robbins, who in his earlier years had been a thorn in the flesh of the Masonic establishment, became a great, if overbearing, President. He was a classic example of poacher turned gamekeeper; but too little thought perhaps is given to how such conversion is regarded by the other poachers, and he probably never quite lived down his past. The story is told—I have it from one of those who voted—of how in some fairly trivial dispute, which provoked one of his long winded speeches, word was passed among the Grand Stewards 'Come on, let's vote the old man down' and they did.

Later Presidents, by their personalities and by their self-evident disinterestedness and ability, have gained the confidence of the Grand Lodge, which seems now to take the sensible view that the matters laid before it have been considered by Board members who collectively have a wealth of experience denied to the individual mason. A good example is the difference of attitude between 1930 when a suggestion of adding six pence to annual dues provoked a descent from the north in a special train—and a subsequent Especial Grand Lodge—and the present era when the Grand Lodge is now content to accept annual recommendations from the Board as to the dues required two years ahead.

THE BOARD OF BENEVOLENCE

I will not attempt an obituary notice of the Board of Benevolence, that oldest of the offshoots of the Grand Lodge and the direct progenitor of the various useful Boards and Committees which Grand Lodge has formed and through which it has worked. It may have been necessary to remove so venerable a feature (one hesitates to use the word 'landmark') in order to maintain the illusion that the Bagnall Report is going to be faithfully and totally implemented, but it is much to the credit of Grand Lodge that, unlike the independent Institutions, it rapidly adjusted itself to the Bagnall framework.

It has already been stated that the Board of General Purposes' parameters[17] are clearly defined in the *Book of Constitutions:* so too are the functions of the Grand Lodge, and though it would be a tidy piece of political theorization to compare them to Cabinet and Parliament, with the whole Craft as the *mobile vulgus* or electorate, it is not so easy to see how exactly the Craft is able to act as such, apart from the fact that each Masonic tier is composed of members of the larger one below it. Again applying the argument that the Craft is composed of persons of good report, and of increasingly sound judgment and experience as they rise in importance through their Lodges, we hope to find that members of Grand Lodge's functioning Boards or special committees combine good reputation and widened experience with a determination to work for Freemasonry, but little hope of self-advancement within the Craft and none outside it.

THE GRAND LODGE AND THE CRAFT

The distinction, to which allusion has already been made, between the Grand Lodge and the Craft underlines that they are two separate entities, just as at Lodge level a meeting of Past Masters differs from the Lodge itself in session. Appeals such as the Duke of Connaught's at the start of the Masonic Million Memorial Fund may be, and were, issued to the Craft as a whole through Grand Lodge, but thereafter Grand Lodge had really very little to do with it: nor indeed had the Board for almost all the detail was carried out by the Peace Commemoration Building Committee which reported regularly to Grand Lodge till it was wound up, *functus officio*, in 1938. The Lodges were used as the vehicle for raising money, and the Grand Secretary's office collected it and generally serviced the Committee: but Grand Lodge's own contribution financially was a minor one, and was more than repaid when the building was handed over in 1938. It is not easy to provide other examples of positive action by the Craft, though when Grand Lodge expels a mason it expels him from the Craft. While such a brother does not cease to be a Freemason, as the ceremonies performed over him and the secrets communicated to him cannot be reversed, he does cease to be a member of the Craft losing his membership of that shadowy but corporate body.

THE GRAND MASTERSHIP

It only remains now, respectfully, to consider the summit of this Masonic pyramid, the Grand Mastership. From the earliest days of the Grand Lodges the office has been elective, none the less so for its having very often and fortunately been repetitive: there has not been any sign of a contested election since 1844, following the death of the Duke of Sussex, and a rather crackpot attempt at opposition some twenty years later by a brother who thought that the system of honours was unsatisfactory:[18] although once, when presiding over his own re-election, the late Earl of Scarbrough jokingly referred to Grand Lodge playing its little democratic game election is no figment. Once elected a Grand Master takes office forthwith and does not have to wait for formal and ceremonial installation[19] like a Provincial Grand Master.

This will be a logical starting point for the consideration of his powers and prerogatives which, unlike the functions of other leading Grand Officers, are not defined in a single place. On a very much wider scale than is the case with any Province, he is the fountain of honour for London Grand Rank and in respect of Past Grand Ranks and Promotions his authority is unfettered. He has power to form any specified area into a Province, District, or Inspectorate, and to rearrange existing boundaries: and with this naturally goes the power to appoint Provincial and District Grand Masters and Grand Inspectors to give effect to his actions. Warrants for new Lodges are granted by him and remain his property, though curiously enough he cannot either erase a Lodge or revoke an appointment to Grand Rank: in each case reference has to be made to the Grand Lodge whose decision is final. Dispensations are issued in his name, though contrary to almost universal belief there is no general power of dispensation: it is only for those cases specifically referred to in the *Book of Constitutions* (a dozen or so in all) that a dispensation can be obtained. He alone can approve the pattern and use of jewels, this being in practice extended to Lodge badges generally and to banners when they include the Lodge badge.

In addition to appointing to Grand Rank, the Grand Master has also powers of appointing scrutineers for the elections in Grand Lodge and of direction, through the Grand Stewards, of the Grand Festival: also he may direct how admission to meetings of the Grand Lodge is to be arranged, ie when tickets need for one reason or another to be issued. In addition to Grand Officers, he also appoints Brethren of other Constitutions, with which the Grand Lodge is in amity, as Representatives and makes suggestions for similar appointments in reverse: these should be, and mostly are, purely honorific, but the appointments are highly prized and much care and consideration goes into the selection of their holders.

   Whether these powers are held to be great or small, too great or not great enough, will be largely a subjective judgment or will depend on theoretical comparisons with other jurisdictions: what stands out however is that in the English system of long-lasting tenure of the Grand Mastership a considerably greater degree of experience will mature, and equally important, there will not be a posse of Past Grand Masters ready and anxious to advise. It would seem therefore that in the English system much more depends on the Grand Master as the apex of its pyramid, and on his relations with the Board of General Purposes and with the massed body of Provincial and District Grand Masters. Sir Alfred Robbins, again, was apt to describe himself as the Prime Minister of English Freemasonry, with the implication that the Board was the Cabinet: he did not, so far as I know, ever proceed to a comparison between the Grand Master and the Crown, or between the Grand Lodge and the House of Commons though he might very well have carried his analogy upwards and downwards [and, for good measure, have worked in a comparison of Provincial and District Grand Masters with Lords Lieutenant or Colonial Governors, of whom in his day there were plenty enough]. What he *definitely* did *not* do was to refer to himself as Lord President of the Council, or designate any Privy Council, yet it is manifest that however long a Grand Master may remain in office he will require advisers in the actual exercise of those prerogative powers already outlined, which are now within the purview of the Board. Hence it is that in the last hundred and forty years the practice has grown up informally and almost imperceptibly of having a Grand Master's Council, all the more useful in that its membership and its meetings are alike unfettered by rules and by-laws. It is however[20] customarily composed of the major dignitaries of Grand Lodge with a sprinkling of Provincial Grand Masters, of experts on the affairs of English Freemasonry overseas, and of Brethren too with an intimate knowledge of problems of the Masonic Charities, on which, as he is their Grand President, the Grand Master stands in need of disinterested advice. Though it is the normal practice not to refer to the Council as such, and even when referring to the members as the Grand Master's advisers we use a small 'a' to avoid any implication of official status, it is pretty widely known that it exists, and there really seems to be no reason why it should not be known: indeed if it were to be abolished something very like it would undoubtedly grow up in its place. Comparison might usefully be drawn to the stages of devolution of power in English History from the Great Council to Parliament, from Parliament via the Privy Council to Cabinet, from Cabinet to Parliament and back to the Privy Council, particularly as so much present day legislation is put into effect by Orders in Council. It must remain clear that in Masonry too there will always be an inner circle of personal advisers, whose advice on matters of Masonic prerogative needs to be sought, and whom it would be unwise to disregard or take for granted.

Students of Plato's *Republic* will have observed that till now there has been no reference to what he considered the lowest form of political life, tyranny. This aspect is covered neatly by rule 15 *Book of Constitutions*, which states the position in quaint but explicit terms. 'If the Grand Master should abuse his power and render himself unworthy of the obedience of the Lodges, he shall be subjected to some new regulation, to be dictated by the occasion; because, hitherto, the Antient Fraternity have had no reason to provide for an event which they have presumed would never happen.' Within the velvet glove there is at least an implied threat, and we should not forget that when Grand Lodge was founded in 1717 it was less than a generation after James II was toppled off the throne following the trial of the Seven Bishops, and then bundled out of Ireland by the tune of Lilliburlero: moreover, the successful 'putsch' by which the Whig Grandees had brought in the Hanoverians was only three years back, while the unsuccessful 1715 rising must have been a very fresh memory. Grand Lodge was born into a Whig Oligarchy, and despite what happened abroad it continued along Whig rather than Tory line.[21]

THE PRO GRAND MASTERSHIP

It would be leaving a large gap if nothing were said about the Pro Grand Mastership, which stands in a peculiarly personal relationship to the Grand Mastership. Our Masonic ancestors saw clearly that the other commitments of a Royal Grand Master would prevent his giving the detailed care and attention to the office that a lesser man might be expected to give; also it is quite possible that they wished to prevent him being exposed to the pressures normally attendant on the office. Hence originated the office of Pro Grand Master, designed to carry out the day to day functions of government,[22] leaving the Grand Master himself unembroiled. The Pro Grand Master is to the Craft as a whole the outward and visible form of the Grand Mastership in action, and just as he will have the confidence of the Grand Master so must he justify the confidence of the Craft in the choice that is made of him by the Grand Master after consultation with his Council. It is reasonable to hold this out as the theory of the matter: to make it work effectively it is essential that the

Grand Master remains outside the usual run of events, approached only by the Pro Grand Master[23] or through him. Any breach of this protocol is likely to lead to the potentially dangerous situation of the Grand Master and Pro Grand Master being given conflicting briefs on the same matter.

THE DEPUTY AND ASSISTANT GRAND MASTERSHIP

I have purposely left out reference to the specific functions of the Deputy Grand Master and the Assistant Grand Master(s) which remain the same whether or not there is a Pro Grand Master. Their appointments derive from the prerogative of the Grand Master, and they may be conveniently looked upon both as manifestations of himself in his absence and as the most senior and responsible of his advisers. It is worthy of note that most formal documents have the Deputy Grand Master's signature on them, and that in the ritual of Grand Lodge he has to answer both for himself and for the Grand Master. (If the Grand Master and the Pro Grand Master are both present it is still the Deputy Grand Master who answers.)

Ideally this little knot of rulers of the Craft, advised by the Board or by the Council in matters of high policy and by the Grand Secretary in routine affairs, will give their directions with one voice, and the Craft as a whole will follow them with unimpaired respect and affection. If however it ever becomes clear that such counsels are divided, as in the case particularly of the Masonic Charities, very deep and lasting divisions will develop in the Craft as a whole; nor will they easily be healed.

THE MASONIC CIVIL SERVICE

Practically nothing hitherto has been said about the Masonic Civil Service: it exists to serve the Craft, whether it be at the Provincial or Grand Lodge level. At the latter it has passed through periods of considerable unpopularity: references to John Hervey and his staff in the Proceedings of Grand Lodge are remarkable for their virulence, even by the uninhibited standards of those days. Since then it seems that the image has improved, and though from time to time there have been objections from one quarter or another to various aspects of their work,[24] by and large we Grand Secretaries have been accepted, if sometimes grudgingly, as doing our best. The staff itself, ever since there has been one of appreciable size, has known its job and done its best to function without fear or favour: its members acquire a very real expertise in Masonic administration, and in many cases in Masonic ceremonial too—the run up to annual investitures and even great occasions such as Albert Hall meetings are taken in their stride. The Grand Secretary himself can rely with confidence on someone in the office, male or female, being able to produce an answer or precedent, which may have slipped his memory or antedated his experience. For almost any problem or question it is then for him to channel it, and the appropriate answer to it, in the right direction for the Grand Master and his advisers or to the Board of General Purposes; often he has to use his own judgment or give the unpalatable answer that it has nothing to do with Freemasonry and its administration.

The Grand Secretary's office is thus the nodal point in the communication system; without having powers in himself but simply by experience and not least by always being available for consultation, he soon acquires that same *auctoritas* that will encourage those whom he meets in person or by correspondence to accept what he tells them as authentic and unbiased.

CONCLUSION

Thus we find at the Grand Lodge level rather more similarity with our British principles of government including the distinction between legislative, administrative and judicial. Bishop Stubbs' insistence on the continuity of development of constitutional organisations helps us to understand that almost everything of significance in our system derives from our Masonic ancestors. Plato gives us invaluable guide lines of definition between, in his vocabulary, aristocracy, oligarchy and democracy: Bagehot guides us to a clearer conception of the different tiers of government in the Craft as a whole.

What must never be lost sight of is that a framework which suits the English Masonic temperament will not necessarily suit others—hence in any consideration of other Masonic Jurisdictions we must be careful not to equate 'different' with 'wrong'. No doubt this lecture could be rewritten on the foundation of American, Latin, Germanic or Scandinavian systems: it is probably true that just as apt a series of comparisons of their forms of government could be made out. It can never be stressed enough that, while Masonic governments may differ, the true principles of Freemasonry do not, whatever may be the temperaments of governors and governed.

It was for the furtherance of knowledge of the Principles of Freemasonry that William Preston, who in his time had been an archrebel against the administration of the Craft, established his lectures: but it is my belief that, if he had ever turned his mind from matters of Masonic ritual to the Government of the Craft, he would have reached empirically the same kind of conclusions as have been laid before you.

NOTES ON APPENDIX I

1. R. 154 *B. of C.*
2. They may be not uncharitably compared to the 'Young Turks' in the last years of the Sultan Abdul in Istanbul, useful at producing evidence of feelings that might not otherwise find expression, but do not necessarily merit acceptance.
3. R. 137 *B. of C.*
4. R. 5 *B. of C.*
5. R. 65 . *of C.*
6. This has become in very large Provinces so lengthy that it is spread over two meetings.
7. A Provincial Grand Master shares with certain other distinguished Masons the right to demand admission to any Lodge within his jurisdiction and preside over it: in this respect it could be argued that he 'overtrumps' the right of the Master of a private Lodge, but in practice it is unlikely that this power will often be invoked for more than purely formal purposes.
8. In 1863 there were 64 Provinces and Districts for 1000 Lodges. Now the figures are 72 and over 8000.
9. This still exists in Rule 95 but is now virtually a dead letter: any holdup nowadays is more likely to be due to (*i*) petitioners who fail to produce all the necessary information when forwarding their petitions or for inclusion in the warrant; (*ii*) the actual writing of the warrant which is largely obviated by its main text being mass-produced and (*iii*) the recurrent difficulty of obtaining the necessary signatures.
10. R. 81(b) *B. of C.*
11. With the curious proviso that the District Grand Master is himself responsible personally for the remittance of dues.
12. Any comparison between such Grand Inspectors and the Inspectors General that are an integral part of the whole organisation of the Ancient and Accepted Rite is pure fantasy: they are a modern (1927) introduction into the Craft's system of government and, having been primarily intended to obviate postal delays, have ceased with the prevalence of air facilities to perform that function: except as a stepping stone to the formation of a new District in a developing area such as Trinidad, Cyprus or the Bahamas, or conversely, as a step down where a District is in process of dissolution (Northern China) their continued necessity is debatable.
13. A very senior Provincial Grand Master of the recent past is on record as having said that even in his highly organised Province he reckoned that never more than 50% of his members supported a festival which he was sponsoring—and that only once in ten years.

14. It would be ungrateful not to refer with appreciation to the valuable help I have received from my immediate predecessor's lecture on the Antients.
15. R. 219 *B. of C.*
16. So says Rule 227, and one is sometimes tempted to ask by what kind of self-denying ordinance or sophistry does it consistently decline to deal with ritual and charitable matters.
17. 'Guide lines' are already out of fashion.
18. He was not a Grand Officer himself.
19. R. 14 *B. of C.* The last three such installations (which have taken place at the Royal Albert Hall) did not in any way increase the Grand Master's power or remove any limitations upon it.
20. Membership is at the personal invitation of the Grand Master and lapses with a change of Grand Master.
21. A close study of John Locke's 'Essay of Civil Government' might well be illuminating; I have not undertaken it.
22. It is significant that the earliest holders of such appointments were described as *Acting* Grand Masters.
23. Logically, if not verbally, R. 17 *B. of C.* applies equally to the Pro Grand Master.
24. Some trivial minds in high places have quoted Dunning's condemnation of the power of the Crown:—'has increased, is increasing and ought to be diminished'. Such fatuity can safely be disregarded: he has plenty to do without looking for more.

Appendix II

The Badges of the Nineteen Red Apron Lodges

No. 1

No. 8

No. 28

No. 91

No. 2

No. 14

No. 29

No. 99

No. 4

No. 21

No. 46

No. 197

No. 5

No. 23

No. 58

No. 6

No. 26

No. 60

No. 259

Appendix II

The list of Red Apron Lodges appears each year in the illustrated menu for the Grand Festival, and is more often than not accompanied with illustrations of their individual badges: most of them are self-explanatory but it may still be of interest to look at them more closely in the light of the further details now supplied.

Grand Masters' Lodge No 1 has as its centre the blazing sun which figures so conspicuously on the Grand Master's apron: heraldically it is known as the Sun in Splendour and was particularly associated with the House of York. The badge is surmounted by an 'antique or Eastern crown'.

Lodge of Antiquity No 2 shows three shields bearing the Arms of the Premier and Antient Grand Lodges and between them the Arms of the Grand Lodge south of the River Trent, of which Antiquity was for a short time the principal, if not the only member. The inclusion of the Grand Lodge supporters and the Ark of the Covenant and 'Holiness to the Lord' occupy every bit of space. The surround refers to its immemorial constitution as one of the founding four Lodges of the Premier Grand Lodge.

Royal Somerset House and Inverness Lodge No 4 shows a Scottish Lion Rampant with the Duke of Sussex label of difference: it is surmounted by a Royal Duke's coronet.

St George's and Corner Stone Lodge No 5 naturally shows the patron saint of England and his victim but the Corner Stone does not appear.

Lodge of Friendship No 6 like Antiquity, refers to its London origin: what shows up generally as an elaborate cross is in fact a clasped hands motif. Above it appears a dove with an olive branch poised on a coiled serpent. The badge includes the motto 'True Friendship' and the earliest appearance in this gathering of the square and compass.

With **British Lodge No 8** we come to the first date of constitution, 1722, and it is interesting to note that the number is given in Roman figures which is the practice also of No IV.

Tuscan Lodge No 14 shows a plain Tuscan pillar adorned with the Lodge number on its base with, like No VIII, the date of constitution.

Lodge of Emulation No 21 shows the beehive, one of the oldest of Freemasonry's symbolic figures. (It was adopted also by Napoleon and is generally held to refer to the industry of the bees rather than their building of honeycombs, though William Shakespeare holds the other view.)

Globe Lodge No 23 shows a globe and almost certainly takes both badge and name from the Globe Tavern in Fleet Street where it was meeting from 1760 to 1768.

Castle Lodge of Harmony No 26 likewise derives both badge and name from the Castle Tavern, Lombard Street, where it met from 1751 to 1763 though it did not formally adopt the Castle name till 1768 and added Harmony in 1776. There seems to be no Beaufort connection as implied by the portcullis.

Old King's Arms Lodge No 28 was meeting at the King's Arms in the Strand as early as 1733 and it adopted the name in 1742 and no doubt the inn-sign, which is the royal arms then current, at the same time to be its badge.

St Alban's Lodge No 29 shows a figure underneath a canopy, rather reminiscent of the Albert Memorial but representing England's Proto-Martyr: it seems, as in the three preceding notes, to have derived its name from the place where the Lodge met at a time when definite names for Lodges were coming into fashion. The canopy is supported by what appears to be sprigs of acacia, the earliest example of these as the sprays in No IV are unquestionably thistles in support of the Scottish Lion.

Old Union Lodge No 46 did not settle for this name till 1816 by which time there were other Unions of later date. It has two pillars of indeterminate design joined by an arch bearing the inscription freely translated as Stability in Union: the tessellated pavement has sprigs of vegetation on it which appears to be acacia like St Alban's.

Lodge of Felicity No 58 has the admirably simple device of three links of chain with 'light and felicity' below them in Latin.

Lodge of Peace and Harmony No 60 introduces new motifs as well as the date of foundation—a three stringed lyre and the all-seeing eye: there is too a wreath rather more suggestive of olive branches than of acacia and it may be surmised that they stand for peace as the lyre does for harmony.

Lodge of Regularity No 91 has the square and compass together with its bicentenary date, at which point the Latin inscription 'It has now flourished for two hundred years' was brought up to date too by W. E. Grey, the Lodge Secretary and the then Deputy Grand Secretary. The scythe and hourglass are familiar emblems of mortality.

Shakespear Lodge No 99 also has square and compass and an hourglass but the central figure is naturally the Bard of Avon surrounded by 'Brotherly Love, Relief and Truth' and the date of its centenary—not, however, amended like Regularity's to the bicentenary.

Jerusalem Lodge No 197 which started life at the Jerusalem Tavern, St John's Gate, shows the St John's Gateway described as its birthplace together with its original number 409 (which Lane's Masonic Records incidentally give as 408) and its current one. The badge, which is in effect a replica of the distinctive jewel authorised in 1871 is surrounded by a coronet commemorating the visit of the Prince of Wales (later Edward VII) on the occasion of its centenary.

Prince of Wales's Lodge No 259 has the Prince of Wales feathers, backed by a 'glory' surrounded by the garter motto and surmounted by a coronet, all emblems so well known as to demand no description.

Appendix III

The following address was given by the author to Supreme Grand Chapter on 9 November 1983 (part one) and 14 November 1984 (part two).

Changes in Grand Chapter 1947 to 1980
(*Part One*)

When I first arrived at Freemasons' Hall in February, 1947, there was a great backlog of work: the permanent Clerks were slowly being disgorged by the Armed Forces as their age and service groups matured and the temporary wartime replacements were beginning to fade out. Nowhere, however, were the arrears greater than in the Royal Arch Department, which had just been taken over by E Comp W. G. H. Browne: it did not seem that any installation returns had been entered for about five years, and I soon became adept at entering four or five successive ones at a time, even when full of yard long Madrassi names. The same must have applied to annual returns which, as there was at that time no money attaching to them, were deemed to be of comparatively little importance: new registrations and certificate issues were on the other hand reasonably up to date.

Both the new Third Grand Principal, Dean Naylor, and the Grand Scribe E were keen upholders of Royal Arch Masonry, laying great and proper emphasis on the spiritual aspects of the Chapter as against the Lodge: also Lord Harewood soon after becoming Grand Master had taken the first steps towards dissociating Craft and Royal Arch Grand Ranks by laying down that some slight degree of merit in the latter beyond having been a First Principal was to be looked for. In spite of this the Royal Arch was still a very poor relation of the Craft and from the official point of view I am afraid that its organisation was negligible.

In the 35 years which followed changes, most if not all for the better, have occurred in various aspects:—

First, ritual: although the Committee of General Purposes like the Board of General Purposes will have nothing to do with ritual arguments nor will it enter into correspondence on the subject, it will not refuse to make suggestions to Grand Chapter in support of a uniform change equally applicable to all the ritual variants known to exist: it will make its recommendations and leave Grand Chapter to decide. This has happened in four cases:

(a) The Installation ceremonies, which excluded the junior Companions for a quite unnecessarily long time and, if they came at all, drove them to any nearby bars, were reorganised in 1960/61 with hardly a word changed, so that the juniors were present for all except the truly esoteric parts of the ceremony—and I would here like to remind Excellent Companions that the point of the scripture readings is not the bible stories, which should be familiar to most of us, but their lead into the esoteric element and the secrets of the various Chairs. As Chapters are divided between the Z first and the Z last methods, two versions had to be prepared: they were accepted as alternatives by Grand Chapter and in my experience are now in pretty general use. I have never indeed heard of a Chapter going back to the old method when it had once adopted the new. Most of the basic work of drafting the new layout was undertaken by Comp. Browne, but the Grand Chapter Committee took the matter on from there and secured the agreement of Grand Chapter.

(b) Secondly, the great penalties debate in Grand Lodge did much to clear the air, but owing to obstinacy (and often I fear the incapacity of Preceptors to change their ways), it has not had as much practical effect as from the overwhelming approval of Grand Lodge might have expected; it rubbed off in a mild way on the Royal Arch ritual. It was just over two years later, in February, 1967, that Lord Scarbrough suggested that consideration be given to a similar reform of the Royal Arch ritual and at the next Convocation himself moved a resolution to that effect which was carried without opposition or argument.

(c) In 1965 the Committee recommended to Grand Chapter that in its view the rendering of all three lectures to every candidate on his Exaltation was unnecessary: the Mystical should always be given in full, but the other two only in the course of the year. Grand Chapter accepted this lightening of the burden, and it thereby became an edict binding on the whole order. I rather doubt if it has been fully implemented, and feel that many Chapters either still do all three, or at the other end of the spectrum do no more than that part of the Mystical which deals, less importantly, with the signs.

(d) Fourthly a matter of more recent date, and one in which the London First Principals Chapter played an important role: it is of course the reorganisation of the Principals' Lectures on a question and answer basis. This stems from the difficulty that there are so few speaking parts and not many actual Officers in a Chapter compared to a Lodge: furthermore the 'efficiency bar' whereby it is not possible to become a Principal until one is an Installed Master is a further limitation on the activities of the junior Companions. Before proceeding further, however, I would like to give expression to my very firm conviction that this same 'efficiency bar', however hardly it may seem to fall upon individuals, has been one of the sources of strength in keeping the Craft and Royal Arch in a close association such as does not exist in some other jurisdictions. Without that compulsory link it might well be found, as it has turned out in Scotland, that the two bodies are to all intents and purposes strangers to each other—a source of weakness in fact to both. Within the Scottish Craft friction is indeed accentuated by the fact that both Grand Lodge and Grand Chapter claim rights over the Mark Degree. This is, however, a diversion from my main theme—that not enough exists for junior members to do: in some Midlands Provinces they try the idea of splitting up the Sojourners' work, which is ingenious, but to my mind far fetched and unrealistic. It seemed to me, thinking about it over a long period, that splitting up the Lectures had much to commend it: in the first place they tend to put off the incoming Principals, who either decline to go forward or shuffle off the Lectures on to other Past Principals who practically appropriate a Lecture as their own: in the second place the Lectures themselves badly delivered can be a positive embarrassment for all parties: in the third place a breaking up of the Symbolical and Mystical Lectures between two or three soloists destroys the sequence of thought. On the other hand, question and answer such as survives in very abbreviated form in the questions after dinner is a much older element of Masonic ritual, I would suppose, than long speeches and exhortations. So I set about what I thought of as a work of restoration, introducing questions at appropriate places in the three Lectures, where, whichever one of the more usual rituals might be employed by a Chapter, the answers could come back in the terms of that ritual. This in itself was a surprisingly simple operation, but it was more complicated to work out where to insert the questions and how long the answer should be before the next question was asked. However, it all came out satisfactorily in the end and after various rehearsals in the Letchworth Chapter, to which the great majority of the Freemasons' Hall Staff belong, the London First Principals Chapter and elsewhere, the culmination came with a demonstration to Grand Chapter itself at what was one of the most interesting and best attended Convocations of recent years. The scheme met with very general approval, and is by now being practised, and one hopes increasingly so, as in the case of the new method of Installation. So much for ritual.

Leaving on one side financial changes, which are continually with us, we now pass on to legislation. Like Grand Chapter itself, *Royal Arch Regulations* have long been closely linked with the Craft: in any matter on which the Regulations were silent, the relevant Rules of the *Book of Constitutions* operated. It will, however, be remembered that the *Book of Constitutions* had been very extensively revised in the years before World War II and that the 1940 edition was from start to finish as different a book from its predecessors as Fenn's revision of 1884 had been from those before it. It is hardly an exaggeration to say that both these constitutional revolutions left the *Royal Arch Regulations* unmoved: while the editions of the early nineteenth century had been expanded with the growing complication and size of the Order, they had remained essentially the same, and the differences between the blue and red books since 1940 had become glaring. In 1954 again with the able assistance of E Comp Browne I rewrote the *Royal Arch Regulations* and submitted them to a sub-committee of the Grand Chapter Committee: many hours of argument took place in Committee under the genial Chairmanship of E Comp. Sir George Boag, but by early 1955 agreement had been reached sufficiently to send a revised draft to all Grand Superintendents. Their comments were all considered, and some were adopted. Then at last, after the necessary constitutional processes had been carried out, the new Regulations came into effect on 1st January, 1956. Though there have been numerous minor amendments since then they remain substantially unaltered as the instrument of government of Royal Arch Masonry. The links with the laws of the Craft have now been consolidated in a practical manner by binding the two sets together, and thus presenting a united front.

It is hardly necessary or appropriate to go back over the details of the changes: while there was a conscious effort to iron out minor differences between Craft and Royal Arch rules in order to simplify administration within Chapters, the historic differences were left untouched. Election of Officers, for example, remained in force unless a Chapter resolved to the contrary—and if it did so the Regulations made clear, as had not previously been the case, that it was the incoming and not the outgoing Principals who made the choice. The number of candidates to be exalted at one meeting was limited as in the case of Craft Degrees, but with a power of dispensation. The use of the tricolour ribbon from which the Royal Arch jewel is suspended was extended to holders of London, Provincial and District and Overseas Grand Chapter Ranks. It was decided too that it was unnecessary to print details of every Chapter's removal in the Paper of Business, and again in the Proceedings. Grand Chapter, however, preserved the right to authorise Charters for new Chapters, Centenary and, proleptically as none were due for a number of years, Bicentenary Charters. Last but by no means least Comp Browne produced an index which for the first time referred to Rules in the *Book of Constitutions* where these applied to the Royal Arch.

When these Regulations came into force it had already been found that the first Wednesday in August, close upon the then Bank Holiday, was an awkward day for Grand Chapter to meet, and the last Wednesday in July was substituted. By 1960 it was found that this meeting hardly justified itself and in a general reorganisation of Quarterly Communications and Convocations it was dropped. At the same time the February and November meetings were transferred to second Wednesdays, like those of Grand Lodge, and the Annual Investiture which was becoming increasingly ill attended by those who were to be invested was moved to the day following the Annual Investiture of Grand Lodge, in the hope that, in some cases at least, one journey could be made instead of two. It still remains rather a moot point whether three meetings in the year are really necessary: to the suggestion that there should be more Lectures or talks in February and November it can only be answered that there is a strictly limited number not only of suitable topics, but also of lecturers who could make them interesting.

One of the last actions of Lord Scarbrough in the Craft was his suggestion that the numbers and relative seniority of Grand Ranks in Grand Lodge should be reconsidered. This was taken in hand and various internal changes were passed by Grand Lodge: some ranks were introduced and rather more of the existing ones were abolished. A few years later when practice had established the benefit of these differences a very similar course was taken in Grand Chapter: it was a good deal simpler as an operation since in the Royal Arch there are fewer gradations of rank and the changes have proved just as satisfactory all round (even if one of the effects was the demotion by four places of the Grand Scribe E and Past Grand Scribe E, a real self-denying ordinance).

At the lower level of Provincial and District Grand Rank also a major restructuring in the Craft has been followed in the Royal Arch, but as it largely took place after my retirement I will leave it to another generation to explain.

I hope, however, it will appear from what I have been saying that Grand Chapter, and the Order generally, has not been idle over the post-war period, and that this brief account has helped to sum up what has been done—and perhaps point to matters which have still to be tackled.

(Part Two)

On a previous occasion I addressed Grand Chapter on what had been happening within its own jurisdiction and domestically from 1947 to 1980: now I would like to say something about its relation with other Grand Chapters—and very briefly where their interests come together about our Chapters overseas.

Some years ago E Comp Haunch addressed us on the superficial differences and underlying unity of purpose of Royal Arch Masonry as practised in England, Ireland and Scotland: I will not attempt to go over this ground again, but will establish straight away the existence of certain principles in our foreign relations which, to judge from correspondence which is still coming to me, are not known or understood abroad.

1. Grand Chapter does not grant formal recognition as Grand Lodge does.
2. Similarly, there is no exchange of representatives, though cases do occur where other Grand Chapters exchange representatives rather incongruously with Grand Mark Lodge.

3. Every Craft Lodge in the English Constitution has an inherent right wherever it is situated to have a Royal Arch Chapter attached to it: there is one exception—where with the idea of bringing a long standing dispute to an end the late Lord Ampthill gave away its birth right of St George's Lodge, Montreal, for a mess of pottage, ie the removal of a ban by the Quebec authorities: whether he had the right to do so is unclear and after so many years have passed, probably immaterial.

4. No Royal Arch Chapter can continue to exist without a Lodge to be attached to.

Over the period now under review most of these points have come to the fore in matters of foreign relations which have by and large been serene, though there has been a little local difficulty with Nova Scotia, which claims with little warrant for so doing, jurisdiction over the adjacent territories of Prince Edward Island, New Brunswick and Newfoundland: its authorities took exception to our chartering a Chapter to be attached to our Royal Standard Lodge No 398, at Halifax as being an invasion of their territory: some pretty strong correspondence ensued, in the course of which E Comp Sir Ernest Cooper, himself a Canadian but no admirer of ME Comp R. V. Harris of Nova Scotia, said that we were going to Halifax and they could go to Hull or its other historic and nautical alternative. The Chapter was duly consecrated by E Comp Sir George Boag and led a fitful and harassed existence till 1978 when, regretfully, it was erased: one hopes with little confidence that the Nova Scotian RA Masons are ashamed of their total lack of Masonic feeling. Mention of this Chapter leads me to a similar but much happier event: after a lot of preparation and correspondence with the Grand Chapter of Victoria a Charter was granted to members of the Combermere Lodge No 752, Melbourne, in 1973: unlike the virtual boycott in Halifax, the Consecration, which I performed with much help from our Companions in Auckland later that year, was attended by the three Grand Principals of Victoria and the Grand Master of the Grand Lodge of Victoria and his Grand Secretary. As against these additions to our strength account must be taken of the considerable loss caused by the formation of the Grand Chapter of India: it will be remembered that the Grand Lodge of India was formed in 1961 when about half the English Lodges in the subcontinent joined it: many of these had Chapters attached to them, and it was only a question of time before they had either to find a surviving English Lodge to which to attach themselves or to set up a Grand Chapter or disappear. A little over half took the second course, and the new Grand Chapter was duly constituted in November, 1963, by Sir George Boag, assisted by Major George Bulman, and Lieutenant General Sir Harold Williams.

This Grand Chapter, however, was not the first or the last to have originated from, or been created by, England in the period under review. Shortly after World War II when Freemasonry was re-established in the Netherlands a number of Dutch Masons, led by their Grand Master, came to London to be exalted: next, my predecessor consecrated a Chapter in Holland, which in due course became the Grand Chapter of the Netherlands in 1950.

The case of Switzerland was slightly different in that the Grand Lodge Alpina was more than a little reluctant to go quite the same way as the Grand East of the Netherlands, but there were not only a good many Royal Arch Masons already in Switzerland who had been exalted elsewhere, but also many interested Brethren, including the Swiss Deputy Grand Master. It was accordingly arranged in 1954, with the full consent and co-operation of Alpina, that a Chapter, to be called Von Tavel after the first Swiss Grand Master, should be attached to our Helvetica Lodge, but should meet in Switzerland, pending Alpina's decision to allow a Grand Chapter to be set up. Three years later Royal Arch Masonry had become firmly rooted in Switzerland and a request came to London to consecrate two more Chapters under the immediate authority of Alpina, the intention being that these three would then at once set up a Grand Chapter. There followed one of the most laborious days of my Masonic life: Sir George Boag, Rev F.J. Dove and I between us consecrated two Chapters, installed nine Third Principals, six Second Principals, three First Principals, created a Grand Chapter and installed its Grand Principals between luncheon and dinner: we were greatly helped, as much of it had to be done in French and German, by E Comp Fulke Radice, now still active at well over 90, and E Comp Hamish Munro who, despite his name and his invaluable occupation as the Chief Brewer in Berne, was 100% an English Mason (incidentally a few years ago I visited his mother Lodge in Assam!). This Grand Chapter flourishes and adds some ballast to the otherwise capsizeable Grand Lodge Alpina.

Before World War II several Finnish Masons had come to London to seek exaltation with a view to setting up a Chapter under their Grand Lodge: owing to the outbreak of War this came to nothing, but after it was over the survivors tried again. Enough were exalted to form Chapters in Finland, and when they were ready they too invited Sir George Boag to constitute them into a Grand Chapter. This was not so hair-raising as the Swiss event as there were no Consecrations and Sir George and I had the assistance of E Comps Major R. L. Loyd, Sir Donald Makgill, G. V. Sinclair, and Rev G. T. Waldegrave, who were all in Helsinki by a happy and not uncontrived coincidence.

That completes the tale of new Grand Chapters formed by us through our own Grand Chapter, but two other acts of expansion should be mentioned. I will not go into the complex question of Craft Masonry in Western Germany: it will be sufficient to say that its various elements are now adequately catered for in the matter of the Royal Arch. The English element obtained authority from its semi-autonomous Grand Lodge to start the English type of Chapter working: I was invited to consecrate on its behalf a Chapter at Dusseldorf which I did with the assistance of E Comp Sir Leonard Atkinson, Jeremy Pemberton, and Rev G.W.N. Groves. It has now formed other Chapters and constituted itself with our full approval but without our assistance into a Grand Chapter. A similar evolution went on in Italy with the powerful assistance of our friends from the Italia Chapter. In some ways this is the most surprising development, for Craft Masonry in Italy has had a rough passage: although clerical opposition there appears to be easing off it was a surprise to have pointed out to us, as a candidate for a Chapter we were asked to consecrate, a monk in his full habit.

So far as Scandinavia is concerned, where a different system from ours prevails, we have reached a mutual agreement that our Royal Arch ceremony more or less agrees with their fourth, fifth and sixth Degrees, and intervisitation can and does take place on this basis.

It is well known that General George Washington was offered and declined a kind of overall Grand Mastership for the whole United States as it then was, and that thereafter each State went its own way. Most, if not all, of them support a Grand Chapter too, but unlike the Craft which took no for an answer, in the Royal Arch a super body has established itself, called the General Grand Chapter. It is not really clear what either its functions or its responsibilities are, but it has extended its ramifications on a world-wide scale far beyond the USA and now has Grand Chapters affiliated to it in three Canadian Provinces, Austria, Germany and Greece. It has extended its ramifications in Central and South America, Taiwan and Japan—as well as Israel and Italy.

Fortunately owing to our policy of non recognition we are not called upon to recognise it or not recognise it: we accept its existence, quietly wondering what, in the modern phrase, it is in aid of—and from time to time we welcome in Grand Chapter some of its leading lights. ·

A word or two in conclusion about our practice in recognitions: if Grand Lodge recognises another Grand Lodge which has jurisdiction over a territory in which a Grand Chapter is operating with its approval, the members of that Grand Chapter are acceptable to us without further ado. I think it is but fair to say that the absence of Grand Representatives has never been felt to be a grievous loss.

Index

Page numbers in *italic* refer to illustrations or their captions
Abbreviations used in this index:
　　　　　　　GM—Grand Master
　　　　　Dist GM—District Grand Master
　　　　Prov GM—Provincial Grand Master
　　　　　　FMH—Freemasons' Hall

Ablett, E. T., Dist GM Transvaal 190, *193-94*, 197
Acacia Study Circle, Madras 188
Adair, Maj-Gen Sir Allan, PDep GM 87, 90, 93, 98, 112, 118, 120, *125*, 127, 131
Adams, A. M., Dist GM Bengal 185
Adams, Col Cecil 83
Adolf VI King Gustaf 93-94
Aims and Relationships of the Craft 56, 63, 137
Aldersgate Chapter of Improvement 149
Aldo, Dr Quinus 200
Allen, R. H. 81
Allerton, Gordon 194
Alexander, Andrew 40
Alington, Rev Hugh 11
Alpina, Grand Lodge of, 144-45, 249
　and Grand Chapter of 249
Amery, G. Douglas, Prov GM Oxon 28, 45, 60, *67*, 117
Ampthill, Arthur, 2nd *Lord* 222
Anderson, J. G., Dist GM South Africa Eastern Division 196
'Antients' Grand Lodge 216, 224
Antigua, visit to 176
Armitage, Bernard, Dist GM Natal 197
Armitage, Norman 110, 111
Ars Quatuor Coronatorum 128
Assistant Grand Secretary 62-63

Atkinson, Sir Leonard 147, 148, 249
Atterbury, Susan *34*
Austen, Godwin 38, 39
Australia, Lodges in 104
Avery, Vernon 179

Bad Oeynhausen 40, 41
Bad Salzuflen 41
Baddeley, C. R. *67*
Bagnall Report 131-33, 232
Bagnall, Sir Arthur 131, 132
Bahamas, visit to, 174-77
Baillieu, Hon Edward L, (GDC), Dep GM, 120, 124, 127, 131, 160, 169
Balliol College 27
Balsdon, Thomas 69
Banks, Dr J. H., Prov GM Middlesex 74
Barbados, Installation of Dist GM for 160, 176-77
Barker, Lt-Col 22
Barkway Vicarage 9, *9*, 10, 11, 12, 18
Bartlett, Lt-Col Harry 37
Barlow, Sgt 50
Barnard, Dennis, 131, 134, 139
Barne, Judge Hume, Dist GM Gibraltar, 93
Barnes, J. Donald, Dep Dist GM Ghana, 199
Barnes, Gordon, Dist GM Newfoundland, 173
Barrett, Cdr R. H. *67*

Bateman, Roland H. 65
Batham, Cyril *171*
Bathurst, W. R. S., Prov GM Gloucs, 66, 67, 71, 79
Bayford, Robin 55
Beckley, A. Z. 200
Belgium, Grand Lodge of 95–96, 146, 147
Belgium, Grand Orient of 95
Bell, John 30, 31, 34, 111
'Belshazzar's Feast', John Martin 69
Bengal, District Grand Lodge of 184, 185
Berry, George 17
Bigge, Augusta 3, 8
Bigge, Ellen 24, 51
Binks, Major 185
Birstwith, William of, 1
Blay, William F., Dep Prov GM Kent 50, 54; development of Gt Queen St 65, 74, 138, 143, 228
Bledisloe, Lord 131
Blockley, Rev Thomas Trotter 27, 28, 29, 128
Boag, Sir George 52, 147, 148, 246, 248, 249
Board of Benevolence (now Grand Charity) 51, 52, 53, 55, 132, 133, 223, 232
Board of General Purposes 51, 52, 55, 80, 136, 148, 150, 166, 168; development of 223–32; personalities 53, 54, 55, 57; on Religion 77; Grand Rank Procedure 140–41; the penalties 150–51; Committee on Committees 229; Colonial, Indian and Foreign Committee (now External Relations) 54, 55, 63–65, 140, 144–47, 226; Finance Committee 54, 61–62, 136–37, 138, 223–31; Library, Arts and Publications Committee 54, 68–69, 136, 137, 227, 228; Officers and Clerks Committee 54, 55, 67–68, 227, salaries and wages 66, 139–40, 228–29; Premises Committee 54, 65–66, 138–39, 227, 228; Procedure Committee 54, 62–63, 140–42, 223, 229, 230
Board of Works 223–25
Boehringer, Oscar 120, 144
Bolton, Geoffrey 11, 12
Bombay, District Grand Lodge of 187–88, Lord Scarbrough as Dist GM of 56
Book of Constitutions 137; Appeals 140; Board of GP 231; dues 136; funerals 78; Grand Master's power 235; Grand Stewards 114; Master's responsibilities 217–18; printing of 166, 228; the Royal Arch 148, 245–46
Börner, Richard Mueller *94*
Botha, Dr 105
Botswana, visit to, 197
Boult, David 73
Bowra, Sir Maurice 17, 54, 132
Boyson, Cleophe 7
Bradburn, John 148
Brasenose College 3, 15, 20–21, 23, 24, 27, 28, 71
Brazil, Grand Orient of, 75, and rival Grand Lodges 64–65
Brett, Bertie 36
British Virgin Islands, lodge in 175
Broad, R. 156
Bromham, William A. C. 56, 128
Brooke, Raymond, GM Ireland 102, 146
Brown, Burnett, Prov GM Middlesex 60, 109
Brown, Howard H. 110
Brown, Hugh, Asst Dist GM Jamaica 175
Brown, Norman Long 156, 157
Browne, William G. H. 59, 243–44
Brunton, Harold D. 52, 59
Brussels 40, 41
Bryant, Rev E.E. 14
Buchan, Alex 151
Buckley, Lt-Cdr Sir Richard *122–23*

Budd, H. O. 46, 54
Bull, Philip C., Prov GM Middlesex (GDC) 55, 59, *67*, 71, 74
Bullen, J. E. 37, 166
Bullingdon Club 26
Bulman, Maj George 248
Bultzo, Cdr Alexander 97–98, 158
Bunting, E. L., Dep Prov GM Worcs 67
Burlington House, Dutch Exhibition 16
Burma, District Grand Lodge of 184
Burrows, Bernard 12

Cadogan, William, *7th Earl*, Dep GM 81, 82, 101, 112, 124, *125*, as Pro GM 127, 131, 133, 135, 154, 155, *162*, *163*
California, Grand Lodge of 94
Camden, London Borough of 48
Canada (in Ontario), Grand Lodge of 101, 124, 174, 226
Canterbury, Archbishop of 75
Carlile, Noel 15
Carmichael, K. 116
Carpmael, Maurice 120
Caron, Dr 65
Carr, Harry 114, 144, 150, 151
Carr, Kitty 8
Cattell, Rev Richard 7
Catterick training course 111
Central London Masonic Centre 160
'Certa Cito', motto of Royal Signals Corp 40, *see also* Lodges, Certa Cito
Chanter, Derrick 49, 136
Chapman family 13
Charing Cross Hospital 167
Charities (*see* Board of Benevolence)
Charterhouse 6, 11–19, 107, 110–12, 156
Charts Edge, Westerham *34*
Cherian, Mrs Tara 188
Chester, Bishop of 6
Chile, Grand Lodge of 64, 75
Chiltern, Henry 50

China, Grand Lodge of 144
Chitty, Jack 207
Christ Church, Oxford 1, 6
Claxton, Rt Revd C. R., Bishop of Blackburn *162*, *163*
Clucas, Sir Kenneth 40
Coates, Joseph 61
Cobb, Cicely 21
Cobban, Sir James 45
Coeur de Lion Preceptory (KT) No 29, Oxford 27, 28, 73
Cole, *Justice* C. O. E. Dist GM Sierre Leone 200
Cole Court, Twickenham 108
Colet Court 30
Colet House 33
Collins, Humphrey 37
Colonial, Indian and Foreign Committee of the B of GP 54, 63, 226 (*see also* External Relations Committee)
Committee on Committees 229
Communism and Freemasonry 63
Connaught, HRH Arthur Duke of 133, 232
Connaught Rooms, London 50, 54, 65, 124, 160, 168, 228
Constitutional History of England, Bishop Stubbs 215
Cooper, John *171*
Cooper, Sir Ernest (President B of GP) 46, 71, *82*, 88, 89, 90, 144, 248; appeal for Westminster Abbey 80; German masonry 85, 87; Jubilee Masters Lodge 108; Lodge dues and finance 61–62; Masonic Fire 62; the penalties 150; precedence of Grand Officers 62–63
Cooper, Dr William E., Dist GM Barbados 177
Corfield, Colin *frontispiece*, *92*
Cornwallis, Fiennes, *Lord*, 78, 112, 131, 132
Corpus Christi College, Oxford 30
Costin, W. C. 82

Cowburn, Herbert, Dist GM South Africa Western Division 195
Crawford, Jock 111
Cromack, E. 120
Crookshank, Harry, *Viscount* 91, 109, 110
Crossman family, the 13
Crosthwaite, Maj Cecil 38
Crowthorne, Berkshire 35, 42
Cuddesdon Palace 6, 7
Curtis, Walter 49, 137
Cyprus, District of 97, 98, 99–101, 102, 158, Othello Lodge room *98*

Daniel, Michael 176
Darell, Brig-Gen William H., Asst GM 56, 57, 74
Darkin, R. A. *115*
Davie, Hugh 111
Davies, Gen Sir Francis, Prov GM Worcs 56
Davies, Robert 174
Davis, Bernard 127
Davis, A. J. 168
Dawney, F. L. *23*
de Bosco, Marie 4
de Rosière, Louis 95
de Wardener, Prof Hugh 167
de Wolfe, Brig Esmond, Dist GM Malta 74, 96
Deputy and Assistant Grand Mastership 236
Derby, Edward John, *18th Earl*, Dep GM 74, 75, 154, *162*, *163*
Devonshire, Edward, *10th Duke of*: general 96, 129; appointed as GM 56, installed as GM 58–60; in 1950 *67*, 71; death of 74–75
Dicker, Col G. S. H., Dep Prov GM Norfolk (now Prov GM) 163
District Grand Lodges 218–21
Dixon, Ewart 174
Dixon, Kenneth N. 13
Doctor, Dora 134
Donnison, Jim 37

Donoughmore, *Earl of*, GM Ireland 124, *125*, 146–47, 161
Douglas, Frank, GDC later Asst GM 60, 74, *82*, 89, 90, 91, *93*, 102, 108, 112, 119, 122, 127, 131, *162*, *163*, 227
Dove, Rev F. J. 249
Dover, Sir Kenneth 30
Dow, James 196
Draffen, George *171*
Dragon School (*see also* Lynams) 6, 12
Driskell, Stanley 49
Dunlop. M 170
Dyer, Colin F. W., *The Grand Stewards and their Lodge* 116
Dymond, E. R., Prov GM Herefordshire 67
Dyson, Richard 14, 15, 17

East Africa, Dist GL of 192–93
Easthampstead Park 30, 33
Easthampstead Rectory *18*, 18
Eaton, F. Owen, PDist GM South Africa Eastern Division, 196
Eisen, G. P. *23*
Edge, Sir Knowles, Prov GM West Lancs, *162*, *163*
Edwardes, Lt-Col the Hon M. G. 98, 102
Egeland, Leif 20, 194
Eglinton and Winton, *17th Earl of*, GMM Scotland, 102
Ellicot, Jack *93*
Elliot, Claude 8
Ellis, Col W. F., PDist GM Gibraltar 93
Emden, The 8
Emulation Lodge of Improvement 149, 151
Emulation ritual working 28, 98, 151
English Constitution, Walter Bagehot 215
Essex, Province of 143
Eton College 6, 7, 12
'Europe', Grand Lodge of 104–105
European Conference 146–47

External Relations Committee (B of GP) 55, 140, 144–47, 226; Communism 63; God and religion 63–65

Fairweather, Brig C. C. 163
Famagusta, Cyprus 99–100
Faridkot, H. H. of, Dist GM N. India 187
Feaver, William, *The Art of John Martin* 69
Ferris, Alan F., GDC, Prov GM West Lancs 142, 160, *162*, *163*, 175–77
Few, Resbury 87
Finance Committee (B of GP) 54; administration of 61–62, 136–37, 138; 223–31
Finland, Grand Chapter of 249
Finsen, George 175
Firth, Brig 42
Fisher, M Revd Geoffrey, *Lord*, of Lambeth 76, 128
Fletcher, Sir Frank 14–17, 20, 111
Fletcher, P. C. 17, 44
Forbes, Alec 30
Forsyth, Johnny 33
Foung, Louk Choon 184
Four Corners, The, Sir James Stubbs 91, 127, 166, 172
France, Grand Lodge of, and GLNF 95, 104, 145
France, Grand Orient of 49, 64–65, 95, 145
Fraser, Rev Charles 10
Frederick Phillips Charity, The 53
Freeman, Merton S. 197
Freemasons' Hall, London 46, 47, 48–51, 54, 55, 60, 126, 138–39, 224, 228; Grand Secretary's office *155*; Restoration and maintenance 65, 138–39; Staff 66
Freemasons' Hall, the Home and Heritage of the Craft, T. O. Haunch and J. W. Stubbs 138
Frere, Alexander Stuart, President B of GP, 55, 91, *92*, 112, 113; installation of GM 119, 120, 124, *125*; 127, 131, 144–45
Fry, Charles 50, 156
Fry, H. A. *162*, *163*

Gamlen, Jack 73
Garrett, K. 163
Garvey, John 194
George VI, *HM the King 5*, 56, 75; installs Duke of Devonshire 58–60
German masonry 84–85, 94–95
Gervis, Nicolette and Paul *34*
Gervis, Ruth 160
Ghana, District of 199, 200–201
Gibraltar, District of *93*, 93
Gill, G. S. 188
Gillanders, Norman 182, 183
Gillmor, Canon F. I. E. 29, 43
Gleadow, Edmund 11
God and Religion 63–64
Goh, Dr Teik Wah, Asst Dist GM Eastern Archipelago 183
Gordon, Lt-Col 'Bungie' 37
Grace, Malcolm 49, 89, 137
Graft-Johnson, WBro 201
Grand Chapter 133, 147–50, 151, 243–50
Grand Chapter Committee 51, 148–49; selection of LGCR 61
Grand Charity (*see also* Board of Benevolence) 170, 206
Grand East of Netherlands 65, 104, 105, 249
Grand Lodge 51, 133, 150; administration 223–32; 250th anniversary 118–26
Grand Lodge 1717–1967 90, 119, 133, 166
Grand Master's Council 51, 167, 234
Grand Mastership 233–35
Grand Orient, use of word 64–65
Grand Rank procedure 140–41
Grand Stewards 114–16, *115*, 149, 150, 234

Grand Stewards' Lodge; in 1983-84 *115*; installation of the Duke of Devonshire as GM 59, 114-16 (*see also under* Lodges)
Grand Stewards and their Lodge, The, Colin F. W. Dyer 116
Grand Treasurer 140-41, 148-49
Grantham, Ivor 50, 138
Great Queen Street, development of 54, 65, 114, 227-28
Greece, Grand Lodge of 97, 98
Greece, Visit to 158
Green, Maj-Gen R., Dep Dist GM Jamaica 175
Gregory, Ivor 173, 201
Grey, W. E. 242
Griffith, John 117
Groom, Sir Victor *162*, *163*
Grose-Hodge, H. 14, 15
Groves, John 138
Groves, Rev G. W. N. 249
Guy, John Ross 134-35
Guyana, District of 177

Haffner, Christopher, Dist GM Hong Kong and the Far East 182, 183
Hagon, John 40, 41
Haig, Miss G. 47, 56, 71, 87, 89, 166; biographical detail, 57; retirement 91
Hainworth, Irene 57, 91, 120, 131, *152*, 153, 163
Hale, J. P. R. 110
Hale, Lionel 15, 25
Halifax, Nova Scotia, 104
Hamill, John *171*
Hannah, Walton, *Darkness Visible* 76
Harbord, A. G. *23*
Harewood Court, RMBI, Hove *132*
Harewood, Henry, *6th Earl of* 46, 47, 55-58, 69, 75, 84, 88, 99, 129, 131, 243; death of 58
Harris, *Lord* 94
Harris, R. V. 248
Harrison, Ron 38
Haunch, T. O. 114, 138, *171*, 247

Hawking, Lt-Col 41, 42
Hayman, P. M. C., Dep Prov GM Gloucs 67
Heaton, Wallace 46, 54
Headlam, Dr, Bishop of Gloucester, 7
Heath, Christopher (Revd) 31
Hecke, Ernest van 95
Herbert, Bishop Percy 150, 207-208
Hervey, John 236
Hewetson, E. P. 25
Hewitt, R. 119, 138
Hierneiss, C. P. 17
Higham, Caroline 47
Higham, Cdr M. B. S. 108, 109, 134-35, 139, 155, 160, *164-65*, 166
Hilbery, Sir Malcolm *82*
Hinett, Leslie 197
Historical Supplement to the Masonic Year Book 85
Hobby, Maurice 117
Hobkirk, Maj 36
Hock, Chan Cheng 184
Hoffmann, Hans 94
Holborn, London 48
Holford Exhibition 6
Holroyd, Michael 20
Hone, R. M. *115*
Hone, Sir Ralph 140, 150, 169, 170
Hong Kong and the Far East, District of 144, 167, 182, 184
Hope, Charles 101, 173
Hopton-Scott, F. W. S. *115*
Horton-in-Ribblesdale 12
Horlock, Wimburn 73
Howarth, Clifford 36
Howe, Ellic *171*
Hunt, John 16
Hutchings, E. K. 191
Hyde, Gordon 199

Ibberson, W. G. 120
Iles, R. W. Bro 174
India, District Grand Lodges of 185, 190
India, Grand Chapter of 248

India, Grand Lodge of 85, 97, 129; inauguration 101-103, 248
Information for the Guidance of Members of the Craft 137, 229
Iran, Grand Lodge of 144
Ireland, Grand Lodge of 102, 124, 146
Irvine, A. L. 15
Italy, freemasonry in 145-46

Jacobs, Aubrey, Dist GM Jamaica 175
Jacobs, HE Sir Wilfred 176
Jaipuria, Saitaram 187
Jamaica, District of 175
James, R. L. 44, 82, 111; OTC officer 23; wedding group *34*
Japan, Grand Lodge of 144
Jennings, Lt-Col C. M. F. 101, 190; and Son 101
Jole, Alan 79, 84, 89, 132, 134, 141
Johnson, R. Gelling, Prov GM Isle of Man *162, 163*
Johnson, John 49
Johnson, Patrick 72
Johnstone, A., Prov GM Cheshire *162, 163*
Jones, Francis 49, 89
Jones, Col H. (Sec RMIB) 81
Joshua by John Martin, 68-69

Kathmandu, Nepal 184, 185
Kay, R. L. *115*
Kell, John 14, 16
Kelway, Col G. T., Prov GM South Wales Western Division 155
Kent, HRH Edward Duke of (GM 1967-); installation as GM 118-24, *122-23, 125,* 126; as GM 133-34; the penalties 150, 207-208; West Lancs installation of Prov GM *162, 163*
Kent, HRH George Duke of (GM 1939-42) 56, 58, 75
Kent, Province of 143

Kenyon, *Lord*, Prov GM North Wales *162, 163*
Kettel Hall 6
Kilravock, Barons of 4 (*see also under* Rose)
Kilravock Castle 4, 7, 9, 10, 12, 16, 69, 158
Kingsway Theatre, Gt Queen St 65
Kitchener of Khartoum, *Earl* 166
Koder, S. S., Dep Dist GM Madras 189
Kyrenia, Cyprus 98, 100

Lane, Sir Peter *115,* 116
Langton, T. B., Prov GM Hants & IoW *93,* 111, 112
Large, K. B., PDist GM Bengal *162, 163*
Larkin, S. 174
Lawson, R. E. *82*
Lee, Richard, Dist GM Hong Kong and the Far East 144, 167, 182, 183
Leeds Clergy School 6
Leeward Islands 176
Leicestershire and Rutland, Province of 148-49
Lenighan, Cdr Maureen 42
Lepper, J. Heron 50, 138
Letchworth, Sir Edward 49, 66, 87, 136
Lewis, Sir Alan 176
Lewis, R., *67*
Lewis, Col William 41, 42
Lewellin, John Jestyn, *Lord*, Prov GM Dorset 109
Ley, Arthur 140
Library, Arts and Publications Committee (B of GP) 54, 68-69, 136, 137-38, 227, 228
Library and Museum, Gt Queen St 50, 228
Limassol, Cyprus 101
Linforth, R. O. *115*
Linklater, John 33
Lodge Dues 61, 136

LODGES: *all English Constitution unless stated otherwise*
Addington, 1937, Natal 197
Alchemy, 7956, Transvaal 197
Alma Mater, 1492, Cambridge 27
Antiquity, 2, London 112-13, 116, 241
Apollo, 7886, Cyprus *98*, 99
Apollo University, 357, Oxford 25-29, 43, 46, 56, 71, 72, 109, 117, 128, 146, 151, 170
Archibald Campbell, 4998, Madras 188
Asanteman, 8351, Ghana 200
Aviation, 7210, London 120
Bard of Avon, 778, Twickenham 108, 113
Berkshire Masters, 3684, Sindlesham 109
British, 8, London 241
Canada, 3527, London 126
Castle Lodge of Harmony, 26, London 241
Centre des Amis (GLNF) 95
Certa Cito, 8925, London 163, 166
Charterhouse Deo Dante Dedi, 2885, London 110, 111, 112
Churchill, 478, Oxford 27, 71, 73, 117
Circle, 8964, Ghana 201
Combermere, 752, Melbourne 248
Cochin, 4359, India 189
Eastern, 8930, Ghana 200
Ellis Robins, 8136, Zimbabwe 191
Federation, 7363, Zimbabwe 191
Felicity, 58, London 242
Fortitude and Old Cumberland, 12, London 113
Friendship, 6, London 241
Gaborone, 8781, Botswana 197
Globe, 23, London 241
Good Hope, 863, S. Africa ED 196
Grand Master's, 1, London 241
Grand Stewards', London 59, 114-16, *115*, 142
Harmonic, 356, BWI 176

Harmony, 3084, E. Africa 192
Helvetica, 4894, London 249
Ideal Endeavour, 7379, Kent *86*
Isaac Newton University, 859, Cambridge 26, 27, 109
Jerusalem, 197, London 242
Jubilee Masters, 2712, London 108, 109, 126, 142
Kitchener, 2998, N. India 187
Lions, 7713, Bombay 188
Lumley, 1893, Skegness 128
Lyceum Lodge of Research, 8682, Transvaal 198
Maseru, 2835, Besutoland 196
Methuen, 631, Marlow 113
Minchin, 2710, Madras 189
Mount Egmont, 670, New Zealand NI 180
Mount Kenya, 5638, E. Africa 193
Okwawuman, 8754, Ghana 200
Old Cliftonian, 3340, London 111, 112
Old King's Arms, 28, London 241
Old Tonbridgian, 4145, London 112
Old Union, 46, London, 114, 116, 242
Othello, 5670, Cyprus *99*, 99
Pacific Lodge of Hokitika, 1229, New Zealand SI 182
Peace and Harmony, 60, London 242
Phoenix, 1860, S. Africa WD 195
Pietersburg United, 2485, Transvaal 198
Pikwe, 8715, Botswana 197
Port Chalmers Marine, 942, New Zealand SI 181
Port of Hercules, 4626, Monte Carlo 97
Prince of Wales's, 259, London 242
Quatuor Coronati, 2076, London 113, 114, 126, 138, 144, 167, 168, *171*
Regularity, 91, London 242
Richard Giddy, 1574, South Africa Central D 196

Royal Alpha, 16, London, 108, 116, 118
Royal Philanthropic, 405, Trinidad 177
Royal Prince of Wales, 1555, Eastern Archipelago 183
Royal Somerset House and Inverness, 4, London 116, 241
Royal Standard, 398, Nova Scotia 173, 248
St Alban's, 29, London 242
St Andrew, 4683, Hull 128
St Blaize, 1938, S. Africa WD 195
St George, 549, Bombay 128
St George's, 8322, Swaziland 194
St George's and Corner Stone, 5, London 241
St John's, 1137, NZ SI 181
St Melyd's, 3840, Prestatyn 43
St Ursula's, 8952, BVI 176
Shakespear, 99, London 242
Singapore, 7178, E. Archipelago 183
Sir John Brand, 3035, Orange Free State 196
Star in the East, 67, Bengal 186
Star of the East, 880, Zante, Greece 97, 98, *99*
Tongariro, 705, NZ NI 180
Turanganui, 1480, NZ NI 179
Tuscan, 14, London 241
University Lodge of Hong Kong, 3666, 183
Victoria Falls, 5327, Zambia 192
Waitemata, 689, NZ NI 179
Wellesley, 1899, Sindlesham 25, 43, 109
Welwitschia, 8768, SW Africa 195
Westminster and Keystone, 10, London 44, 56, 109, 128, *164-65*, 183
London Grand Chapter Rank, appointments to 60-61; Senior London GCR 142
London Masonry 143-44, 222
London Grand Rank 233; appointments to 60-61, 141-42; Senior LGR 142
London Grand Rank Association 53, 142, 168
London Grand Rank Fund 53
Lord, Leslie, Dist GM Otago & Southland 181
Lorimer, RW Bro 174
Loyal Order of Moose 229
Loyd, Maj Robert Lindsay 29, 62, 73, 141, 170, 249
Lucea, Jamaica, Masonic Hall 175
Lunn, Arnold 9
Lynam, C. C. 6
Lynam's 6, 11

McCain, J. L., GM Pennsylvania *96*
MacDonald, A. 74
MacGillivray, D., Dist GM Newfoundland 119
MacGillivray, Doris 173
McKenna, Michael 12
McLaren, Russell, 57
McIntyre, F., PDist GM SA WD 194
McMahon, Sir Henry 226
Macphersons, I. A. C. *115*
Madon, Mr Justice, GM India 103
Madras, District Grand Lodge of 188
Magdalen College, Oxford 11, 27, 30, 128
Magdalen College, Cambridge 8
Makgill, Sir Donald, Viscount of Oxford 113, 249
Mallory, George 8
Manekshaw, Bro 185
Marfell, George 22
Mark Grand Secretary 57, 207
Mark Masonry 169
Mark Masons' Hall 54, 65, 207, 228
Marsh, Ben, Prov GM Worcs 67
Martin, Sir Alec 68
Martin, John 68-69
Martin, T. 111
Martin, William 68-69
Masonic Civil Service 236-37
Masonic Fire 62

Masonic Funerals 78
Masonic Million Memorial Fund 49, 68, 87, 232
Masonic Year Book 49, 69, 136-37, 166, 228
Master of Lodge 216-17
Matthews, Sir Trevor 52
Matthey, George 74
Matson, A. J. *115*
Mavor, Revd Ivan 43
Meikle, George, Dist GM Cyprus 100, 101, 158
Mena, Anthony, Dist GM Gibraltar 93
Mendoza, Harry 169, *171*
Mercantile Credit Building 65
Middlesex, Province of 55, 108, 143
Miller, Sir Stephen 160
Mitre, the, Hampton Court 85, 108
Monie, Revd Peter 11
Montgomery, Lt-Col Robin 36
Montreal, Canada 104
Moore, Norman, Prov GM Mddx 74
Morgan Affair, the 207
Morgan, James 21, 25
Morgan, Maj J. Vaughan 38
Morris, Sir Harold 55
Moss, Jock 157
Morton, Douglas 14, 15
Munro, Hamish 249
Murphy, Arthur 140, 150
Murray, Angus 173

Nairn, River 10
Natal, District Grand Lodge of 197
Naylor, Revd Dean of Bath, PGM Sussex 243
Netherlands, Grand Chapter of 249
Netherlands, Grand East 65, 104, 105, 249
Nevill, Rev Tom 98, 157
New College, Oxford 8, 27
Newfoundland 173; District of 104
Newsells 13
Newson-Smith, Sir Frank 227
Newson-Smith, Sir John *162, 163*
Newton, J. G. *115*

New Zealand, District of 101, 104, 178-82
New Zealand, Grand Lodge of 180-81, 101-104
Nicolaides, Costas 100
Norris, Frankie 40
Northern India, District Grand Lodge of 187-88
Nova Scotia, Grand Lodge of 173

Oakeshott, Sir Walter 34, 44, 45
Officers and Clerks Committee (B of GP) 54, 55, 66-68, 139-40, 227, 228-29
Orange Free State, District Grand Lodge of 196
Order of Service to Masonry 55
Orr-Ewing, Sir Ronald, GMM Scotland 124
OTC Camp 17, 21-23, 31
'Ousels' 35, 42
Owles, J. R. *115*
Oxford Masonry 25-29, 117
Oxford Ritual 28
Oxford University RAM 55, 73, 117
Oxford University Boat Club 53
Oxford University Press 166
Oxfordshire, Provincial Grand Lodge of 27, 28

Palmer, Peter, Prov GM Northants & Hunts 132
Paphos, Cyprus 100, 101
Parish, Geoffrey 12
Pascho, David 112
Pask, Sydney 31
Paterson, D. L. *162, 163*
Patiala, HH the Maharajadhiraj of, DGM N. India *82*
Paw, S. W. 184
Platres, Cyprus 100
Pearson, *Lord* 131
Peel, Maj J. E. 51
Pemberton, Jeremy, President B of GP 36, 39, 109, 135, 136, 139, 142, 145, *164-65*, 166, 167, 249

INDEX

Penalties, the 150-51, 207-208
Penang 183
Pennsylvania, GM of *96*
Penny, Maj-Gen 45
Pensioners Court, Charterhouse 156, 157, *157*
Peters, Rev William 69
Peterson, Vic, PDist GM Zambia 198
Philip, Peter 158
Phillips, Frederick 53
Piccadilly Hotel 110, 120
Pirie Gordon, Christopher 146, 204
Pirie Gordon, Patrick 170, 204
Platnauer, Maurice 20
Plooy, A. L. du, Dist GM Orange Free State 196
Pooke, N.C. 196
Pope, Rev Arthur F 1, *3*, 9
Pope, Ebenezer 1
Pope, Ven Edward 3
Pope, Harold 8
Pope, James 8
Pope, Kate *3*
Pope, Margaret *34*
Pope, Muriel 7
Potts, Howard, Prov GM Cumberland & Westmorland 103, 110, 111, *162*, *163*
Powell, A. M. 110
Powney, Lt-Col du Pre 29
Pratt, Solomon 200
Premier Grand Lodge 216, 223-24
Premises Committee (B of GP) 54; 65-66, 138-39, 227
Prestatyn 36, 44
Preston, William 237
Prestonian Lecture 69, for 1982 167-68; *The Government of the Craft* 211-39
Price, F. B. 180
Princess Royal, HRH the (*Countess of Harewood*) 46, *132*
Private Lodges 216-18
Pro Grand Master 56, 235-36
Procedure Committee (B of GP) 54; 62-63, 140-41, 229-30

Provincial and District Grand Lodge 218-21, 233
Provincial Grand Masters 219
Provincial Grand Rank, promotions to 62, 141

Queen's College, Oxford 3, 27
Queen Elizabeth the Queen Mother, HM *82*

Radford, Peter 191, 192
Radice, Fulke 249
Rampur, HH the Nawab of 102, 103
Ramsay, A. R. 16
Randall, Maj 'Day' 36
Randolph Hotel, Oxford 28, 73
Rangoon, Burma 184
Ranina, H. J. 188
Rathcreedan, *Lord* PPGM Oxford 109
Rav, Krishna 188
Read, R.G. 174
Read, William 171
Red Apron Lodges 240-42
Rees, Brian 111
Reeves, Rev J. 166
Reeves, R. R. 180
Regalia; Gauntlets 79, use of full dress 78-80
Reid, N. C. R. W. *115*
Relationship of Masonry and Religion 77-78
Religion and Freemasonry, 63-65, 75-78, 207
Republic Plato 215
Richardson, G. 166
Rickard, Col 144
Ridler, Vivian 166
Rivers, Ned 174
Robertson, Sir Stuart 51, 149
Robbins, Sir Alfred 49, 141, 231, 234
Robins, *Lord* Dist GM Rhodesia 109
Rodway, Gilbert 183
Roe, Robin 98
Roper, Hugh Trevor, *Lord Daker* 18
Rose, Catherine I. E. 1, 7

ROSE CROIX CHAPTERS
  Adams Peak, 133, Sri Lanka 190
  Mount Calvary in the East, 47, Singapore 183
  Namirembe, 307, Kenya 192
  Oxford University, 40, Oxford 73, 117
  St Mary Magdalene, 73, Hong Kong 183
Rose family, early history 4
Rose, Col Hugh, 24th Baron of Kilravock *5*
Rose, Maj James, 23rd Baron of Kilravock 3, *4*
Rowland, R. *115*
Royal Albert Hall, installations of Duke of Devonshire 58-60; Lord Scarbrough 75; installation of Duke of Kent 118-26
Royal Arch, the 147-50, 243-50; chapters of instruction 149-50
ROYAL ARCH CHAPTERS
  Apollo University, 357, Oxford 51, 73, 116, 117
  Cana, 116, Colne 154
  Carthusian, 2885, London 117
  Harmony and Fidelity, 438, Bengal 186
  Italia, 2687, London 146, 250
  Letchworth, 3505, London 245
  London First Principals, 2712, London 117, 244-45
  St George, 549, Bombay 128
  Unity, 3406, Bengal 186
  Westminster and Keystone, 10, London 117, 118
Royal Arch Regulations 148, 245-46
Royal Corps of Signals 21-23, 31, 33, 36-42, 163
Royal Masonic Benevolent Institution 54, 57, 68, 80, 83, 168, 205-206
Royal Masonic Hospital 54; opening of Wakefield Wing *82*; 83, 126, 131, 134, 137, 158, 205-206
Royal Masonic Institution for Boys 80, 81-83, 125, 206

Royal Masonic Institution for Girls 80-81, 83, 126, 206
Rundle, Philip (Rundell) 8
Rutherford, David 53
Rutter, Edgar, Dep PGM SW ED 52, 54; and B of GP 55; opposed to increase in dues 61, salaries and wages of staff at FMH 66; the RMIB 81-82; installation of GM 120; External affairs 144; 179
Rutter, G. 179

Sabine, Neville 21
Sackey, Dr E. A., Dist GM Ghana 199, *199*
St Albans, Bishop of 7
St John Ambulance Association 59
St Paul's Cathedral 112, 128
St Paul's School 30-35, 40, 42, 45, 111
St Thomas' Hospital 34
Salisbury, *Marquess* 6
Salvini, Lino 146
Sandler, Prof M. 116
Sargeant, Frankie 41
Savill, J 155
Savill, L. E. M. *23*
Saxton, Clive 72
Sayer, Anthony 113
Scandinavian Grand Lodges 85
Scarbrough, Lawrence Roger, *11th Earl of*, 71-72, 85, 87-90, 133, 154, *162*, *163*; biographical details 56, 128-30; the Church 75-78; and Sir Ernest Cooper 53; death of 118, 127-30; as Dep GM 56; in France 95; as Grand Master 74-75, *122-23*, *125*, 233; Grand Rank 141, 247; GL of India 101-103; Jubilee Masters 108; other Lodges 109, 113; the Penalties 150-51, 244; Royal Masonic Hospital *82*; Royal Masonic Institution for Boys 81; in Stockholm 93-94; 250th Anniversary celebrations 118-26

INDEX

School of Military Administration 38
Scotland, Grand Lodge of 78, 102, 108, 124, 146
Scutt, R. W. B. *115*
Semple, L. G. 42
Seychelles, visit to 101
Shannon, Richard, *9th Earl of* 142
Sharnock, Margaret 35
Shenley Mental Hospital 39
Shepherd-Jones, G. S. 149
Si, Lao-Htin, Dist GM Burma 184
Sierra Leone, District of 199
Simes, Erskine 103, 121
Simmons, Leo, PDist GM SA ED 196
Sinclair, G. V. 249
Sinclair, Norman 81
Sinclare, Leslie 160
Singapore, visit to 183–84
Singh, Brig Sant 187
Skelly, John 168
Skinner, John 137
Smale, A. 180
Smart, Col F. W. B. 13–14
Smith, Alex 193
Smith, Cecil 30
Smith, Sir Colville 25–26, 47, 57, 84, 87, 88, 109, 111, 112, 128, 136
Smith, Eynon 30
Smith, Glen, Dist GM SW Africa 195
Smith, H. Clifford, Prov GM Yorks WR *162, 163*
Smith, Maj (Sir) Thomas Lumley 57, 169
Smyth, C. E. 12
Smyth, Frederick *171*
Soane, Sir John 225
South Africa, Grand Lodge of 104–105
South Africa, visit to 190, 193–98
South Africa Central Division, District of 196
South Africa Eastern Division, District of 196
South Africa Western Division, District of 194–95
South African Freemasonry 104, 105

South Wales, Eastern Division, Province of 52, 55
South West Africa 195
Spiers, R. J. 27
Sri Lanka, visit to 101, 189–90
Staff Committee, B of GP (*see* Officers and Clerks)
Stallybrass, Dr W. T. S. 20
Stebbings, Sir John 170, 174
Stein, G. E. *115*
Stilgoe, T. 25
Stradbroke, John, *4th Earl of* 155
Stratford sub Castle *70*, 72
Streatfeild, Noel 167
Streatfeild, R. K. T. (*see* Stubbs, Richenda)
Strong, L. A. G. 11
Stubbington, George 49
Stubbs, Barbara *34*
Stubbs, Catherine 1, *2*, 4
Stubbs, Sir Edward 100, 203
Stubbs family background 1–10
Stubbs, Revd Wilfrid Thomas 4, 6, *9*, 10, *70*
Stubbs, Muriel Elizabeth 7, 8, 10, *70*
Stubbs, Hugh (*brother*) 10, 107, 204
Stubbs, Hugh (*son*) 43, 44, 93, 107, *107*, 112, 116, 156, 203
Stubbs, Sir James W.; *frontis*, application to Grand Lodge 46–47; Assistant Grand Secretary 62–63, 67; Barkway 13; Birth and early years *9*, 9–20; Board of General purposes 51–56, 136–40; Board of Benevolence 52–54; Brasenose College 20–21, 23, 24; in Brussels, *39*, 40–41; the Charities 81–83, 205; Charterhouse School 12–19; Control Commission, 40–42, Germany, *94*; Cyprus 97, 98, *99*–101, 102, 158; Ghana *199*, 200; Grand Chapter, lecture to 243–50; Grand Lodge of India 101–103; appointed Grand Secretary 88–89 and at desk *155*; Grand Rank precedence 140–41;

Stubbs, Sir James W.—*cont.*
as a Grand Steward, *115*, 116; Great Queen Street 48-51; Gibraltar *93*; initiation to Fmy 21, 25-27; installation of the Duke of Kent as GM *122-23*, *125*, 133-34; at Kilravock with Hugh *107*; Knighthood 158, *159*; Lodges in general 107-117; London Grand Rank appointments 60-61; Mark and Rose Croix 169, 170; Marriage to Richenda Streatfeild 33, *34*; membership index at Grand Lodge 66, 68; overseas visits 91, 93-105, 172-202; the penalties debate 207-208; in Pennsylvania *96*; Prestonian Lecture 167, 211-39; with HRH the Princess Royal *132*; Provincial and LGR 141-43, 154-55; Quatuor Coronati Lodge *171*; religion and Fmy 207; retirement 134-36, 156, 160-67; Royal Corps of Signals 21-23, *23*, 31, 33; Royal Masonic Hospital; opening of Wakefield Wing *82*; views on 205-206; St Paul's School 30-35, 44; salaries and wages at Freemasons' Hall 66; Lord Scarbrough 127-30; 250th anniversary of UGL 118-126; Upjohn Report 81; with Wendell Walker *157*; West Lancs installation of Prov GM *162*; Westminster and Keystone Lodge *164-65*; with Sir Sydney White *86*, tribute to 87-88

Stubbs, Jack E. C. 52, 54, 74
Stubbs, Janet *35*, 35, 42, 43
Stubbs, *Lady* Richenda K. T. 33, 34, 35, 43, 44, 47, 72, 100, 106-107, 121, 126, 135, 167; at Charterhouse *157*; at Frankfurt *94*; Ghana *199*; with Janet *35*, 42; portrait *32*; wedding day *34*
Stubbs, William 21

Stubbs, Dr William, *Bishop of Oxford*, 1, *2*, 203, 215
Studd, Sir Eric 112-13
Studd, Sir Kynaston 112-13
Sullivan, Dean Martin 160
Summer Fields 11, 12, 13
Sundaram, P. M. 103
Supreme Council, England and Wales 91, 169-70
Supreme Councils (USA) 64
Surrey, Province of 143
Sussex, HRH Augustus Frederick Duke of 56, 228, 233
Sutton, S. N. V. 17
Sweden, visit to 93-94
Swedish Rite 95
Switzerland, Freemasonry in 144-45, 147
Sydney, HMAS 8

Tantia Topi 3
Tawney, J. A. 28
Taylor, N. 177
Temperton, Dr 155
Thomas, Maj-Gen G. I. (Sir) 37
Thompson, W. J. 110
Thomson, Rev C. E. Leighton *164-65*
Thomson, D. *115*
Thorpe, C. H. 54
Tinney, Ernest 49
Tortola, B., BVI 175-76
Townshend, George, 7th Marquess 78
Toye, Kenning & Spencer Ltd 119
Transvaal, District of 194, 197
Tressler, Alfred 18
Trethowan, Michael 37, 38
Tribe, W. J. 50, 51
Tring, Herts 1, 3, 4, 6-10, 12
Trinidad, District of 102, 177-78
Trinity College 1, 6
Trinity Hospice 168
Trumper, Frank 140
Tryon, George, Prov GM Bristol *67*
Tubbs, Kingsley 59, 112, 113
Tuckwell, Sir E. G. 15, 16, 158
Turner, George 81, 111

Index

Twemlow, Anna Maria 3
Twistington-Higgins, Mr 42
Tyson, Maurice 34
Tzazopoulos, Alexander, GM Greece 98, 120, 124, *152*

United Grand Lodge(s) of Germany 85, 94-95, 145
University Mark Lodge No 55, Oxford 73
Upjohn, the Hon Sir Gerald (*Lord*) 81
Upjohn Report 81
Uruguay, Grand Orient of, unrecognised by UGL 64-65, 75
Usborne, Richard 11, 12

Vaisey, Mr Justice 4, 8
Valley Forge, Pennsylvania *96*
Van Oss, Oliver 12, 111, 157
Vickers family 13
Victoria, Grand Chapter of 248
Vieler, Douglas 197
Vincents Club 26
Vogel, Dr Theodore 85, 94, *94*, 147
Von Heidenstam, Count Rolf 85

Wagemanns, Charles, GM Grand Lodge of Belgium 95, 146
Wakefield, Sir Wavell 91
Waldegrave, Rev G. T. 249
Walker, George 41
Walker, Wendell *157*
Wallace, Dr J 109
Walpole, Horace 208
Wanklyn, Neville 33
War Office 38
Wasbrough, John 147, 148
Washington, George *96*, 250
Weeden, Charles 23
Welch, Sir Cullum 87, 90, 127
Welch, Sir John *164-65*, 166
Weldon, T. D. 26
Wellington College 30
Wells, Roy *171*
Wesley, John 6

West Africa, visit to 198-202
West Heath School 8
West Kent, Province of 102
West Lancashire, Province of 161, *162*
Western Australia, GL of 71
Westminster Abbey 80
Westminster School 1, 3, 12
Weyland, Capt Mark Ulick, Prov GM Oxon 27, 29
Wheeler, John 37
White, Maj-Gen C. M. F. 40
White, Eric 64
White, Jack 112
White, 'Nanny' 43
White, Sir Sydney 46, 47, 69, 74, 84, 95, 134; appointed Grand Secretary 57, 169; Boards and Committees 51, 54-55; death of 85-89, 90, 146; Duke of Devonshire 59; Freemasons' Hall matters 48, 50, 137, 138, 139, 143, 160; installation of Grand Masters 59, 122-23; Lodges 108, 111, 112, 116; Sir Trevor Matthews 52; overseas visits 71 72, 92; Religion and Fmy 76-77; RMIG 80-81; Edgar Rutter 55; Salaries and wages at FMH 66; selection of LGR nominations 61; with Sir James Stubbs *86*
White, William JNR 136, 226
Whitting, Philip 24, 30
Whittington, Michael 16, 17
Widgery, *Lord Chief Justice* 110
Wigglesworth, Walter 122
Wild, Cyril 17
Williams, Lt-Gen Sir Harold 102, 129, 248
Williams, Watkin 170
Wilson, A. B. *115*
Winchester College 6, 7
Winslade, Gerald 49
Wodehouse, P. G. 11
Wolfenden, Jack F., *Lord* 26, 81
Wolfit, Sir Donald 120

Woodman, Andy 59
Woods, Hersey 49, 52, 60, 58–59, 151
Worcestershire, Province of 56
Worsdell, R. J. *115*
Wragge, J. D. 197
Wren, Sir Christopher 112
Wren Maul 121
Wright, Dr 191
Wyatt, Dorothy 173

York, HRH the Duke of, *see* George VI

York Minster 127
Young, Douglas 33
Young, James 121
Young, Geoffrey Winthrop 9

Zambia, District of 102, 191–92, 197
Zante, Greece 97–98
Zetland, Lawrence, *3rd Marquess of* 94, 155, 225
Zimbabwe, District of 191

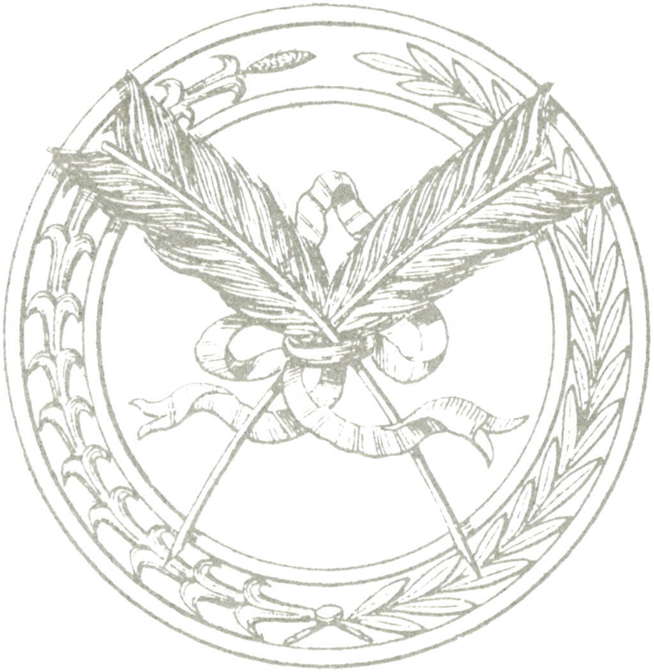